ASSET DEDICATION

ASSET DEDICATION™

How to Grow Wealthy with the Next Generation of Asset Allocation

STEPHEN J. HUXLEY

J. BRENT BURNS

McGraw-Hill

New York   Chicago   San Francisco   Lisbon   London   Madrid
Mexico City   Milan   New Delhi   San Juan   Seoul
Singapore   Sydney   Toronto

"Asset Dedication" is a trademark of Asset Dedication, LLC.

1 2 3 4 5 6 7 8 9 0 DOC/DOC 0 9 8 7 6 5 4

ISBN 0-07-143482-8

This publication is designed to provide accurate and authoritative information in regard to the subject matter covered. It is sold with the understanding that the publisher is not engaged in rendering legal, accounting, or other professional service. If legal advice or other expert assistance is required, the services of a competent professional person should be sought.

—From a declaration of principles jointly adopted by a committee of the American Bar Association and a committee of publishers.

McGraw-Hill books are available at special quantity discounts to use as premiums and sales promotions, or for use in corporate training programs. For more information, please write to the Director of Special Sales, McGraw-Hill Professional, Two Penn Plaza, New York, NY 10121-2298. Or contact your local bookstore.

 This book is printed on recycled, acid-free paper containing a minimum of 50% recycled, de-inked fiber.

Library of Congress Cataloging-in-Publication Data

Huxley, Stephen J.
    Asset dedication : how to grow wealthy with the next generation of asset
    allocation / by Stephen J. Huxley and J. Brent Burns.
        p.   cm.
    Includes index.
    ISBN 0-07-143482-8 (hardcover : alk. paper)
    1. Asset Allocation.   2. Portfolio management.   3. Investment analysis.   4.
    Investments.   5. Finance, Personal.   I. Burns, J. Brent.   II. Title.
HG4529.5.H95   2004
332.6—dc22

                                                                              2004004062

This book is dedicated to all those people who want to do the right thing for themselves, their families, or their clients in managing financial investments and who prefer to think for themselves.

The King will reply "I tell you the truth, whatever you did for the least of these brothers of mine, you did for me."

—Matthew 25:40 (NIV)

CONTENTS

PREFACE

This book is designed to shift investors and those who advise them to a new paradigm for personal investment. Asset allocation has reigned supreme in the marketplace of financial ideas since the 1980s. It has become such a dominant paradigm that it is no longer possible to have a conversation about finances without hearing something about asset allocation.

Asset allocation has had a good run, but it is beginning to show its age. Its flaws are becoming more apparent with each passing year. The primary flaw of classic asset allocation is the lack of a defensible way to determine the optimal formula for allocating the funds in a portfolio to stocks, bonds, and cash. In simple terms, classic asset allocation says, allocate X percent to stocks, Y percent to bonds, and Z percent to cash. The problem is that there is no easy way to determine exactly what X, Y, and Z should be.

This flaw becomes obvious if you go to three different brokers and give them the same personal financial information. You will fill out a "risk-tolerance" questionnaire for each broker to make the process appear mathematically precise, but you will get three different allocation recommendations—three different formulas for where to put your money. This should be the warning sign: Why are the three allocations different?

If you went to three different optometrists, you would be very puzzled if you got three different prescriptions for eyeglasses. The formulas for correcting vision are not arbitrary. They are based primarily on the scientific laws of optical behavior. The formulas for asset allocation, however, are not based on science. They are based on the opinions of each broker.

Brokers and their research departments rely on asset allocation as a selling tool, hoping to make you believe that their process is completely scientific and objective. They will point to their questionnaires and charts as evidence that they are customizing the perfect portfolio to fit your needs. What they are really doing is making you fit into one of their predetermined categories of investors ("Conservative," "Aggressive," or whatever).

They then try to get you to sign up for their services and buy a model portfolio that is based on a fixed XYZ percentage allocation to stocks, bonds, and cash that is said to be best for your type of investor. And they will tell you to rebalance your portfolio to that allocation formula in case your percentages deviate from it by more than what the broker deems appropriate.

But if you listen carefully to their prognostications, they will not be able to explain why their particular XYZ formula is different from any other broker's XYZ formula, or why it is better for you. They can't explain it because there is no explanation. No one has been able to prove that a particular set of percentage values for the XYZ formulas is optimal for any particular person. The bottom line here is that with classic asset allocation, there is neither true optimization nor true customization of your portfolio.

It is time to take asset allocation to the next level. Asset dedication does that.

Asset dedication is based entirely on customization and mathematics. If you go to three different brokers that use asset dedication, they will give you the same prescription for how to allocate your money, a prescription that is specifically designed to fit your needs and your financial situation. This book explains why asset dedication works and provides evidence of its superiority to the asset allocation paradigm.

The idea of asset dedication is not revolutionary. It is better described as evolutionary because it is based on the concept of *dedicated portfolios*, a device that is commonly used by corporations and institutions as a financial management tool, generating precisely timed cash flows out of large portfolios involving millions or hundreds of millions of dollars. The difference is that modern technology now makes it feasible for small, personal investors to use the same methods. This is especially important for retirees, who face the same problem of generating cash flows from their portfolios. They had no way to get access to this high-end approach—until now.

By focusing on long-term performance, asset dedication takes advantage of the unique investment characteristics of stocks and bonds. Each has its own fundamentally different purpose. Historically, stocks have been proven to outperform other assets for long-term growth. Bonds, on the other hand, pay a predictable income stream and return of principal, but sacrifice long-term growth. In asset dedication, stocks and bonds are utilized to do what each of them does best in the precise quantities needed for an investor's specific situation—no more, no less. The investment portfolio flows directly from the investor's needs rather than fitting the investor into a prefabricated, arbitrary investment plan.

It has been suggested that many brokers will not like asset dedication because it cuts out excessive transactions that generate commissions. Asset dedication offers the possibility of a "set it and forget it" portfolio that generates predictable income over a chosen time horizon with no active management required. Hopefully, this will encourage a new, low-cost form of financial management, following the footsteps and philosophy of discount brokers and index funds.

In addition, asset dedication provides the best opportunity for long-term growth, nullifying the turbulence and risks of short-term market movements. With a single stroke, individual investors who prefer the do-it-yourself route can set up a portfolio that will run for up to 10 years (or even more in special cases) with no further need for active management unless that is desired. To top it off, this strategy outperforms all portfolios that have up to 70 percent invested in stocks, based on the historical record going back to 1926.

The chapters in this book were designed to be read in sequence, as each one builds on the others. The chapters in Part 1 describe asset allocation and its flaws and demonstrate how asset dedication contrasts with asset allocation. The final chapter (Chapter 4) presents the heart of the evidence in favor of asset dedication, using comparisons over four historical time spans—back to 1990, 1976, 1947, and finally 1926.

Part 2 introduces the idea of the critical path and shows how younger investors who followed it could have avoided the kinds of problems that many investors faced when the market declined in 2000. Tracing the financial projections of a couple from age 56 to age 102, these chapters demonstrate how personal investors can use asset dedication both before and after retirement. It includes step-by-step instructions on how to use the web site that accompanies this book. Finally, Chapter 9 ends Part 2 by describing how asset dedication can be used for lumpy withdrawals, structured settlements in legal cases, charitable foundations, and other situations in which predictability and stability of income are important without sacrificing the opportunity for growth.

Finally, Part 3 is for those who are newer to the world of investing or who somewhere along the line missed some of the fundamentals. It examines some of the theory that underlies personal investing, along with a number of economic, legal, financial, and portfolio management fundamentals. It also covers the good and the bad when it comes to forecasting financial markets, describing some of the problems market timers face and the scams that financial con artists use to take advantage of naïve investors.

Individual investors, institutional investors, professional advisers, money managers—anyone who needs to generate predictable cash flows for him- or herself or others—will benefit from reading this book. As you come to understand asset dedication, you will discover the power of building completely customized portfolios and why asset dedication performs better over the long run. You will see how to apply asset dedication in real-world situations and become a better-informed consumer of financial information.

Most books on personal financial management carry the warning that while the authors and publishers believe that the data from various sources relied upon to reach conclusions were accurate, valid, and reliable, there can be no guarantees in this regard. The same is true for this book, and its conclusions regarding asset dedication. No one should consider financial advice from any book as necessarily the best for their particular situation. Just as each patient must be examined individually before the appropriate medical steps can be taken, each person's financial situation must be considered individually to make certain all the relevant information has been integrated into the recommendations.

A final note: Although the research for this book was done by both Stephen and Brent, most of the text was written by Stephen. Whenever a first-person singular pronoun is used (I, my, mine, and so on), it refers to Stephen.

ACKNOWLEDGMENTS

We would like to thank everyone who helped in the preparation of this book:

Betty, Steve's mother-in-law, who provided the original impetus to find a better way to help people find financial security without sacrificing growth. In fact, our initial name for the research project that led to this book was Grandma's Portfolio. Patti and Kim, our wives, who read (and reread) drafts and provided valuable suggestions based on their own professional training (Patti O'Healy Huxley is a CFP, and Kimberly Burns is an attorney). They also put up with husbands who were grumpy from countless late nights and early mornings. The entire Huxley clan—Ryan (and Kim), Geneve, Jason, Colleen (and Abilio), Kevin (and Michelle), and Conor (and Nicole)—for their support. Ryan deserves special thanks for reviewing first drafts with his incredible engineer's instinct for attention to detail, as does his wife, Kim, also an attorney, who reviewed the book for legal issues at the same time she was carrying their first child, Grace. The Burns boys, Tyler and Kyle, who seemed to know when their Dad needed some peace and quiet and who will one day be able to point out their names here to friends. Robert Burns (no relation), a true friend who developed the web site that supports the book (www.assetdedication.com) while teaching his own computer programming classes at Diablo Valley College, and who is one of those quiet geniuses who just gets the job done. Manual Tarrazo and Rich Puntillo, colleagues who teach finance at USF and reviewed early portions of the manuscript; in addition to providing valuable comments, they also provided invaluable encouragement and support. Larry Wiens and Mark Welch, the first professionals in the financial industry to use asset dedication for clients. Larry especially provided many insights that led to improvements. John Dorfman, former analyst for the *Wall Street Journal* and a true scholar whose clarity of thought, style of presentation, and thoroughly professional attitude were not only helpful but actually inspiring. Ron Judson, Jim Collins, George Coughlin, and Mike Ricinak, friends who are also finance professionals and who provided insightful guidance and suggestions. Christine Dispaltro, the dedicated MBA research assistant who entered reams of data, performed many calculations, and proofread pages of material with unerring accuracy and without a whimper. The staff at McGraw-Hill for their thoroughly professional attitudes and actions, specifically Alice Manning, who copyedited the manuscript in its entirety with an uncanny ability to spot better ways to get ideas across and Kelli Christiansen and Pattie Amoroso, who must be the most responsive and patient editors on the face of the planet.

Finally, our thanks to our many friends, acquaintances, and familiy members who endured our ups and downs (specifically Ann, Rawley, Hank, Steve, Shirley, Jan, Ofelia, Andrew, Jack, Barbara, Russ, Vicki, Pat, and Fred). They may not realize how much their words of support and encouragement helped our resolve to bring the book to completion.

Any errors are entirely the responsibility of the authors.

ASSET
DEDICATION

PART 1

Asset Dedication—
The Next Step
in Asset Allocation

Every single dollar in a portfolio should be where it is for a specific reason. If it has no reason, it should not be there. It should be somewhere else.

New ideas often take a long time to replace old ideas. Max Planck and Albert Einstein, two of the greatest minds that ever blessed the human race, faced similar resistance when they put forth their new theories about how atomic particles behave and how the universe works. Most of the scientific community was suffering from intellectual inertia and scoffed at their ideas. Acceptance often takes several decades to achieve. J. H. Northrop, 1946 Nobel Laureate in Chemistry, in attempting to explain why it takes so long, quoted Max Planck as saying, "Scientists never change their minds, but eventually die."[1]

This book presents a new idea for personal investing that challenges the dominant paradigm, asset allocation. Whether it will face the same sort of resistance as Planck's quantum mechanics or Einstein's relativity theories remains to be seen. The financial industry moves quickly if it sees something that looks like it might be in its best economic interests. However, much of the industry is dependent upon the asset allocation paradigm, and changing its tune may be a slow and arduous process. Asset allocation means different things to different people, and the way it is practiced today is often only remotely related to the way it was originally envisioned.

Many financial planners have taken the extensive training needed to acquire the title of Certified Financial Planner, the premier credential in the industry. But many stockbrokers who work for large mainstream brokerage houses like Morgan Stanley or Merrill Lynch are little more than salespeople, paid to attract customers. Their primary focus is on selling services that make money for themselves and their company. It is not on looking out for the best interests of the people who invest with them. Recent scandals reported in the media suggest that such behavior is rampant in many parts of the financial community. The former chair of the Securities and Exchange Commission is quite blunt about it: "Investors today are being fed lies and distortions, are being exploited and neglected."[2]

The purpose of this book is to introduce a new idea: asset dedication. To some financial theorists, asset dedication is simply the natural next step in the evolution of asset allocation. To others, it appears to be the first step in "post-modern portfolio theory," an entirely new way to handle the common issues faced by individual investors. The vast majority of people are not financial theorists, of course, and are not particularly interested in how asset dedication is perceived to fit into financial theory. They simply want a financial strategy that they can understand and that works. This book will provide the evidence, based on the actual historical record of the stock and bond markets since 1926, that asset dedication is both.

If you start more books than you finish, Part 1 is for you. It summarizes the fundamentals of asset dedication and explains why it appears to be superior to asset allocation. If you already know something about investing, Part 1 may be enough to give you a sufficient understanding of this new investment strategy, and Part 2 will provide more specific details. If you are relatively new to investing, then Parts 1 and 2 will get you started, and you can arm yourself with Part 3, which describes the theories and conventional wisdom that underlie financial markets and the economics of investment.

Before we get started, it needs to be pointed out that personal financial planning has many different elements. This book does not cover them all. For example, it does not cover estate, trust, or tax planning. You can be the best stock or bond picker in the country, but when the IRS gets through with you, it won't matter. Consultants and attorneys who specialize in the highly technical details of these matters need to be involved. Different states have different legal provisions, the laws governing such matters change periodically, and every person's situation must be examined individually. Getting the job done professionally may cost several thousand dollars, but this is cheap compared to the additional taxes, probate fees, internal family conflicts, and so on that are likely to ensue without it.

On the other hand, knowing the legal regulations concerning trusts, wills, charitable giving, IRA accounts, and other such things does not make an attorney or even a financial adviser a superior investment policy strategist. In fact, psychologists have a name for the fallacy of believing that just because a person is good at one thing, that person will also be good at something else. They call it the *halo effect*, and it tends to color our perceptions of the people who give us advice. This book assumes that the legal and tax issues associated with different types of accounts have already been settled. What is needed next is a way to preserve and enhance the performance of the funds in those accounts. That is where asset dedication comes in.

Do not think that this book will lead to quick riches. Books that promise that are usually designed to attract readers who are devoid of discernment. This book describes a strategy that offers a simple way to take advantage of the best things the market has to offer to most individual investors, either by themselves or with the help of ethical, competent advisers. It is a strategy that works. The evidence is here. You be the judge.

NOTES

1. J. H. Northrop, Nobel Laureate, Chemistry, 1946, "There is a complicated hypothesis which usually entails an element of mystery and several unnecessary assumptions. This is opposed by a more simple explanation which contains no unnecessary assumptions. The complicated one is always the popular one at first, but the simpler one, as a rule, eventually is found to be correct. This process frequently requires 10 to 20 years. The reason for this long time lag was explained by Max Planck. He remarked that 'Scientists never change their minds, but eventually die.'" Reported by Dr. Robert Baffi in "Design vs. Darwin: A Scientific Controversy," *The Light Bulb,* Volume II, Issue 1, Summer, 2003 (*www.ideacenter.org*). The Max Planck statement to which Northrop was referring is as follows: ". . . a new scientific truth does not triumph by convincing its opponents and making them see the light, but rather because its opponents eventually die, and a new generation grows up that is familiar with it." From *Scientific Autobiography and Other Papers* by Max Planck (Nobel Laureate, Physics, 1918), translated by F. Gaynor (New York, 1949), pp. 33–34, as reported in *The Structure of Scientific Revolutions* by Thomas S. Kuhn, 2nd Ed. (Chicago: The University of Chicago Press, 1970), p. 151.

2. Quoted from the jacket cover of Arthur Levitt, *Take on the Street* (New York Pantheon, 2002). Levitt was chair of the Securities and Exchange Commission (SEC) from 1993 to 2000.

1

Asset Allocation— the Dominant but Procrustean Paradigm

In Greek mythology, Procrustes was a thief along the road to Athens who offered travelers a magical bed that would fit anyone. He then either stretched his guests or cut off their legs to make them fit the bed.

Asset allocation became the dominant paradigm of investment strategy in the late 1980s. A research paper in a respected academic journal suggested that over 90 percent of the variation in a portfolio's return could be explained by the way the funds were allocated among the three major asset classes: X percent to stocks, Y percent to bonds, and Z percent to cash.[1] This was widely misinterpreted to mean that if you follow an asset allocation strategy, you will capture 90 percent of whatever returns are available. In fact, the misinterpretation spread so quickly and widely that later researchers referred to it as the "universal misunderstanding."[2]

Academic researchers understood the true meaning of the 90 percent, and a number of them tried to set the record straight.[3] But it was too late. The mainstream brokerage community had already headed down the asset allocation path, and asset allocation remains the preeminent model used throughout the investment industry today. In a nutshell, financial advisers classify investors in broad categories (such as "conservative," "moderate," or "aggressive,") and allocate percentages of their assets to the basic asset classes following simple, prefabricated formulas. When clients come into an office, they fill out a questionnaire that is supposed to place them in the right category. An "XYZ" formula for that category is then recommended and, bingo, on to the next client.

Investors are also told to rebalance their portfolio allocations at least annually, using the original formula or some other formula that the company claims is better this year (better for whom—itself or its clients—is sometimes open to question). It is very much a cut and dried, wholesale approach to investment advising. Large brokerage firms were attracted to the idea of asset allocation because it allowed them to control the advice their employees were giving to prospective clients. It ultimately evolved into a very procrustean paradigm.

A new challenger has appeared, however, that may unseat the champ: asset dedication. Based on computer and Internet technology that was not widely available until the 1990s, asset dedication looks at the personal investor's problem from a different angle. The name and principles of asset dedication grew out of the same concept of dedicated portfolios that institutions have been using for years to match the flow of cash coming in with the flow of cash going out.[4]

Asset dedication applies the same idea to each investor's individual situation. It dedicates specific assets to his or her specific goals. By customizing the dedication of assets for each individual, it provides an inherently better fit than the "off-the-rack" approach. Research also demonstrates that it delivers superior returns while simultaneously insulating investors from short-term market declines (see Chapter 4). It may well become the first major shift in investment strategy since the advent of asset allocation.

With asset dedication, allocations are no longer based on fixed, arbitrary formulas, so there is no longer a need to rebalance the portfolio to maintain arbitrary XYZ proportions. The allocation proportions actually change over time in a dynamic fashion that depends on the length of the planning horizon and the target goals. Some people may see asset dedication as a strategic shift in portfolio management theory. Others may see it as a tactical shift in how portfolios are engineered. Still others may see it as filling gaps in asset allocation and simply the next step in its evolution.

Regardless of its perceived niche in the theory of personal finance, the real issues are how asset dedication attacks the problems faced by investors who are seeking to take care of themselves financially and how it differs from asset allocation. To comprehend the differences, however, the approaches of both strategies must be understood. We will start with asset allocation.

THE ROOTS OF ASSET ALLOCATION

Why the Brokers Loved It

We begin with the way asset allocation was originally intended. The theory is easily understood, which probably explains its wide acceptance within the financial community in spite of the questions raised against it (one critic even called it a hoax).[5] Most advisers embrace asset allocation wholeheartedly because they do not have enough technical training to understand the criticism. In fact, if you start a serious conversation with someone in the financial industry, you will generally hear the words "asset allocation" within a minute or two. (If the person you are talking to seems to think that this is the first time you have ever heard the phrase, my advice is to terminate the conversation as politely but as quickly as you can. You are being set up for a sales pitch.)

The current popularity of asset allocation began with a 1986 paper by Brinson, Hood, and Beebower (BHB).[6] They examined the performance of 91 pension fund managers over the 10-year period from 1974 to 1983. The managers were seasoned professionals who were supposed to know how to actively manage portfolios for maximum performance. They were supposed to know which stocks and bonds to select and how to time the market (when to buy low and when to sell high). They earned their living by convincing clients that they were worth their fees because they consistently beat the market as a result of their tinkering. Conventional wisdom at the time agreed with them. Index funds were not yet widely researched.

BHB challenged the conventional wisdom. The researchers compiled what is known as an *attribution study* to see how much of each portfolio's performance could be attributed to active management (timing and selection) and how much could be attributed to the simple percentage allocations to stocks, bonds, and cash over the 10-year period.[7]

The results were bad news for the professional pension managers. The study suggested that their stock selection and timing decisions had actually *hurt* rather than helped the overall performance of their portfolios. If they had simply invested their portfolios in index funds for stocks and bonds (and U.S. Treasury bills for cash) and had not changed their underlying average allocation percentages, their portfolios would have returned an average of 10.1 percent per year. But their active involvement in trying to pick winners and time the market actually *reduced* the return to only 9.0 percent. In other words, their active management *lost* an average of 1.1 percent per year! The numbers would have been even worse if the fees the managers charged had been included. The difference between 9.0 and 10.1 percent per year may seem small, but because of the power of compounding, the difference over time can become significant. For example, assume that Mr. and Ms. Brown (whom we will meet later) were 10 years from retirement and had already accumulated a nest egg of $275,000 in their 401(k) retirement fund. At 10.1 percent, this would grow to $719,790 by the time they retired, but at 9.0 percent, it would grow only to $651,025, a deficit of $68,765. If this difference does not seem like a significant amount of money to you, you are probably in a different league from most people who read (or wrote) this book.[8]

BHB concluded that what mattered most was the managers' basic allocation decisions. When BHB correlated actual quarterly returns with the returns that would be generated from passively investing in generic index funds, they found that, on average, 94 percent of the variation in quarterly returns could be explained by the allocations alone. The impact of the managers' selection and timing decisions was trivial by comparison, contributing only the remaining 6 percent.[9] Later work by the same authors with data covering 1977 to 1987 and additional research by other academics reached the same conclusion.[10]

The fact that portfolio returns were strongly correlated with stock returns is not too surprising from a statistical standpoint. Stocks are much more volatile than either bonds or cash. That means that stocks are the component that introduces most of the variability into any portfolio, whether they represent a large or a small portion of the overall value. It therefore makes intuitive sense that movements in the quarterly returns of any portfolio will closely follow the quarterly returns of a stock index, unless the particular stocks selected are totally out of synch with the market.

Nevertheless, BHB startled the investment community. Most people had thought that actively managed portfolios were superior. But now it appeared that active management of portfolios was a waste of money. The research was interpreted to mean that it was much better to follow an asset allocation formula and leave the portfolio alone than to tinker with it. Theoretically, there was no need for active professional managers once the allocation decision had been made. All that was needed was an XYZ formula, where X was the recommended percentage to put into stocks, Y the percentage to put into bonds, and Z the percentage to put into cash.[11] This became the foundation underlying the theory of asset allocation, which was touted as a whole new approach to investing.

With the BHB study behind them, the major brokerage houses swung into action. They quickly mobilized to make asset allocation the cornerstone of their investment recommendations. They began to publish their own XYZ formulas. Soon the single formula gave way to a family of formulas, each one designed for a different investor category. All their brokers had to do was administer a "scientific" questionnaire to diagnose what type of investor the client was and prescribe the standard formula. Enter Procrustes.

It is easy to see why the financial community seized on the results of the BHB research to justify the XYZ fixed-formula approach to investing. Here was evidence that any attempt to select the right stocks or the right time to buy and sell them was futile or even damaging to their clients. In fact, once the basic asset allocation decision was made, other aspects of active management did not matter much. Branch office brokers could be turned into selling machines, focusing their attention on getting more customers, while the big decisions on investments were made at headquarters.

So the crux of financial advising became asset allocation recommendations. The central office would devise "official" policy recommendations on the percentages for X, Y, and Z, and all the representatives would follow these simple formulas when dealing with clients. From an administrative standpoint, it was a dream come true: The head office would have an easier time managing its far-flung advisers and less fear of rogue advisers generating terrible investment advice and creating potential fiduciary liabilities for the company. It was the perfect cookie-cutter approach that large corporations love.

BASING ALLOCATIONS ON HISTORICAL AVERAGE RETURNS

A Fact No One Disputes: Stocks Yield Higher Returns

The research departments at the head offices claimed to base their allocation formulas on historical average returns such as those shown in Table 1.1. Six types of financial securities are listed, along with their long-term total returns over various spans:[12]

Table 1.1

Annualized Returns for Basic Asset Classes

Asset Class	Source	Details	Approximate Maturity	Average Annualized Returns		
				1926–2002	1947–2002	1976–2002
1. Small cap	The Center for Research in Security Prices (CRSP File), U. of Chicago (*See Note 1*)	Approximately the smallest 20 percent of publicly traded companies	—	12.1%	12.3%	14.8%
2. Large cap	Same as above	S&P 500—Approximately the largest 500 publicly traded companies	—	10.1%	11.8%	12.7%
3. U.S. Treasury bills	Same as above	Includes only "normal" U.S. Treasury bills (excludes callable, nonnegotiable, etc.)	30 days	3.8%	4.8%	6.5%
4. Intermediate-term government bonds	The Center for Research in Security Prices (CRSP File), U. of Chicago and Global Financial Data, Inc. (*See Notes 1, 2*)	Includes only "normal" U.S. Treasury bonds (excludes callable, nonnegotiable, etc.)	5 years	5.5%	6.2%	9.1%
5. Long-term government bonds	Same as above	Includes only "normal" U.S. Treasury bonds (excludes callable, nonnegotiable, etc.)	20 years	5.2%	5.8%	9.9%
6. LT corporate bonds	Global Financial Data, Inc. (*See Note 2*)	Includes only "normal" corporate bonds (excludes callable, nonnegotiable, etc.)	17.5 years	6.8%	7.2%	10.8%

Sources:

1. © June 2004, CRSP® Center for Research in Security Prices, Graduate School of Business, The University of Chicago; used with permission. All rights reserved. www.crsp.uchicago.edu. Data provided as follows:

    Asset Class 1. 1925-2002, CRSP Cap-based 9-10 File,

    Asset Class 2. 1925-2002, CRSP S&P 500 Value-weighted Index File

    Asset Class 3. 1925-2002, CRSP 30 Day T-Bill Index File

    Asset Class 4. 1942-2002, CRSP 5-Year Treasury Bond File (see Note 2)

    Asset Class 5. 1942-2002, CRSP 20-Year Treasury Bond File (see Note 2)

2. © June 2004, Global Financial Data, Inc. (www.globalfindata.com)

    Asset Class 4. 1926–41, 5-Year U.S. Treasuries (TRUSAG5M File)

    Asset Class 5. 1926–41, Estimated from regression analysis of CRSP 20-Year Treasury Bond data and GFD 10-Year U.S. Treasury Bond data (TRUSAGVM File)

    Asset Class 6. 1926–2003 Dow Jones Corporate Bond Total Return Index (_DJCBTM File)

11

1. Small-company stocks (as measured by a large sample of the smallest 20 percent of publicly traded companies)[13]
2. Large-company stocks (as measured by Standard & Poor's Index of 500 large company stocks, known as the S&P 500)
3. Treasury bills (as measured by 30-day U.S. Treasury bills, considered to be closest to the rate usually paid on cash held in money market funds.)
4. Intermediate-term government bonds (as measured by U.S. Treasury bonds with 5-year maturities)[14]
5. Long-term government bonds (as measured by U.S. Treasury bonds with 20-year maturities)
6. Corporate bonds (as measured by the Dow Jones Corporate Bond Index of 96 bonds with varying maturities averaging 17.5 years)[15]

A quick glance at these figures makes it clear that on average, stocks have provided higher returns than either bonds or cash. Figure 1.1, which plots the returns as they accumulate over time, makes this even more evident. The top two lines,

Figure 1.1

Stocks versus Bonds versus Cash, Linear Scale, 1926–2002

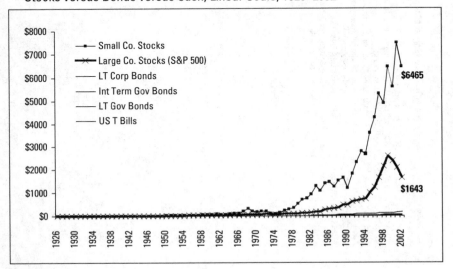

Source: Table 1.1.

Figure 1.2

Stocks versus Bonds versus Cash, Logarithmic Scale, 1926–2002

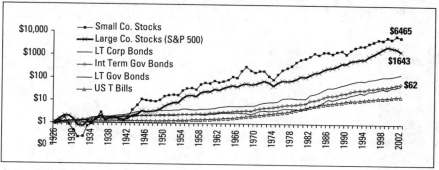

Source: Table 1.1

small-co. stocks and large-co. stocks (S&P 500), show significant growth (12.1 percent and 10.1 percent respectively). But you cannot see the bond and cash plots because they rise only microscopically from the bottom of the chart. To make them visible, Figure 1.2 uses a logarithmic scale that distorts the true relationship between stocks and bonds, but allows the bond returns to be visible.

Figure 1.3 demonstrates just how much better stocks are than bonds at making money grow. It plots only large-company stocks and intermediate-term government bonds on a linear scale and shows the ending value in 2002 of $1 invested in 1926. The return on stocks was nearly double the return on bonds (10.1 versus 5.5 percent per year).[16] The difference this makes over 77 years is dramatic. A dollar invested in large-company stocks would have grown to $1643 (or $6465 for small-company stocks). A dollar invested in bonds would have grown to only $62. Both of these end figures include the major decline that began in early 2000.[17]

From the brokers' perspective, these simple observations made their recommendations easy. Investors who were looking for faster growth through higher returns (i.e., "aggressive" investors) should put more of their money into stocks and less into bonds. The charts for the postwar era and even going back to pre-Depression times were crystal clear. The historical record was unassailable on this point: Stocks produce higher returns in the long run.

Figure 1.3

Large-Company Stocks (S&P 500) versus Intermediate Government Bonds, Linear Scale, 1926–2002

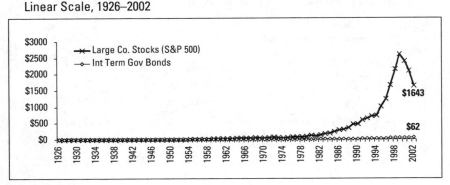

Source: Table 1.1.

WHY NOT 100 PERCENT STOCKS?

Volatility—The Dark Side of Higher Returns

The question is, if stocks offer so much better returns, why should anyone invest anything in bonds? Why not put 100 percent into stocks and forget about bonds?

The standard reply is volatility. You can begin to see the bumpiness in stocks in Figure 1.2. Stock returns fluctuate much more widely than bond returns, especially over the short run. The actual year-to-year returns are shown in Figure 1.4, and they follow a random, almost violent up and down pattern. Bond returns, by comparison, are much steadier. Some fluctuations are still present from the before-maturity changes in the value of bonds, but the magnitude is far less than with stocks.[18]

These observations again made the brokers' recommendations easy. Any investor who wished to avoid volatility and the associated risk ("conservative investors") should put more in bonds and less in stocks. Again, the charts and the historical record supported this without question.

There is a flaw in the volatility argument, however. Volatility by itself does no harm. It becomes harmful only when it creates risk, which is the product of three factors. The first factor is, indeed, variations in the value of the portfolio resulting from fluctuations in stock prices (bonds are also guilty, but much less so than

Figure 1.4

One-Year Returns, Large-Company Stocks (S&P 500) versus
Intermediate Government Bonds, 1926–2002

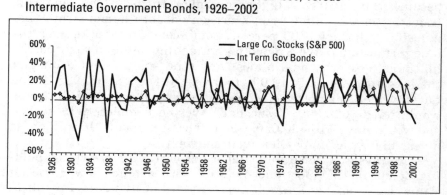

Source: Table 1.1.

stocks). The second factor, however, has nothing to do with the market. It is the probability that funds will have to be withdrawn from
the portfolio for some reason (for an emergency, a regular withdrawal, or whatever). The third factor is probability that the stocks
have to be sold at just the wrong time, when the market is down
(whatever "down" means). If all three of the factors line up against
the investor often enough, it could gradually consume the capital
in the portfolio. This is a legitimate fear of someone who has highly
probable or definite cash flow needs that must be met by the portfolio. But volatility is only one of the three critical ingredients and
by itself is not harmful.

For example, someone who is saving money for retirement by
depositing funds in a retirement account such as a 401(k) or a similar plan has a very low probability of needing to withdraw funds
from this account. This means that there is very little risk associated with the fluctuations in a retirement account during most of a
person's life. There is, therefore, little reason to include bonds in
a preretirement portfolio. An argument could be made that someone who is within 5 years or so of retirement should consider bonds
to avoid the fear of a significant decline, but prior to that time, 100
percent in stocks is a winning strategy. The research presented in
Chapter 4 will verify what the charts make obvious: At the end of
the day, it is better to get a higher return than to worry about
volatility unless you are withdrawing funds.

In fact, a number of academic researchers have pointed out that fluctuations are actually the long-term investor's friend because they generate higher overall returns in the long run. Indeed, the table and figures presented here demonstrate that investors who held 100 percent small-company stocks over the long term would have a much higher ending value in their portfolio than those who held almost any other investment. Consider the investor who had $10,000 to invest at the end of 1925. If she had invested completely in bonds, then by the end of 2002, she would have $620,000; if she had invested completely in stocks, she would have $16,430,000. The difference, about $16 million, is a very high price to pay for avoiding volatility.

An investor who dilutes his or her portfolio's growth by holding bonds in that portfolio ends up with a much lower ending value. He or she suffers a lower standard of living as a result of needlessly avoiding fluctuations that are irrelevant and harmless. Such people will have lost far more money from the lower return than they would have lost if they had taken other steps (insurance, loans, or whatever) to cover themselves.

Yet most financial advisers blindly and slavishly advise their clients to follow the asset allocation formulas put out by their managers and supervisors. In the long run, their clients end up worse off. They may have suffered less volatility, but was it worth it? It is a little like advising drivers to carry around 10 spare tires just in case they have 10 flat tires on a trip. Would it be worth it?

To summarize, the theory of asset allocation suggests that the proportion of money invested in various asset classes explains a large part of why portfolios move the way they do. Primarily for this reason, most financial advisers recommend that their clients follow an asset allocation plan based on an XYZ formula. For investors who fear the risks of short-term volatility more than they fear long-term loss, the generic recommendation is to put more in bonds and less in stocks. For aggressive investors who can better tolerate volatility, the reverse is recommended: Put more into stocks and less into bonds. The financial community embraced asset allocation because it promised significant advantages that were especially compelling in the adviser/client interface:

1.   It was easy to understand (on the surface).
2.   It promoted uniformity in recommendations.

3. It appeared to explain 90 percent of the variability in returns.

4. It was a great sales pitch.

The next chapter explores the down side of asset allocation as an approach to personal investing. For large, multimillion-dollar portfolios (such as pension funds and mutual funds), asset allocation may make sense as a way of dealing with the problems faced by their managers. But the rest of this book challenges its efficacy for the investment issues faced by individual investors who are not concerned with managing millions of dollars. They simply want guidance to avoid major blunders in managing their retirement funds so that they can live normal lives free of financial fear. Asset dedication will provide that guidance.

NOTES

1. Gary P. Brinson, L. Rudolph Hood, and Gilbert L. Beebower, "Determinants of Portfolio Performance," *Financial Analysts Journal*, July-August 1986, pp. 39–44.
2. Ibbotson Associates, *SBBI 2003 Yearbook: Market Results for 1926-2002: Stocks, Bonds, Bills, and Inflation (Stocks, Bonds, Bills and Inflation Yearbook, 2003)*, p. 116.
3. Roger G. Ibbotson and Paul D. Kaplan, "Does Asset Allocation Policy Explain 40, 90, or 100 Percent of Performance?" *Financial Analysts Journal*, January-February 2000, p. 26.
4. William F. Sharpe, Gordon J. Alexander, and Jeffery V. Baily, *Investments*, 5th ed. (Englewood Cliffs, N.J.: Prentice-Hall, 1995), p. 478.
5. William W. Jahnke, "The Asset Allocation Hoax," *Journal of Financial Planning*, February 1997, pp. 109–113.
6. Brinson, Hood, and Beebower, "Determinants of Portfolio Performance."
7. The generic term for stocks is equities and that for bonds is fixed-income securities. Cash means any liquid investment, such as a money market account, a savings account, Treasury bills, or any equivalent security that can be quickly converted into cash.
8. This is why financial advisers tend to focus on annual rates of return. Minor differences in rates can make major differences in dollar amounts over time.
9. The statistical tool used was regression analysis, and the 94 percent comes from the measure known as R Squared. It is beyond the scope of this book to go into the statistical merits and caveats regarding the Brinson study. Interested readers are referred to the papers in the next note.
10. Gary P. Brinson, Brian D. Singer, and Gilbert L. Beebower, "Determinants of Portfolio Performance II: An Update," *Financial Analysts Journal*, May-June 1991, pp. 40–48. Many other articles have been written comparing the absolute or relative performance of mutual funds to index funds or to each other, but a sampling would include the following: (1) E. J. Elton, M. J. Gruber, and C. R. Blake, "The Persistence of Risk-Adjusted Mutual Fund Performance," *Journal of Business* 69,

April 1996, pp. 133–157. (2) W. N. Goetzmann and R. G. Ibbotson, "Do Winners Repeat? Patterns in Mutual Fund Return Behavior," *The Journal of Portfolio Management* 20, Winter 1994, pp. 9–18. (3) M. Grinblatt and S. Titman, "The Persistence of Mutual Fund Performance," *Journal of Finance* 47, December 1992, pp. 1977–1984. (4) M. J. Gruber, "Another Puzzle: The Growth in Actively Managed Mutual Funds," *Journal of Finance* 51, July 1996, pp. 783–810. (5) D. Hendricks, J. Patel, and R. Zeckhauser, "Hot Hands in Mutual Funds: Short Run Persistence of Relative Performance, 1974–1988," *Journal of Finance* 48, March 1993, pp. 93–130. (6) R. D. Henriksson, "Market Timing and Mutual Fund Performance: An Empirical Investigation," *Journal of Business* 57, January 1984, pp. 73–96. (7) M. C. Jensen, "The Performance of Mutual Funds in the Period 1945–1964," *Journal of Finance* 23, May 1968, pp. 389–416. (8) Jeffrey M. Laderman, "The Stampede to Index Funds," *BusinessWeek*, Apr. 11, 1996, pp. 78–79. (9) B. G. Malkiel, "Returns from Investing in Equity Mutual Funds 1971 to 1991," *Journal of Finance* 50, June 1995, pp. 549–572. (10) W. F. Sharpe, "Mutual Fund Performance," *Journal of Business* 39, January 1966, pp. 119–138. (11) Marlene G. Star, "Active Investing vs. Indexing: The Bogles Disagree," *Pensions and Investments,* Feb. 19, 1996, p. 3. (12) R. A. Strong, *Practical Investment Management* (Cincinnati, Ohio: South Western College Publishing, 1998), p. 432. (13) Vanguard Corporation, *Vanguard Index Trust: A Broad Selection of U.S. Stock Index Funds* (Valley Forge, Pa.: Vanguard Marketing Corporation, 1998). (14) E. T. Veit and J. M. Cheney, "Are Mutual Funds Market Timers?" *The Journal of Portfolio Management* 8, Winter 1982, pp. 35–42. (15) D. A. Volkman and M. E. Wohar, "Abnormal Profits and Relative Strength in Mutual Fund Returns," *Review of Financial Economics* 5, January 1996, pp. 101–116.

11. The percentage allocated to cash, by the way, usually plays a minor role in the decision-making process. This is due to the fact that cash traditionally offers a very low return. It tends to be used primarily for emergencies or as a temporary parking place for stock or bond money (or, as some cynics suggest, a convenient source for paying adviser's fees). The real decision point is the split between stocks and bonds.

12. The terms *small cap, large cap,* and so on have technical definitions that will be discussed in Chapter 11, but the intuitive interpretations are correct. "Cap" stands for capitalization. Small cap companies are those with annual sales of less than $1 billion, whereas large cap companies have over $10 billion. The terms *small-cap, small-company, large-cap,* and *large-company* will be used interchangeably.

13. The Center for Research in Security Prices (CRSP®) is one of the premier providers of high quality data for research. Statistics on the performance of small cap stocks are compiled by Dimensional Fund Associates. Its principals include Eugene Fama and Kenneth French, who wrote the original papers that led to the classification scheme for public companies, such as small-cap growth, small-cap value, mid-cap growth, mid-cap value, and so on (http://www.dfaus.com/).

14. ©June 2004, CRSP® Center for Research in Security Prices, Graduate School of Business, The University of Chicago; used with permission. All rights reserved. www.crsp.uchicago.edu. Data provided as follows:

    Asset Class 1: 1925-2002, CRSP Cap-based 9-10
    Asset Class 2: 1925-2002, CRSP S&P 500 Value-weighted Index
    Asset Class 3: 1925-2002, CRSP 30-day T-Bill Index
    Asset Class 4: 1942-2002, CRSP 5-year Treasury bond (see Note 2)
    Asset Class 5: 1942-2002, CRSP 20-year Treasury bond (see Note 2)

15. © June 2004, Global Financial Data, Inc., Los Angeles, CA 90042 USA. All rights reserved. www.globalfindata.com. Data provided as follows:
    Asset Class 4: 1926-1941, 5-year U.S. Treasuries (TRUSAG5M File)
    Asset Class 5: 1926-1941, estimated from regression analysis of CRSP 20-year Treasury bond data and GFD 10-year U.S. Treasury bond data (TRUSAGVM File)
    Asset Class 6: 1926-2002, Dow Jones Corporate Bond Total Return Index (DJCBTM File)
16. Many times people do not really know where their portfolio ought to be at each point in time if it is to have a particular growth rate. Chapter 4 will introduce the critical path concept, which shows what a portfolio should be worth at each point if it is to reach a specified target. Chapter 5 will explain the critical path in detail.
17. These figures are slightly off because of rounding errors. Also, inflation would reduce these figures by a significant amount but would not change the relative position. As prices rise, the ending value of the portfolio has to be discounted by whatever amount prices have increased. Between 1926 and 2002, inflation averaged 3.0 percent per year. So items that cost $1 in 1926 would have risen to $10.09 in 2002. This means that the stocks' ending value of $1643 is worth only $163 in real purchasing power ($1643/10.09 = $162.83), and the bonds' $62 is worth only $6 ($62/10.09 = $6.14). These are a better reflection of the true value of each portfolio and illustrate that both stocks and bonds beat inflation, but stocks do so by a far greater margin.
18. Forecasting these year-to-year fluctuations is a challenge to statisticians and economists who are trying to provide accurate projections. Day-to-day fluctuations are even more violent in relative terms. Much of a year's total gain is typically achieved in just a few trading days, with bland returns the rest of the year. This "biggest days" impact drives forecasters to the brink of insanity. No one can forecast them (see Chapter 14).

CHAPTER 2

Asset Allocation: The Gaps

To treat your facts with imagination is one thing, to imagine your facts is another.

—JOHN BURROUGHS

Asset allocation is not without its critics. As pointed out in Chapter 1, a number of researchers have challenged the methodology and conclusions of the original paper published by Brinson, Hood, and Beebower (BHB). It remains a topic of debate among financial theorists. More damaging, however, is the way in which asset allocation has been applied in the real world by people who should know better.

THE EMPEROR'S NEW CLOTHES

The Worst-Kept Secret: The XYZ Formulas Are Arbitrary; Brinson's Clarification

One obvious problem in asset allocation is the XYZ formula itself: X = ? Y = ? Z = ? That is, what should the values of X, Y, and Z be? To simply say that aggressive investors should invest more in stocks and conservative investors should invest less is not really very specific. How much more? How much less?

The original paper never dealt with the problem of finding the specific XYZ formula for any particular investor. Neither BHB nor anyone else could predict the ideal percentages for stocks, bonds, and cash. All formulas were arbitrary. Broker A might recommend an 80/20 split between stocks and bonds for an aggressive investor, whereas Broker B might recommend a 60/40 split for the same investor. Which was best? Since 1986, theorists and practitioners alike have been searching for a scientific way to determine the optimal values for X, Y, and Z for any given case. To date, that search has proved fruitless. Everybody has opinions, but nobody really knows how to mathematically derive the best X, Y, or Z.

In the finest tradition of herd mentality, however, the financial community ignored this major theoretical gap in its stampede to asset allocation. Asset allocation quickly became the dominant paradigm. To his credit, Brinson himself pointed out the problem. He wrote directly regarding the gap:

> *This analysis made no effort to judge the merits of various policies, but rather focused on the importance of policy versus active management decisions irrespective of the specific policies.*[1]

It is important to understand why he felt compelled to point this out: Determining the best values for the XYZ formula is precisely the problem that investors and their advisers face. Formulating an asset allocation plan without a way to determine the correct XYZ values is like building a house without blueprints, cooking without a recipe, or driving without a steering wheel. The key component is missing!

BHB simply showed what would have happened if the money managers had followed a passive XYZ allocation policy based on their average allocation decisions over a 10-year period. That is, BHB calculated the overall average (mean)[2] percentage invested in stocks after the fact ("ex post"): what percentage, X, each broker had put into the stock market on average over the 1974 to 1983 period. BHB then did the same for bonds and cash. BHB then applied the average percentages to stock, bond, and cash indexes and compared the resulting returns to what actually happened. The pension fund managers had tried to beat the market by the selection and timing of particular stocks, but what happened was that the market beat them. The brokers with higher allocations in stocks did better in terms of long-term return, but that was nothing new. Everyone already knew that stocks outperformed bonds or cash.

THE PSEUDOSCIENCE OF RISK-TOLERANCE QUESTIONNAIRES

Try Explaining "Risk Tolerance" to Your Mother

It gets worse. Not only is there no science to back up specific values for the XYZ formulas, but there is little agreement within the industry. Investors with higher risk tolerance should put more in stocks—that is about as far as the consensus goes. Anyone who interviewed several brokers would probably find them all sounding very much alike. In the standard recipe, you are asked to fill out a questionnaire "to determine your goals and your risk tolerance." Your responses determine which category you fall into, conservative or aggressive or somewhere in between. You are then sold the particular model portfolio (or XYZ formula) that the head office claims is best for your category of investor. The portfolio you are sold is not really based on your own specific, individual goals. The situation is actually the reverse: You are shoehorned into a category and then told that this is the best portfolio for that category. It is equivalent to buying a pair of shoes from a store that has limited sizes: The salesperson is selling you the products they have on the shelves. There is no real customization—the salesperson will simply squeeze you into whatever the store has. When you think about it, most people do not buy shoes based on how nice the shoe salesperson is, but they often choose a portfolio based on how nice the financial adviser is and buy whatever he or she says is the best fit.

If you have ever filled out one of the risk-tolerance questionnaires used by brokers, you probably had a hard time providing realistic responses to the questions. Most people want maximum return with minimum risk. That is about as deep as their understanding goes. Giving responses to questions when respondents do not really comprehend the significance of their answers leads to what statisticians call *response bias*. The answers cannot be trusted as a true indicator of the person's feelings, attitudes, or needs because the person does not understand the true consequences of the answers. He or she is being forced to give a response to a hypothetical situation, and the response may not really reflect how he or she would feel if this situation actually happened. The dissatisfaction and anger that people felt toward their brokers during the market decline that began in the year 2000 testifies to the fact that they really did not know what "risk tolerance" meant when they filled out those questionnaires. Planning a person's financial future based on uninformed answers is a dubious practice, to say the least.

The basic XYZ formula becomes even more complicated when other asset classes are considered. Brokers enjoy tossing around terms like "small-cap growth" or "mid-cap value" or "domestic versus international." But regardless of the number of asset classes considered, the core idea of asset allocation remains the same. Brokers have replaced individual stock selection with asset class selection. They sometimes hint that they utilize very sophisticated analytical tools that give them prescient powers to forecast the market. They imply that by looking at the money supply or the deficit or some other esoteric macroeconomic variable, they can discern the future. They seldom have any hard numbers to back up these claims, but they are well armed with lots of excuses later on. A few fund managers can point to a string of past successes. With thousands of coin flippers, however, some are bound to be lucky enough to get ten heads in a row.[3]

What is misleading is the implication, direct or indirect, that this whole procedure is scientific and objective. If it were truly scientific, then presumably you would get the same prescription for the same XYZ formula no matter who did the analysis. It would be like visiting optometrists, who rely on real science. You get the same prescription for eyeglasses no matter which optometrist you visit. But if you visit several brokers, you are likely to get different formulas, leading to different allocations and, consequently, different results.

The disparity among brokers on the best allocation again points up the same unpleasant fact: No one really knows the ideal XYZ values for any given situation. There are only so many ways you can slice up 100 percent and make any real difference.[4] The truth is, most people pick their financial advisers the same way they pick their friends: on the basis of friendliness, trustworthiness, conscientiousness, availability, location, and so on. Competence, unfortunately, does not often play a major role. Years later, when the consequences of poor planning come home to roost, it may be too late to recover. But that will not be the broker's problem. It will be your problem.

ACTIVE VERSUS PASSIVE MANAGEMENT: HAVE BROKERS LEARNED?

The Abysmal Record of Brokers' Recommendations in the 1990s

As indicated earlier, the primary research that popularized asset allocation concluded that stock selection and market timing—the hallmarks of active management—lead to worse performance than passive index investing over the long run. The evidence was quite clear on this point.

One would think, therefore, that after the implications of the Brinson, Hood, and Beebower 1986 study were realized, analysts and decision makers in the major brokerage houses would have learned not to make the same mistakes the pension fund managers did. They would have learned not to toy with their policies. But subsequent research suggests that they did not learn that lesson. Even with the presumed superiority of asset allocation, brokers still attempt to actively manage portfolios and still continue to do poorly compared to passive management. Any mutual fund that is not an index fund is probably actively managed, and if you own it, you are paying extra fees for this active management (you can check how much you are paying on the Internet at www.personalfund.com).[5]

When you see their advertisements on TV, the brokers sound very wise and savvy. Just give them your money, they say, and they will invest it to help you achieve your goals, to get maximum return with minimum risk, to produce optimal results and make all your financial dreams come true—the yada, yada, yada goes on and on. They are, after all, in business to make a profit, and they know the honeyed words that investors want to hear. In other words, they know how to market the stuff they sell.

What does the record show about how well their predictions and prognostications performed? A study of major brokers' performance from 1988 to 2000 is very revealing, and the results are not pretty.

All major brokerage houses have research departments that feed information to "investment policy committees." These committees consist of highly paid money managers who make asset allocation recommendations based on the company's research and their own expertise. Once these recommendations are set, brokers down the line are expected to follow them when providing portfolio advice to their customers. The individual brokers are not paid to think or analyze for themselves—they are paid to find customers and sell the product.

The investment policy committee usually issues its recommended allocations for each type of investor at least once every quarter, and these recommendations often change from one quarter to the next. The committee may recommend 60 percent in stocks for the coming quarter, then 70 percent 3 months later because it believes the market is heading up.

What this means, of course, is that these committees persist in trying to time the market—exactly what BHB showed to be harmful! They may even recommend different funds or stocks each quarter, meaning that they are trying to select specific stocks, also contrary to the research conclusion. But once they publish their recommendations, those recommendations become a matter of public record. Anyone who has patience and tenacity can keep score.

John Dorfman had that patience and tenacity. As senior special writer for the *Wall Street Journal* from 1986 to 1997, Dorfman initiated an asset allocation survey to track the quarterly performance of a sample of mainstream brokerage house recommendations shortly after the asset allocation juggernaut arrived.[6] He reported each broker's asset allocation recommendations for the coming quarter and its results for the previous quarter, year, and 5 years. The recommendations reported were the percentage allocations for stocks, bonds, and cash, the classic XYZ fixed-formula approach. Dorfman rebalanced the portfolios based on the latest recommendations. He footnoted any other assets that were recommended, but the big three in XYZ accounted for the vast majority of cases. The newspaper had all calculations performed by independent research agencies, Wilshire Associates and Carpenter Analytics. It published the articles faithfully every 3 months over a period of 12 years. It was very solid work.

Table 2.1 lists the average allocation recommendations by the brokers that had the longest track records during the span, along with the maximum and minimum allocations.[7] Most tended to stay below 70 percent in stocks, above 20 percent in bonds, and close to 10 percent in cash. Only the last 10 years are shown (40 quarters, beginning with the third quarter of 1990) because the list of brokers in the study changed early in the series as a result of mergers and additions.

Dorfman provided one additional piece of crucial information: He reported the gain or loss in each of the asset classes to serve as a benchmark. With perfect foresight, the best investment over the past quarter would have been whichever asset class had the highest return. If stocks were the best, put 100 percent in stocks; if bonds were the best, put 100 percent in bonds; if cash was the best, put 100 percent in cash. With these additional data, it becomes easy to judge each broker's performance with 20/20 hindsight. In theory, if the asset allocation approach was the ultimate investment panacea, and if the brokers were as wise and prescient as they would like their prospective clients to believe, their results should be pretty close to perfection.

Table 2.1

Asset Allocation Recommendations by Brokerage Houses Tracked by the *Wall Street Journal*, 1990–2000

	Mean Stocks	Mean Bonds	Mean Cash	Max Stocks	Min Stocks	Max Bonds	Min Bonds	Max Cash	Min Cash
Morgan Stanley D.W.	62%	28%	10%	85%	45%	50%	15%	25%	0%
Goldman Sachs	67%	27%	6%	84%	35%	55%	15%	11%	0%
Lehman Brothers	65%	29%	6%	80%	40%	40%	0%	30%	0%
Prudential Securities	67%	22%	11%	87%	40%	55%	0%	40%	0%
PaineWebber	59%	33%	8%	77%	48%	47%	17%	17%	0%
Salomon Smith Barney	53%	36%	11%	60%	45%	45%	25%	25%	0%
A.G. Edwards	54%	36%	10%	70%	40%	45%	25%	25%	0%
Merrill Lynch	49%	42%	9%	65%	40%	58%	25%	20%	0%
Raymond James	63%	20%	17%	75%	45%	33%	12%	40%	5%
Mean	60%	30%	10%	76%	42%	48%	15%	26%	1%
Max	67%	42%	17%	87%	48%	58%	25%	40%	5%
Min	49%	20%	6%	60%	35%	33%	0%	11%	0%
Robot Blend	55%	35%	10%	55%	55%	35%	35%	10%	10%

Source: John Dorfman, "Your Money Matters," (data from a series of articles published in the *Wall Street Journal* beginning in 1988). *Wall Street Journal*, Western Edition [Staff Produced Copy Only], by Dorfman, John. Copyright 1988 by DOW JONES & CO. INC. Reproduced with permission of DOW JONES & CO. INC.

It turns out that over the 10-year period, perfection would have achieved an average compounded return of 26.7 percent per year. This is based on simply investing in the asset class (index funds for stocks, bonds, or cash) that did the best over the next quarter. So how did the brokers score compared to perfection? Would you guess that they scored 90 percent of the optimal? 80 percent? 70 percent?

Table 2.2 lists the scores. A pure stock portfolio of 100 percent of the S&P 500 beat all the brokers, with a return of 17.9 percent per year or 67 percent of the optimal (Score 1 in Table 2.2). The best any broker did, however, was a return of 14.8 percent, or about 56 percent of the optimal (Lehman Brothers). The worst (Raymond James) provided recommendations that yielded a return of 11.0 percent, or 41 percent of the optimal.[8] Dorfman also included a "Robot Blend" that always used 55 percent stocks, 35 percent bonds, and 10 percent cash. The Robot earned about 13.4 percent, or about 50 percent. Figure 2.1 charts the returns.

By this yardstick, the overall average for the brokers as a group was only about 51 percent, little better than the Robot. All of these returns exclude management fees, transaction costs, taxes, or any other such charges. If they had been included, the results for the brokers would have been even worse.

The brokers did manage to beat 100 percent bonds (7.8 percent) and 100 percent cash (5.0 percent). But that is not much to boast about, especially during the great bull run of the 1990s.

To see how much difference these rates of return mean to an investor, consider someone who had invested $10,000 in 1990 (see Figure 2.2). If this person had received perfect advice over the next 10 years, his investment would have grown to $106,304. If he had invested 100 percent in stocks, he would have ended with $52,065, or 49 percent of the optimal (Score 3 in Table 2.2). If he had followed the advice of the best broker, the portfolio would have grown to $39,775; with the worst, it would have grown to $28,413. These represent only 37 and 27 percent of the optimal, respectively. Overall, the brokers' ending values averaged only $35,854, or about 33.7 percent of the optimal. Such a record does not seem very impressive for those who claim to be the best in the world at managing money.

Perhaps the optimal based on hindsight is an unfair yardstick. No one is prescient. If a portfolio of 100 percent stocks is used, based on the S&P 500, then the brokers look better. Score 2 in Table 2.2 represents each broker's performance compared to 100 percent stocks. Investing a portfolio completely in an S&P 500 index fund may not sound very exciting, but it certainly provided better long-run returns than any of the brokers. Using its return of 17.9 percent

Table 2.2

Comparison of Portfolio Returns and Ending Value of a $10,000 Investment, 1990–2000

Portfolio Design	Total Return	Score 1 = % of Optimal	Score 2 = % of 100% Stocks	$10,000 Initial Invest	Score 3 = % of Optimal	Score 4 = % of 100% Stocks
Optimal	26.7%	100%		$106,304	100%	
100% stocks	17.9%	67%	100%	$52,065	49%	100%
Lehman Brothers	14.8%	56%	83%	$39,775	37%	76%
Goldman Sachs	14.7%	55%	82%	$39,522	37%	76%
Morgan Stanley D.W.	14.5%	54%	81%	$38,608	36%	74%
Prudential Securities	14.2%	53%	79%	$37,749	36%	73%
PaineWebber	14.1%	53%	79%	$37,557	35%	72%
A.G. Edwards	13.7%	51%	77%	$36,204	34%	70%
Robot Blend	13.4%	50%	75%	$35,302	33%	68%
Salomon Smith Barney	13.1%	49%	73%	$34,199	32%	66%
Merrill Lynch	11.9%	44%	66%	$30,663	29%	59%
Raymond James	11.0%	41%	61%	$28,413	27%	55%
100% bonds	7.8%	29%	43%	$21,190	20%	41%
100% cash	5.0%	19%	28%	$16,349	15%	31%
Average—All brokers	13.6%	50.9%	75.6%	$35,854	33.7%	68.9%

Source: John Dorfman, "Your Money Matters," (data from a series of articles published in the *Wall Street Journal* beginning in 1988). *Wall Street Journal*, Western Edition [Staff Produced Copy Only]. By Dorfman, John. Copyright 1988 by DOW JONES & CO. INC. Reproduced with permission of DOW JONES & CO. INC.

Figure 2.1

Average Annual Rates of Return, Optimal versus Broker Allocations,
1990–2000

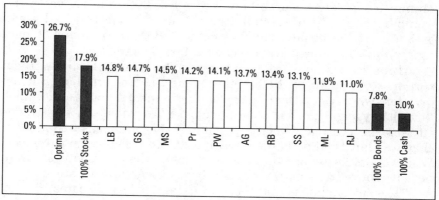

Source: Table 2.2.

Figure 2.2

$10,000 Invested, Optimal versus Broker, 1990 to 2000

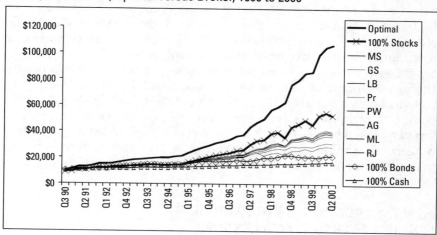

Source: Table 2.2.

as the yardstick, the best, average, and worst brokers were capable of only 83 percent, 75.6 percent, and 61 percent of the return generated by 100 percent stocks (Score 2 in Table 2.2). Score 4 in the final column in Table 2.2 shows how well a $10,000 initial investment would have faired with each portfolio. The best, average, and worst broker portfolios achieved only 76 percent, 68.9 percent, and 55 percent of the 100 percent stocks result after 10 years.

Brokers will no doubt squeal about the lower volatility of their portfolios compared to the optimal or pure stock portfolios. But for investors who lock up their money in a retirement account and cannot touch it anyway, what does volatility matter? We will discuss the trade-off between return and volatility and how they are measured in later chapters, but the fluctuations mean nothing to long-term investors. What counts for them is the ending value of the portfolio when they need it—for retirement, their kids' college expenses, or whatever.

The bottom line is that those who claim to be advocates of asset allocation appear to have missed the primary conclusions of the original BHB research. They continue to try to time the market and pick the best stocks, but they now do it in the context of asset allocation. The problem is compounded by recommendations to rebalance every quarter or every year to match whatever formula they currently recommend. Procrustes must be chuckling in his grave.

Cynics might suggest that it is the brokerage companies' own bottom line that they are most concerned about rather than their clients' bottom line. In fact, Arthur Levitt's book, mentioned earlier, is a stinging commentary on the investment industry.[9] As an insider, Levitt saw abuses and corrupt practices that harmed investors by taking advantage of their ignorance and trust. The pervasiveness of this so appalled his sense of decency that he felt compelled to write the book, and will probably be a marked man in the financial community forever. Most whistle-blowers are. The recent and continuing scandals concerning trading violations by major players and mutual funds in the industry suggest that Levitt and the other cynics are right.[10]

ASSET ALLOCATION IS NOT ALL BAD— IT'S JUST OVERSOLD AND MISUSED

A Few Socially Redeeming Qualities

The basic asset allocation approach does not deserve a blanket condemnation. Asset allocation does have socially redeeming features, and everyone can thank its developers for the following:

1.   It forces investors to think in terms of the big picture for their investments by making them aware of the various types of asset classes that they can use to meet their investment goals.

2.   It explicitly recognizes the differences and trade-offs among the various types of asset classes in terms of risk and return and the inherent volatility of the market.

3.   It promotes diversification of investments, so that the investor's eggs are in different baskets. Diversification is one of the cornerstones of modern portfolio theory.

Likewise, this critique of asset allocation is not intended to suggest that all financial advisers who utilize asset allocation are acting in bad faith. By asking deep questions about a person's life goals, assembling facts and figures, and guiding funds into the right sorts of accounts to take advantage of tax laws, many advisers provide valuable service to their clients. The reason they attempt to fit their client's needs into the formula-based asset allocation model is because it is the only model available from their research departments. There is no other choice. It operates as a conceptual monopoly.

This is the real problem: Asset allocation has been oversold. It commits a "one-size-fits-all" fallacy. Honest, hard-working financial planners, looking for help from their research departments, theoreticians, and academics to deal with the hopes and fears of their clients, have been led to believe that asset allocation is the panacea for all investors. It is treated as if it were the only honest game in town to justify and add value to the services they provide to their clients. Unfortunately, as the old saying goes, when the only tool you have is a hammer, every problem becomes a nail.

In the next chapter, we will look at a new tool, asset dedication. It addresses a number of the gaps in asset allocation. One of its primary advantages is the fact that it truly customizes a portfolio for each person instead of trying to force-fit that person into an arbitrary category.

NOTES

1. Gary P. Brinson, in Robert G. Ibbotson and Gary P. Brinson, *Global Investing: The Professional's Guide to the World Capital Markets* (New York: McGraw-Hill, 1992), p. 58.

2. The arithmetic average that most people know is what statisticians call the *mean* (the number calculated by adding a list of numbers and dividing by how many numbers are on the list). Chapter 12 will cover statistical concepts in greater detail.

3. The tables of probabilities found in any statistical textbook show that the probability of getting 10 heads in 10 flips of a fair coin is .001, or 1 in 1000. With over 10,000 mutual funds, it could be expected that, even if the probability of success in any one year is only 50 percent, there will at any one time be 10 fund managers who can point to successful market calls over the past 10 years.
4. A web site that will calculate the expected returns for 20 different asset allocations ranging from 5 to 100 percent stocks can be found at http://www.ifa.tv.
5. The group that runs www.personalfund.com offers a number of articles and tools on evaluating mutual funds. The recent scandals involving malfeasance on the part of mutual fund managers suggest that these managers' subpar performance may be due to more than simply an inability to forecast the market.
6. Dorfman initiated the project and ran it for 9 years before leaving the *Journal* in 1997. Other journalists continued the articles until 2000, when they disappeared from the paper. Compiling and maintaining the statistics required a significant amount of effort, and perhaps no one else has the perseverance to continue the study. After he left the *Journal*, Dorfman became a money manager and now runs his own investment company (www.dorfmaninvestments.com).
7. The allocations shown are for the 40 quarters from Q3 1990, through Q2 2000. Although the study actually began in 1988, mergers of brokerage companies and missing data prevented a complete tally of all 48 quarters. Estimates from the complete series of 48 quarters are not significantly different from the results shown here.
8. Results for two of the brokers, Goldman Sachs and Raymond James, had to be adjusted slightly because a few data points were missing and had to be estimated by extrapolation or interpolation.
9. Arthur Levitt, *Take on the Street* (New York: Pantheon, 2002). Levitt was chair of the Securities and Exchange Commission (SEC) from 1993 to 2000.
10. Allan Sloan, "Cleaning Up a Dirty Business," *Newsweek,* Oct. 13, 2003, p. 49.

3

Asset Dedication— How It Works

Thinking is like living and dying. You must do it for yourself.

—Anonymous

It is always easy to criticize existing systems and procedures, especially when they are the work of others. Providing a better solution is something else. The last chapter explained asset allocation and the weaknesses of its fixed-formula approach to personal investing. It also explained why asset allocation is so appealing to the mainstream brokerage houses. It offered them a great sales tool, promoted administrative control, and they could ignore its primary message about avoiding active management. If the shortcomings of asset allocation are enough to raise doubts in your mind, the next thought is, what alternative approaches are available? The answer is asset dedication.

THE ASSET DEDICATION APPROACH

Dedicated Portfolios Migrate from the Elite to the Masses

Asset dedication is based on what financial theorists call dedicated portfolios. They are designed for investors who face the "matched-funding" problem. Matched funding means that the portfolio must generate the precise amount of cash that is to be withdrawn each month or each year in order to pay commitments, obligations, and/or expenses. This is not a new or novel problem. As one author put it, "Matched funding is a basically simple (and relatively ancient) concept."[1]

But what makes asset dedication new is its application to personal investors. Pension fund managers, corporate controllers, and treasurers have faced the matched-funding problem for years. It has provided a lucrative market for financial consultants because setting up dedicated portfolios takes a degree of effort and expertise that was difficult to justify for small accounts.

That was before the advent of the desktop computer and the Internet. These new technologies mean that a dedicated portfolio can be constructed quickly and easily by or for anyone who wishes to dedicate his assets to match his personal funding needs. It can be customized for each individual investor rather than forcing an investor to fit into some predefined broad category.

The most obvious example of a personal investor who needs a dedicated portfolio is the retiree. The demographics of the baby boomers suggest that they are likely to be the fastest-growing group of investors in the next 10 years.

Most retirees will probably receive monthly social security checks. They may also receive income from a few other sources (other pensions, part-time work, and so on). And many will withdraw funds from their accumulated savings in 401(k) or other retirement plans. They need a secure and stable source of cash inflows from their portfolios to replace their monthly paychecks and pay their ongoing living expenses. Because most research on constructing dedicated portfolios has focused on large portfolios, such as pension funds where millions of dollars are involved, the advantages and benefits of asset dedication are only now becoming available to the small individual investor.

If retirees follow customary allocation advice, they will probably increase their allocation to bonds by selling stocks. More bonds mean more stability but less return. The critical questions are, of course, how much to put in bonds and how much is too much? The asset allocation approach cannot answer these questions objectively. But asset dedication can.

THE RIGHT ASSETS IN THE RIGHT PLACES FOR THE RIGHT REASONS

Best Uses of Stocks, Bonds, and Cash

Asset dedication answers these questions by attacking the problem from a different perspective. It splits the portfolio into three parts, cash, bonds, and stocks, but dedicates each part to a specific goal. This sounds a lot like asset allocation at first. But the allocation is not based on an arbitrary XYZ fixed-formula approach. Rather, it allocates the precise amount needed to achieve each goal—no more and no less. The rationale for how much to have in each asset class becomes definable and defensible.[2] The goals are made specific as follows.

CASH

The first goal is to dedicate enough cash to handle unexpected and immediate emergencies. Whether this is 3 months', 6 months', or a year's worth of cash, the point is to have enough so that random needs and minor emergencies can be taken care of without interfering with the other parts of the portfolio. Any personal financial strategy should allow for this.

Cash and cash equivalents are money that can be accessed almost immediately, such as checking accounts, savings accounts, and money market accounts. Nearly all financial institutions, including banks, credit unions, and stockbrokers, offer such accounts. Any highly liquid investments count as cash. Most carry the lowest rates of return as investments. The banks and others often invest funds deposited in these accounts in U.S. Treasury bills. Their returns are therefore highly correlated with "T-bill" rates.

Some people prefer to keep cash at an absolute minimum by opening avenues of quick-access credit, such as unused higher credit card limits or a home equity line of credit. Financial planners often discourage such lines of credit because of the temptation to use the credit for purposes other than emergencies and because annual fixed costs are often charged. But unused credit remains a very common option that many people use as the first line of defense in emergencies.

BONDS

The second goal is to dedicate enough to bonds (or similar fixed-income assets) to provide a steady stream of income over a specified length of time called the *holding period* or planning horizon. The key idea for this portion of the portfolio is to buy only enough bonds to generate the target cash flow stream (interest and principal) over the planning horizon at minimum cost. This protects the income stream from the volatility of stocks by bridging over their fluctuations for the length of the planning horizon. A 5-year planning horizon is probably the most common length, but it can vary from 3 to 10 or more years depending on each individual's specified income need and desired time horizon.

Bonds (or *fixed-income securities*) are loans that pay a specified amount of interest usually twice a year until maturity, when the borrower must pay back the amount printed on the face of the bond. Interest on bonds is higher than on cash equivalents but lower than the returns on stocks over the long term. There are many types of bonds, and Chapter 11 will explain them. Buying bonds does *not* mean buying a bond mutual fund. Rather, it means buying a precise set of individual bonds designed to provide exactly the income stream needed—no more, no less. One of the unique features of a bond as a financial instrument is that you will never suffer a loss of capital if you buy the bond itself and hold it to maturity.[3] But bond funds destroy this unique feature of bonds. Bond fund managers attempt to predict the future movements of bond prices by predicting changes in interest rates. They often do not hold the bonds they buy to maturity. They treat them more like sluggish stocks. In so doing, they undermine the true security that bonds can provide. They believe that their clairvoyance can do better.

At this point, some advisers will sniff that asset dedication is nothing more than a bond ladder, which they have been building for years. They already buy bonds with spaced out regular or irregular maturities. But there is a big difference. They do ladders without a goal or purpose other than to achieve diversification and coupon interest. They are trying to blindly obey the XYZ fixed-formula approach that asset allocation imposes. Like most bond fund managers, they also treat bonds as sluggish stocks. The process is formula-driven rather than goal-driven and results in an aimless bond strategy. Comparing the traditional bond ladders used in the XYZ asset allocation formulas to the precision-guided bond bridges used in the asset dedication approach is like comparing a Chevy sedan to a Ferrari sports car. True enough, they are both cars, but that is about all they have in common. Another analogy might be a camping trip versus a luxury cruise. Both may be categorized as a vacation, but they do not provide the same sort of experience.

To be realistic, the target income stream ought to increase steadily each year to allow for inflation of 3 or 4 percent. Also, extra needs that arise irregularly, such as vacations every other year, special gifts to relatives, or donations to charities, can be added to the target income stream. But the key idea is to buy only enough bonds to satisfy these cash flow needs for the desired planning horizon. The investor should minimize the amount allocated to bonds because the historical record shows that bonds give lower returns than stocks over longer time horizons. The point is to buy only the specific set of individual, mathematically efficient bonds needed to do the job of supplying a specific set of future cash flows. If you buy more, you are overinvesting in bonds and needlessly earning less than you could on your portfolio.

STOCKS

The third goal for the portfolio is growth. All remaining funds are dedicated to this goal. Emergency and cash flow needs have been secured over the planning horizon with cash and bonds. Stocks are the obvious choice for this goal because of their historical performance compared to other financial instruments as pointed out in Chapter 1. Leveraged real estate or any other investment that an adviser specializes in can be used if it promises a higher return. Asset allocation policies or other equity investment strategies can even be applied within the growth portion of the portfolio if it can be demonstrated that they can beat 100 percent stocks. But they are restricted to this portion only.

Stocks (or *equities*) are fundamentally different from cash or bonds. They represent a share of the profit (or loss) of a company. A company may issue a million shares, with each one representing only a tiny fraction of the total company, namely one millionth. A share's price may go up or down depending on the fortunes of the company, investor psychology, and many other factors. There are many types of stocks, as Chapter 11 will explain.

The simplest policy—and, according to research on attribution, the best policy—is to invest the growth portion in generic index funds that have the best historical track record for growth over the horizon length. Short-term volatility in stocks is no longer a threat as it is in asset allocation. This is especially true if the investor is rebalancing the portfolio regularly to match some arbitrary formula. The key idea is to buy stocks that will yield the highest expected returns over the planning horizon. With asset dedication, the growth portion has been isolated from any withdrawals. There will be no need to sell anything until the end of the time horizon. All dividends can be immediately reinvested to achieve "total return."[4] Because asset dedication mathematically minimizes the allocation to cash and bonds, it automatically maximizes the amount allocated to stocks and their higher growth. Hence, it maximizes growth subject to the income stream that must be generated over the horizon to match the investor's individual need. Mathematicians call this "constrained optimization."

THE PRECISE ELEGANCE OF ASSET DEDICATION

Matching and Protecting the Target Income Stream at Minimum Cost

The challenge in constructing the portion of an investor's portfolio dedicated to providing the income stream is finding a suitable collection of bonds to match the needed cash flows at the lowest cost. William Sharpe, 1990 Nobel Prize winner in Economic Sciences, states in his recent text:

> . . .cash matching is not so easily accomplished. This is because the promised cash outflows may involve an uneven stream of payments for which no zero coupon bonds exist. Indeed, it can be difficult (if not impossible) and expensive to exactly match cash inflows with promised outflows.[5]

Fortunately, mathematical algorithms have now been developed that render that statement essentially obsolete. No longer are matched-funding portfolios restricted to zero-coupon bonds. A variety of fixed-income instruments, including Treasury bonds, agency bonds (such as those of the Federal Home Loan Agency), corporate bonds, and municipal bonds can be used.[6] To protect the income stream, only bonds rated double A or better by the Moody's or S&P rating service should be used.[7] The portfolio is designed to precisely match any specified, inflation-adjusted target income stream or cash flow over any planning horizon up to 30 years into the future or longer. Asset dedication represents a form of structural engineering within a portfolio to reduce or eliminate the primary risks associated with bond investing and maximize long-term growth potential.

Another way to contrast asset dedication with asset allocation is to consider how most brokers look at bonds. As mentioned earlier, most brokers tend to view bonds as sluggish stocks. They tell clients to buy bonds to achieve less volatility. In essence, their allegiance to asset allocation leads them to sacrifice return only to reduce volatility. Ask most asset allocators why they have Y percent in bonds, and they will typically answer something about avoiding risk or increasing stability. They can never give you a better answer because asset allocation is devoid of rational specificity.

Asset dedication, on the other hand, takes a very proactive approach to bonds. It dedicates them to a specific purpose, namely, to produce a steady stream of income that is matched to the investor's needs. Ask an asset dedicator why he owns the bonds he does, and he will produce a list showing each bond earmarked for a specific purpose: a precise amount of income at a precise time so that he no longer has to worry about the daily, weekly, monthly, or even quarterly ups and downs of the market. The checks will arrive right on time in the right amounts as the bonds pay interest or mature in a preordained sequence over the planning horizon. Whatever funds are not needed for this purpose are dedicated to growth (except for the small allocation to cash for emergencies).

By using the "just-in-time" concept that has worked so well in industrial supply chains, asset dedication produces higher returns and lower risks in portfolio management. Chapter 4 provides the historical evidence.

ASSET DEDICATION STEP BY STEP

Investing with Ms. Smith

To illustrate asset dedication, consider Ms. Smith, a typical small investor who is just starting retirement. We will follow step by step how she implements an asset dedication strategy tailored specifically to her own individual needs, rather than trying to force-fit her into some preordained category set up by an anonymous committee in a generic mainstream brokerage house.

STEP 1: FORECAST INCOME OR CASH FLOW NEEDS

Assume that Ms. Smith needs $70,000 a year for her retirement living expenses. To keep it simple, we will assume that this includes an allowance for taxes. She already receives $18,000 from Social Security plus another $22,000 from a pension. She must withdraw the rest, $30,000, from her portfolio (an IRA or some other retirement account).

The decision as to how much can be withdrawn from a portfolio depends on how long Ms. Smith wants her money to last. Obviously, withdrawing it too fast runs the risk of depleting it too soon, running out of money before running out of life, so to speak. The decision also depends on how much she wishes to leave in her estate. If she has $600,000 on the day she retires, does she wish to leave exactly $600,000 in her estate when she dies? Attorneys call this "preserving the corpus." Does she want to leave even more to allow for inflation? Or does she simply wish to avoid going broke by depleting it entirely?

These are questions of policy that advisers must ask their clients because different answers lead to very different outcomes. Research suggests that preserving the corpus itself requires withdrawing less than about 4 percent of the total value in the portfolio.[8] Not going broke would allow about 8 percent to be withdrawn. Preserving the corpus plus inflation is not really very realistic for most people because the portfolio would have to grow faster than inflation plus withdrawals. This is not an easy thing to do unless withdrawals are practically zero (or negative, meaning that additions are needed, not withdrawals) for a long period of time. Chapter 5 will discuss how life expectancies and other factors also enter into this decision. For now, assume that she is satisfied with the 5 percent withdrawal rate of $30,000 per year.

STEP 2: SPECIFY A PLANNING HORIZON

How far ahead should Ms. Smith look in planning her finances? How far ahead should any of us look in planning our finances? There's no easy answer here. But this question is inherently easier to comprehend and answer than the questions that are typically asked on asset allocation questionnaires. For instance, if you ask retirees about their risk tolerance, most of the time their answers contain response bias, as explained in Chapter 2. They give an answer, but they don't really understand the consequences of their answer because risk tolerance is an alien concept for most people.

Defining a planning horizon, on the other hand, involves a more understandable idea. People are used to thinking about life in terms of time spans. Many factors come into the investment planning horizon decision: the vagaries of day-to-day living, actuarial probabilities, market predictability, current interest rates, and so on. But everyone is used to dealing with the impact of time on personal decisions.

In his original 1952 paper (which led to what is called *modern portfolio theory*), Harry Markowitz called the planning horizon an investor's "holding period," the length of time that money will be invested.[9] Any span in the range of 3 to 10 years is acceptable to most people. In the absence of compelling reasons to do otherwise, many financial professionals use 5 years as the standard planning horizon. Bear markets seldom last longer than 5 years. It is a number that many people are comfortable with and find acceptable.

There are several options for planning horizons:

Fixed horizons: For this simple example, we will use a fixed horizon of 5 years. That is, we will focus on setting up a portfolio based on the asset dedication strategy covering a 5-year period. At the end of 5 years, the portfolio will be "reloaded" for the next 5 years, and the same every 5 years thereafter.

Rolling horizons: A rolling horizon begins with 5 years, but at the end of the first year, it sells enough stock out of the growth portion of the portfolio to buy a new 5-year bond. The horizon is thereby extended out to 5 years again. At the end of each year, it repeats this extending process by buying a 5-year bond. This results in a perpetual 5-year horizon. That is, it keeps the horizon 5 years out by automatically extending it another year as each year passes. Yields on 5-year bonds are nearly always higher than on shorter maturity bonds. Therefore, once the dedicated bond bridge is set up, the bonds purchased to maintain the horizon would nearly always have higher interest rates because they are at the high end of the yield curve. This rolling asset dedication procedure can be done for any horizon, of course, not just 5 years.[10]

Flexible and other horizon options: Rolling horizons open the door to many other options. For instance, there is nothing mandatory about extending the horizon by only 1 year. Flexibility in terms of extending the horizon is easy to see. Market conditions or investor circumstances may suggest extending it for more than 1 year by buying bonds with 6- or 7-year maturities to convert the 5-year horizon into a 6- or 7-year horizon. Or, they may suggest waiting until later in the current horizon before making any extensions.

The down side of trying to guess where the market is headed gets back into the problem of forecasting again. So it may be prudent to simply follow the mechanical 1-year extension unless there is some compelling reason not to. The near-historic low interest rates beginning in 2002 is an example of a situation in which it would probably be better to wait before reloading.

Yet another possibility would be to have the horizon extension triggered by gains in the growth portion of the portfolio. If stocks make the growth portion reach a point where the gains can be cashed in to buy bonds that extend the horizon, this is done automatically. The system becomes almost self-regulating, extending the horizon indefinitely. Taxes, minimum distribution requirements, and so on may play a role in this decision, of course.

For Ms. Smith, we will keep it simple and assume a fixed planning horizon of 5 years. A note on describing time horizons: The current year is sometimes counted in the planning horizon and sometimes not. So when someone says 5 years, this sometimes means 5 years including the current year and sometimes means 5 years beyond the current year, or up to 6 years total. In this example, we will assume that the planning horizon means the span beyond the current year. So you will see a reference to Years 0 through 5 when we discuss 5-year horizons. Year 0 will be the current year in full, but, in practice, it may represent whatever part of the current year remains until January 1 of the next year.

STEP 3: ALLOW FOR INFLATION

Inflation is a fact of life. Worries in 2003 about deflation proved short-lived. Prices tend to rise over the long run, and this must be factored in. Assume that Ms. Smith wants to play it safe and uses the long-term average of 4 percent.

If it is January 1, she will need to set aside $30,000 in cash for the current year. Treasury bills or a money market account—anything liquid that allows easy access—is equivalent to cash. If it is July 1, she will need to set aside half that amount, but to keep it simple, we will assume that she needs the full $30,000. For the next year, she will need 4 percent more, or $31,200, and so on. She now has a target income stream after inflation for Years 1 through 5 as shown in Table 3.1 and Figure 3.1. The total cash flow over the entire period will amount to $198,989 to cover all 6 years, the current year plus 5 years out. Without inflation, she would need $180,000 over the entire 6 years, but inflation adds $18,989.

Table 3.1

Year	Target Income
0	$30,000
1	$31,200
2	$32,448
3	$33,746
4	$35,096
5	$36,500
Total	**$198,989**

Figure 3.1

Target Income Stream Starting at $30,000 Plus 4 Percent Annual Inflation

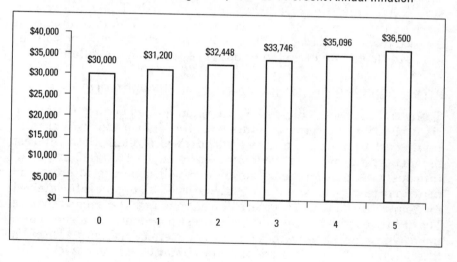

STEP 4: BOND RESTRICTIONS

We now need to set up the portion of her portfolio that will generate this stream of income for Ms. Smith. Call this the *income portion* of her portfolio.

In this day and age of sophisticated bond funds, many investors and even advisers seem to have forgotten the important distinguishing characteristic of bonds as financial instruments: Bonds are legally required to repay principal if they are held to maturity. This makes them fundamentally different from stocks. If you buy a $1000 U.S.

Treasury bond due in 5 years with a coupon interest of 6 percent, it will pay you without fail $60 each year over the next 5 years plus $1000 when it matures. These cash flows are predictable, and both interest and principal are guaranteed. It is this feature of individual bonds that allows asset dedication to reduce risk and provide a better investment strategy. It nullifies risk where it counts: protection of income. This is not true for most bond *funds*. Funds frequently trade bonds rather than hold them to maturity because the managers are trying to time the market by predicting future interest rates (which is precisely the type of active management that the original BHB research warned against).

The technicalities of bond categories and rating scales do not make for stimulating reading, so the details are skipped here (see Appendix 1). Let us assume that Ms. Smith wants to play it super safe and restricts the income portion of the portfolio to U.S. Treasury bonds only, the safest investment on earth. This makes sense because the purpose of this portion of the portfolio is to provide a protected source of income. The only bonds that should be considered are those rated triple A or double A, the safest available.[11]

STEP 5: DEDICATE THE INCOME PORTION OF THE PORTFOLIO

The secret to asset dedication is precision-guided bonds: buying the right bonds in the right amounts with the right maturities at minimum cost to match the target withdrawal stream. Both interest payments and principal redemptions must be factored in simultaneously. Bonds purchased for Year 5 will generate interest and principal to pay for Year 5 itself, but will also generate interest for Years 1 through 4. Therefore, fewer bonds will be needed to fund Years 1 through 4 because of the interest payments from the Year 5 bond. The Year 4 bond will have the same effect on Years 1 through 3, and so on. This is where the mathematics can get tricky. Ms. Smith needs to invest just enough in bonds maturing in each year for each year's income need to be satisfied by the maturing bond principal plus the interest on the bonds remaining in the portfolio. The asset dedication web site (www.assetdedication.com) uses computerized techniques to find the minimum-cost bonds to accomplish the trick.

By following the asset dedication strategy, Ms. Smith or her adviser almost completely eliminates the four major risks of bonds:

1. *Default risk.* This is gone because Ms. Smith chose U.S. Treasury bonds. If she had purchased lower-quality bonds,

such as corporates or munis, some slight risk of default would remain. How much depends on the quality of the bonds purchased, their maturity date, and so on.

2.   *Reinvestment risk.* This is gone because the interest and principal are not reinvested. They are used for income.

3.   *Inflation risk.* This is almost gone because we factored in 4 percent inflation over the entire planning horizon. If inflation on the items that Ms. Smith buys averages 5 percent, then Ms. Smith will have lost 1 percent in terms of purchasing power, so we cannot claim that this risk is entirely gone. She could have selected a higher inflation rate, of course.

4.   *Market risk.* This is gone because all bonds are held to maturity. There is no need to worry about their intervening values in the market. They will not be sold before they mature.

To demonstrate the actual flow of funds for Ms. Smith, we will assume that all bonds pay exactly the same coupon rate of interest, namely 6 percent, and all are selling at par. That is, they pay exactly $6 per year per $100 invested, and their current price is exactly $1000, making their yield 6 percent also. Ms. Smith will collect the interest from all bonds each year and will hold each bond until it matures.

By dedicating just enough of her assets to bonds, she will supply her income needs over the next 5 years—no more, no less. The first year's funding would take $30,000 cash, and the bonds for the following 5 years would cost $141,720, a combined total of $171,720 (see Table 3.2 and Figure 3.2). Recall that her overall need was for $198,989 including inflation. The principal repayments will cover 86 percent of this, and interest will cover the other 14 percent.

Note that the allocation to bonds is no longer based on some arbitrary percentage, as it is in the XYZ asset allocation formulas. It has a rational foundation. It is dedicated to guaranteeing an income stream over the next 5 years. Ms. Smith's investment strategy is not based on her like or dislike of her financial adviser, on faith in some faceless research department somewhere, or on an arbitrary formula.

Note also that the XYZ formulas become meaningless with asset dedication. The percentage allocations to stocks, bonds, and cash now depend on the length of Ms. Smith's planning horizon, the income she wants, and the size of her portfolio. For example, her initial allocation to cash is enough to fund her initial withdrawal of

Table 3.2

Dedicated Portfolio Cash Flows
from Interest and Principal

Year	Target Income	Interest	Principal
0	$30,000		$30,000
1	$31,200	$8,503	$22,697
2	$32,448	$7,141	$25,307
3	$33,746	$5,623	$28,123
4	$35,096	$3,936	$31,160
5	$36,500	$2,066	$34,434
Total	$198,989	$27,269	$171,720
As %	100%	13.70%	86.30%

Figure 3.2

Dedicated Portfolio Cash Flows from Interest and Principal

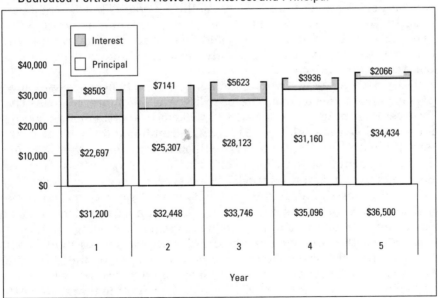

$30,000 for her first-year support, which we assumed to be a full year. If her portfolio had a total of $600,000, then this $30,000 allocation to cash would represent 5 percent; her $141,720 allocation to bonds would be 23.6 percent; and the remaining $428,280 allocated to stocks, 71.4 percent. So in asset allocation terms, she would initially have X = 71.4 percent in stocks, Y = 23.6 percent in bonds, and Z = 5 percent in cash (see the left pie chart in Figure 3.3).

If, however, she had a $1,000,000 portfolio and withdrew the same income stream starting at $30,000, her allocations would be X = 82.8 percent in stocks, Y = 14.2 percent in bonds, and Z = 3 percent in cash. Notice that under asset dedication, her goals become the driving force in her asset allocation, not a formula based on arbitrary percentages. And these dedications are customized to her individual needs, not to the imagined needs of a generic class of investors.

This example assumes bond yields of 6 percent for all the bonds in the portfolio regardless of their maturity, i.e., a flat yield curve. In the real world, 1-year bonds usually have lower interest rates than 5-year bonds. The *yield curve* that charts yield against maturity date is usually positively sloped. So the actual cost of the income portion of a portfolio and corresponding allocations will differ from case to case. Indeed, the cost will change minute by minute, as the prices of bonds fluctuate just like the prices of stocks.

Furthermore, the percentage allocated to any single asset class changes over time. As the years pass, and Ms. Smith progresses along the time line of the planning horizon, bonds mature and the proceeds are used for income. This means that the percentage of

Figure 3.3

Initial Asset Allocation Percentages Depend on the Size of Ms. Smith's Portfolio

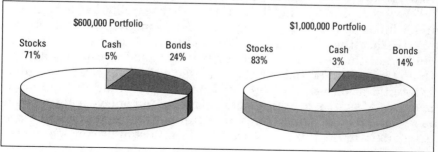

$600,000 Portfolio				$1,000,000 Portfolio		
Stocks 71%	Cash 5%	Bonds 24%		Stocks 83%	Cash 3%	Bonds 14%

the portfolio invested in bonds becomes less and less as she approaches the end of her fixed planning horizon (under a rolling or flexible horizon, it might not). Asset allocation becomes dynamic under asset dedication because it is driven by goals rather than by fixed formulas.[12]

To understand fully how this all fits together, the interested (and mathematically comfortable) reader is referred to Chapter 7. There are other complexities involved, but the main purpose here is to demonstrate the basic concept of asset dedication.

STEP 6: DEDICATE THE GROWTH PORTION OF THE PORTFOLIO

Once income needs have been guaranteed, the balance of the portfolio can be dedicated to growth. The objective is to make this portion grow as large as possible over the planning horizon. It can now be invested independent of income needs because the bonds have already been dedicated to doing that job. In a sense, this growth portion of the portfolio represents the truly "investable funds" that Ms. Smith has available for taking care of her future needs. The income portion has been taken off the table, removed and dedicated to another purpose, namely providing the income for her living expenses over the next 5 years.

How the growth portion is invested is up to Ms. Smith and her adviser. Serious academic researchers are practically unanimous that investing in index mutual funds is the best recommendation that advisers can give their clients (see Chapter 11 for a fuller discussion of mutual funds and index funds). Small-company index funds have historically provided the best return, as listed in Table 1.1. Large-company index funds are the next best choice, although within each of these categories, subcategories of other types of index funds can be found. Probably the most popular of all index funds is the venerable Vanguard 500, which tracks the S&P 500 (www.vanguard.com). They are not very sexy, but in the long run, index funds beat the vast majority of actively managed mutual funds.

In fact, there is a deep and broad inventory of studies that conclude that the performance of actively managed mutual funds lags that of index funds. Indeed, that was the whole point of the original asset allocation premise in Chapter 1. The few mutual fund managers who beat their corresponding index fund one year by random luck seldom beat it the next year, meaning that repeat winners are extremely rare.[13] But that does not seem to stop brokers from recommending these funds for their clients, especially funds that pay the highest commissions.

The final section of this chapter will discuss further the advantages that asset dedication brings to the growth portion of Ms. Smith's portfolio. For now, we will assume that she invests in a fund like the Vanguard 500 in order to provide the funds that will allow her to replenish her income portion at the end of 5 years. This becomes the final Step 7 in the asset dedication process.

STEP 7: REVIEW, RELOAD, AND REPEAT

Assuming that Ms. Smith follows the asset dedication strategy just outlined for her $600,000 retirement portfolio, she first set aside $30,000 to cover her expenses in the current year, which we called Year 0. She used $141,720 to buy U.S. Treasury bonds for the income portion of her portfolio to supply the exact stream of income she needs for the 5 years following the current year. And she allocated the remaining $428,280 to the growth portion of her portfolio for whatever investment will make her funds grow the fastest. Maximizing returns will be her goal for that portion. She has thus planned her financial life for the next 6 years beginning today.

Some time before the end of her planning horizon, Ms. Smith will need to review her progress to date and her goals for the future, and repeat essentially the same strategy she followed here. If she started her first plan with a total of $600,000, then her 71.4 percent initial allocation to growth was $428,280. How much this will have grown over her planning horizon will depend on the stocks she purchased.

Assume that the adviser chose an index fund of small-company stocks such as the one listed in Table 1.1. Over all 6-year periods since 1926, small-company stocks have averaged a remarkable 13.7 percent annualized rate of return.[14] If her stocks grow at this average rate, the growth portion of Ms. Smith's portfolio will reach about $ 925,000. For large-company stocks like the stocks in the S&P 500, comparable figures would be 10.9 percent growth, making the growth portion of her portfolio nearly $800,000. To match her current $600,000 in 6 years in real terms (i.e., including inflation at 4 percent per year), the ending value would need to be $759,171 or more.[15] The $428,280 in the growth portion of her portfolio would need to earn a total return of about 10.0 percent per year to reach $759,151 in 6 years. Thus, 10.0 percent becomes the target rate of return that her growth portfolio needs to achieve if she wants her portfolio to be self-sustaining.[16] If returns on either small- or large-company stocks meet or beat their averages, she will have more than enough to reload the income portion of her portfolio for another

5 years, after which she can start all over again. This process can continue indefinitely.

This assumes that the prices of the bonds in 6 years will be the same as they are today, meaning the interest rates will continue to be 6 percent. If rates were significantly lower than 6 percent, then the cost of the bonds needed to provide the next income stream would be higher, and she might not have enough. Or her stocks might not have achieved the average growth rate. As always, there can be no guarantee of ultimate sustainability. She could increase the likelihood of sustainability by reducing her withdrawal to something less than the initial 5 percent. But these risks are simply facts of life and will always be there for either asset dedication or asset allocation.

If we assume that her portfolio does achieve the averages, and that she is comfortable with 5-year horizons, then at the end of each 5 years, she will continue to repeat this process. Figure 3.4 presents a schematic diagram illustrating four consecutive 5-year planning horizons for Ms. Smith, assuming that she invests in large-company stocks. Notice the sawtooth pattern at the very bottom of the chart. This represents the cash in her money market account that she withdraws at the beginning of each year for annual income expenses. Directly above the bottom cash line is the bond line, which

Figure 3.4

Value of Portfolio over Four Consecutive 5-Year Plans (20 Years Total)
$600,000 Portfolio, 5% Initial Withdrawal

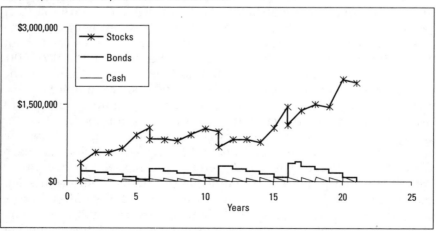

drops in a stair-step fashion each year as bonds mature and the funds are transferred to cash.

The value of the stock portion of her portfolio is tracked as the upward-sloping line at the top of the chart above the bond line, assumed to be growing randomly at the average rate of 10.1 percent per year, the same as for large-company stocks. The randomness of stock market movements creates the volatility, which is displayed as the irregular pattern of fluctuations shown. This is only one of many different possible patterns that the stock portion could follow. Under other circumstances, it would follow a different pattern. But these temporary fluctuations do not affect her steady stream of income. Only once every 5 years are stocks sold to buy a new dedicated bond bridge for the next planning horizon. (This assumes a fixed horizon. With a rolling horizon, the pattern would be different in that the bonds would not drop steadily as shown.)

ADVANTAGES OFFERED BY ASSET DEDICATION

Using Stocks and Bonds to Do What They Do Best

By splitting the portfolio into portions dedicated to performing specific tasks—providing income or providing growth—the asset dedication plan represents a sort of division of labor. Each portion of the portfolio does not interfere with the other portion's purpose. The provision of income with bonds automatically reduces risk by holding the bonds to maturity. It also uses just enough bonds to do the trick—no more and no less. By keeping the cost of providing the income to the lowest possible level, the remaining funds dedicated to portfolio growth are pushed to the highest possible level.

By following the asset dedication approach and dedicating the assets that are not needed to provide income to growth for the length of the planning horizon, Ms. Smith will enhance her overall portfolio performance in at least four ways.

1.   *Total return earned.* No withdrawals will be made from the growth portion. All dividends can be automatically reinvested. This means that this portion will earn what is called *total return*—appreciation plus dividends. Without automatic reinvestment, dividends sometimes end up in cash, earning little return.

2. *No rebalancing.* No periodic rebalancing is needed because there is no predetermined XYZ fixed formula as the driving force behind the investment strategy. If the stock portion is growing rapidly, the funds can be left there to continue to grow. Under the forced-rebalancing discipline of fixed-formula asset allocation, investors are told to pull money out of the fastest-growing assets and put it into slower-growing assets. In bull markets, this is obviously a harmful strategy. It demonstrates the fallibility of asset allocation and how it can harm those who follow it blindly.

3. *Impact of volatility diminished.* Volatility is no longer an issue (at least short-term volatility). Not only does asset dedication remove nearly all the risks associated with bonds, it also lowers the actual and perceived impact of volatility on the growth portion.

    To understand why this happens, it is important to know that volatility in rates of return has historically been lower over longer terms because there are both good and bad years to even things out. This is one of the key advantages of asset dedication as an investment strategy. Longer periods are inherently less volatile and thus less risky. The volatility of quarterly or even annual returns becomes irrelevant to someone who has a 5-year perspective.

    One of the simplest ways to see this is to examine the range of returns from best to worst over longer spans of time (see Table 3.3). The first two columns show the range of returns for the prices of large-company stocks for 77 years, from 1926 to 2002. The best and worst years occurred in two successive years in the early part of the Great Depression: a gain of 54.8 percent in1932–1933 and a loss of –45.8 percent in 1930–1931. Equivalent figures for small-company stocks were a maximum gain of 187.0 percent (1932–1933) and a loss of –52.8 percent (1936–1937).

    Figure 3.5 plots the best and worst returns for all time spans from 1 to 34 years that were possible during the 77-year period 1926–2002. The primary observation to make from Figure 3.5 is the fact that the range from best to worst narrows as the time span gets longer. This is evident in the funnel effect as longer and longer spans are included. A narrower range means less volatility, less uncertainty, and therefore less risk the longer the investment horizon or holding period.

Table 3.3

Best and Worst Annualized Total Returns for Small- and Large-Cap Stocks, 1-Year to 34-Year Spans, 1926–2002

	Range of Average Annualized Total Returns			
	Large-Cap Stocks		Small-Cap Stocks	
Span	Best	Worst	Best	Worst
1 yr	54.8%	−45.8%	187.0%	−52.8%
2 yr	41.7%	−36.8%	88.8%	−48.5%
3 yr	31.5%	−28.7%	82.5%	−49.0%
4 yr	31.0%	−23.9%	83.0%	−38.2%
5 yr	29.1%	−14.1%	65.2%	−26.7%
6 yr	25.2%	−10.7%	40.2%	−21.7%
7 yr	24.2%	−4.9%	35.1%	−17.8%
8 yr	21.8%	−4.7%	34.1%	−3.9%
9 yr	21.1%	−5.0%	34.1%	−2.8%
10 yr	20.5%	−2.0%	29.6%	−0.4%
11 yr	19.7%	−2.1%	28.3%	−0.3%
12 yr	19.4%	−2.9%	30.4%	−1.3%
13 yr	19.0%	−3.3%	33.8%	−2.3%
14 yr	19.1%	−1.8%	31.9%	0.5%
15 yr	19.1%	−0.1%	28.3%	2.3%
16 yr	18.3%	1.1%	26.1%	1.5%
17 yr	18.5%	2.9%	24.6%	3.9%
18 yr	18.7%	2.2%	25.7%	5.4%
19 yr	17.9%	2.4%	24.8%	5.3%
20 yr	18.0%	2.5%	24.0%	6.1%
21 yr	18.1%	3.2%	23.1%	8.1%
22 yr	17.5%	4.4%	23.9%	6.1%
23 yr	16.7%	5.2%	23.8%	7.6%
24 yr	17.2%	5.7%	23.2%	7.7%
25 yr	17.4%	5.4%	22.3%	9.0%
26 yr	16.2%	6.5%	22.7%	8.5%
27 yr	15.1%	7.5%	22.8%	8.8%
28 yr	14.2%	7.7%	22.0%	8.3%
29 yr	14.2%	7.1%	21.7%	7.5%
30 yr	13.8%	8.1%	21.3%	9.2%
31 yr	13.8%	8.3%	19.9%	10.1%
32 yr	13.6%	8.1%	19.9%	9.3%
33 yr	13.6%	8.6%	20.4%	10.0%
34 yr	12.8%	8.0%	20.1%	9.2%

Figure 3.5

Small- versus Large-Cap Stocks: Best and Worst Annualized Total Returns
over 1- to 34-Year Spans, 1926–2002

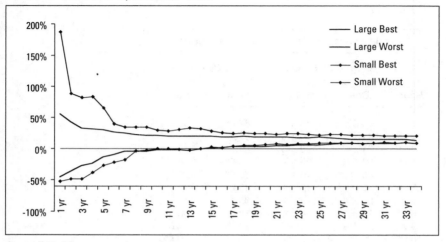

Source: Table 3.3.

The second key observation from Figure 3.5 is that
small-company stocks have a wider range than large-company stocks, meaning they are somewhat more volatile,
but the difference becomes very small for longer periods.
It seems a small concession to make for the higher returns
that small stocks offer over longer periods. For spans
longer than 18 years, the worst possible return that has
ever happened to funds invested in small-company stocks
(–3.9 percent) was higher than the worst possible for
large-company stocks (–4.7 percent).

Table 3.4 and Figure 3.6 exclude the Great Depression and World War II years. They cover the period 1947
to 2002. The fluctuations are less extreme when the most
distant past is removed. Only 1- to 11-year spans are
included to provide a closer view of the funnel effect. For
large-cap stocks, the best single year gain was 52.8 percent
(1953–1954) and the worst loss, -26.3 percent (1973–1974),
or a range of 79.1 percent. For 5-year spans since 1947, the
highest annualized return was 29.1 percent, and the worst
loss was 2.3 percent per year (which totals an 11.1 percent

Table 3.4

Best and Worst Annualized Total Returns for Small- and Large-Cap Stocks, 1- to 11-Year Spans, 1947–2002

| Stocks | Return | Span Length (Planning Horizon) in Years | | | | | | | | | | |
		1 Yr	2 Yr	3 Yr	4 Yr	5 Yr	6 Yr	7 Yr	8 Yr	9 Yr	10 Yr	11 Yr
Large-cap	Best	52.8%	41.7%	31.5%	31.0%	29.1%	25.2%	24.2%	21.8%	21.1%	20.5%	19.7%
Large-cap	Worst	−26.3%	−20.8%	−14.3%	−6.4%	−2.3%	−3.3%	−1.4%	1.4%	0.1%	1.2%	2.6%
Small-cap	Best	103.1%	74.8%	47.4%	40.7%	41.3%	40.2%	35.1%	34.1%	34.1%	29.6%	28.3%
Small-cap	Worst	−40.8%	−34.3%	−24.8%	−15.8%	−17.3%	−19.0%	−11.5%	−3.9%	−2.6%	0.9%	2.4%

erosion of capital over the entire 5 years, 1969–1974). It should be noted that over spans of 8 years or longer, there has never been a loss of principal (if inflation is ignored). Therefore, longer spans of time are historically better in terms of volatility.[17]

For small-company stocks, shown in the two bottom rows of Table 3.4, the same is true. Overall, the volatility is higher than that of large-company stocks, but the narrowing effect is still unmistakable. The best 1-year return for small caps was 103.1 percent (1966–1967). The worst was a loss or negative return of -40.8 percent (1972–1973). The range from best and worse is 140.9 percent. This is greater than the range for large-cap stocks, as expected. But the range gets smaller and smaller as the spans lengthen. There are no 10-year spans with negative returns at all since 1947 in small-company stocks. Ms. Smith should end up with at least as much in the growth portion of her portfolio as she started with even if she invested entirely in small-company stocks over a 10-year horizon (excluding inflation[18]).

Figure 3.6

Small- versus Large-Cap Stocks: Best and Worst Annualized Total Returns over 1- to 11-Year Spans, 1947–2002

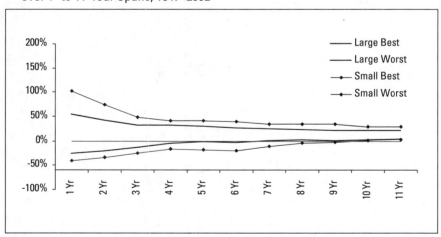

Source: Table 3.4.

It should be clear that investors using the asset dedication approach with 5- or 10-year planning horizons face much greater protection against volatility than investors who are worried about quarter-to-quarter or year-to-year horizons. This effect is true for all asset classes. Riskier investments can be made in the growth portion of the portfolio so that even conservative investors can capture higher returns.

4. *Sequence risk reduced.* There is another form of risk that asset dedication reduces that is often hidden by long-term averages: sequence risk. Few brokers take the time and trouble to explain it to their clients, even those who fully comprehend its danger. Sequence risk is covered in Chapter 14, but the main idea is not difficult to understand.

In a static situation, where no external funds are being added to or withdrawn from a $100,000 portfolio, the end result will be the same regardless of the sequence of returns. For example, it does not matter if the portfolio grows 10 percent the first year and 20 percent the second year or the reverse. Both will end up at $132,000. The present value will be higher under the "quick start" situation, where the 20 percent return occurs in the first year, but the end value will be the same either way. The sequence of returns does not matter to the ending value. Mathematicians call this the commutative law of algebra: A times B equals B times A.

But in a dynamic situation, where funds are being withdrawn from the portfolio periodically (as they typically are in most retirement situations), then the sequence of returns can make a big difference. Consider a simple example of only 2 years. Assume that $50,000 is being withdrawn from the $100,000 portfolio each year. If 0 percent is earned the first year and 20 percent the second, then at the end of the second year, after the withdrawal of the second $50,000, the account will have $10,000 left in it. But if it grows 20 percent in the first year and 0 percent in the second, the ending value will be $20,000, double that in the first case. The additional $10,000 comes from the extra money in the portfolio at the end of the first year produced by the higher initial return. Table 3.5 shows the calculations for this simple example. Reversing the order makes quite a difference, even though the average growth rate is the same.

Table 3.5

Impact of Sequence Risk

$5,000 Withdrawal at End of Each Year	Slow-Start Growth	Quick-Start Growth
Portfolio value at start of first year	$100,000	$100,000
First-year return	0%	20%
Portfolio value at end of first year	$100,000	$120,000
Withdrawal	$50,000	$50,000
Portfolio value at start of second year	$50,000	$70,000
Second-year return	20%	0%
Portfolio value at end of second year	$60,000	$70,000
Withdrawal	$50,000	$50,000
Portfolio value at start of third year	$10,000	$20,000

The intuitive explanation of sequencing is simple: You would rather have your money grow faster before you take it out, not after. The opposite is true when funds are being added. Younger investors who are still accumulating their savings would rather have their money grow faster after they put it in, not before. Older investors who are withdrawing want their money to grow faster before they take it out, not after. For the older investors, this possibility of slower growth (or loss) before they take their money out is sequence risk.

Asset dedication reduces sequence risk because it insulates the growth portion of the portfolio from withdrawals. That is, the growth portion becomes a static environment, with no external withdrawals to create the sequence problem. The ending value will be the same whether gains occur early or late in the planning horizon.

Figure 3.7 illustrates in a visual manner how asset dedication manages volatility in a portfolio by making use of bonds to smooth out the fluctuations that stocks create. Stocks move in an irregular fashion, and the bonds serve as a bridge over the volatile fluctuations of stocks. The bonds provide a "safe passage" for income, while stocks romp around, but generally in an upward direction, to provide growth. This captures the essence of how asset dedication uses the best features of both stocks and bonds as financial instruments.

Figure 3.7

Asset Dedication Bridges the Volatility of Unpredictable Stock
Market Fluctuations

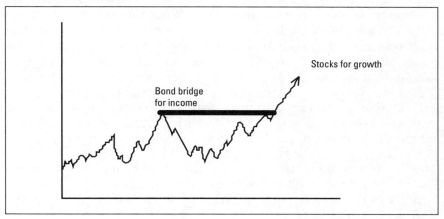

Asset dedication cannot remove sequence risk entirely because there will always be some probability, however slight, that a person may enter the market at the very beginning of a long down market that extends beyond the planning horizon. If the planning horizon is at least 8 years long (10 years for small-cap stocks), it is unlikely this will happen (at least it never has happened since 1947). If it does, then it will create financial problems for anyone who must withdraw funds before the market has a chance to recover its losses. An asset allocation strategy would face the same problem, of course.[19]

It should be noted that if the withdrawals are a strict percentage of the value of the portfolio, then sequence risk is not a problem. But restricting withdrawals to a flat percentage of the portfolio's value is not very practical. During bear markets, retirees would have to cut their spending to match the declines in their portfolio. From the year 2000 to 2002, this would have meant a 30 to 40 percent cut. Most monthly living expenses, such as housing payments, insurance, and so on, are fixed dollar amounts, not percentages. A strict percentage withdrawal rate would put retirees in a very tough spot. It is not a very realistic scenario.

CONCLUSION

In summary, asset dedication allows Ms. Smith to achieve her goal of providing income for herself and removing the worry associated with short-term swings in the market. What matters to her now is not what happens in a day, a month, a quarter, or even a year. The only volatility she needs to be concerned with is volatility over 5-year spans, which is always less than volatility over shorter periods. With a 10-year planning horizon, her volatility would be even less. It allows her to retain total control over the portfolio.

Unlike an annuity, the bonds in the income portion have no restrictions or conditions or any of the other encumbrances that usually accompany annuities. Because she owns the bonds outright, she can sell them or trade them at any time. In a sense, the dedicated bond portion of the portfolio represents a type of self-annuitization. Because a rolling horizon maintains a perpetual income stream, it eliminates the need to purchase an annuity and avoids the high fees and rigid regulations.

Asset dedication thus reduces or eliminates most types of portfolio risk on both portions of the portfolio, growth and income. It focuses on longer planning horizons and can generate better results because it effectively nullifies volatility where it can do the most damage, namely where income withdrawals are involved. Once Ms. Smith implements an asset dedication strategy, she can follow a passive management style and simply turn her attention to other retirement matters. It allows for a passive portfolio management strategy—a true "set-it-and-forget-it" type of investing.

In the next chapter, we will examine the historical record of how asset dedication has performed compared to asset allocation strategies applied to the same data set. As we shall see, it provided superior performance against any asset allocation strategy that used 70 percent or less in stocks. Most mainstream brokers would never recommend 70 percent stocks for conservative investors like Ms. Smith. If you examine their model portfolios for conservative investors (as of this writing in late 2003), you will seldom see more than 50 percent in stocks. If you remain skeptical of asset dedication but are willing to get into the numbers from the historical record that had to be crunched to reach this conclusion, the next chapter is for you.

NOTES

1. Martin L. Leibowitz, "The Dedicated Portfolio in Pension Funds—Part 1: Motivations and Basics," *Financial Analysts Journal*, January-February 1986, pp. 68–75.

2. This may sound like another sales pitch, but this book and the accompanying web site (www.assetdedication.com) provide historical data to support the claim. The evidence will speak for itself.

3. This is 100 percent true for U.S. Treasury bonds. It is over 99 percent true for bonds issued by corporations, state or local governments, municipal agencies, and other public entities when they have investment-grade ratings of A or higher. See Chapter 14 for more details and the historical record on bond default rates.

4. Total return consists of the two main components of return, appreciation resulting from a rise in price and yield resulting from dividends. Various definitions of returns will be covered in Chapter 12 on quantitative fundamentals.

5. William F. Sharpe, Gordon J. Alexander, and Jeffery V. Baily, *Investments*, 5th ed. (Englewood Cliffs, N.J.: Prentice-Hall, 1995), p. 478. Technically, Sharpe is right if the word *exactly* means to the penny. Because many bonds can be purchased only in $1000, $5000, or $10,000 increments and bond prices fluctuate minute to minute, it is nearly impossible to get an exact match. But precision to within 1 percent of the target income stream and cumulative errors of less than a few hundred dollars over entire 10-year periods are attainable. Examples of this can be found at www.assetdedication.com.

6. Under some circumstances, certificates of deposit (CDs) or collateralized mortgage obligations (CMOs) can be used, but these are more complicated financial instruments that are best left to sophisticated investors with very large portfolios. Most investors should stick to the standard types of bonds—government, corporate, or municipal.

7. See Chapter 11 for further explanations of bond types and Appendix 1 for a definition of bond ratings.

8. Phillip Cooley, Daniel Walz, and Carl Hubbard, "Retirement Savings: Choosing a Withdrawal Rate That Is Sustainable," *The AAII Journal*, February 1998. This study was called the Trinity study (the authors were professors of economics at Trinity University in Texas) and will be described in greater detail in Chapter 10. Their research was later embellished by the Zunna Corporation (www.zunna.com). Whereas the Trinity study used predefined asset allocations, Zunna finds optimal asset allocations using a computational technique known as simulated annealing, available in the software Zunna sells, called WATS. Three of Zunna's major studies, which it provides free of charge on its web site, are

> Study 1: "Maximum Sustainable Withdrawal Rates with Varying Historical Success Rates Using Large Cap Stocks, Corporate Bonds and US T-Bills. Ending Value Goal: *Above Zero (Don't Go Broke)*." Data from 1946 to 2000.

> Study 2: "Maximum Sustainable Withdrawal Rates with Varying Historical Success Rates Using Large Cap Stocks, Corporate Bonds and US T-Bills. Ending Value Goal: *Equal or Greater than Original Corpus*." Data from 1946 to 2000.

> Study 3: "Maximum Sustainable Withdrawal Rates with Varying Historical Success Rates Using Large Cap Stocks, Corporate Bonds and US T-Bills. Ending Value Goal: *Equal or Greater than Inflation-Adjusted Corpus*." Data from 1946 to 2000.

9. Harry M. Markowitz, "Portfolio Selection," *Journal of Finance* 7, no. 1, March 1952, pp. 77–91.

10. One investment adviser, Bert Whitehead of Cambridge Advisors (www.bertwhitehead.com), uses 15 years because long-term U.S. Treasury bonds have traditionally earned interest in the 5 percent range, and at 5 percent, money doubles every 15 years. Thus, at the end of each year, 2 years are added to the ladder.

11. There are three primary categories of bonds based on source: federal government, corporate, and muni bonds. Corporate bonds are issued by corporations, and munis are issued by state and local government agencies. Munis are free of federal taxes and of state taxes in some states. See Chapter 14 for a table of historical default rates on various bond ratings.

12. Zero-coupon bonds ("strips") pay no interest, only principal. So strips whose face values match the income stream needed will do the trick quite neatly. There is a catch, however (as always). First, interest-rate yields on strips are sometimes a little less than on regular bonds, so strips sometimes cost a little more. Second, taxes must be paid on the accrued interest in accounts that are not tax-deferred even though the interest has not actually been paid. That means that if your strips accrue $1000 this year, you will have to pay taxes as if you had received the $1000, even though you did not really receive it. Therefore, money will have to be set aside to pay these taxes. These two factors can make strips (or other zero-coupon bonds) a second-best solution, but do-it-yourselfers may like the idea anyway.

13. Part 3 of the book discusses the challenges faced by anyone who is trying to forecast the market and the probability of getting 10 heads in a row. It is not that mutual fund managers are necessarily inept or fraudulent (some are, no doubt). Their poor performance relative to the index funds is due to the higher costs they face (transactions costs, marketing expenses, fees, taxes, and so on), which average roughly 1 to 3 percent more than the costs incurred by index funds. Thus, they need to beat the index funds by more than this to come out on top. They may get lucky in some years and do this, but as a group, they cannot do it consistently.

14. The year-to-year compound annualized rate since 1926 for small-cap stocks is 12.1 percent, but over 5- year periods, the average is a bit higher. The mathematics of annualized versus average annual growth rates is somewhat nonintuitive and will be explained in Chapter 12.

15. The figure of $759,151 is simply the value of $600,000 growing with inflation at 4 percent per year over the entire span of 6 years (the current year plus 5 additional years). If interest rates on bonds were the same then as now, she could in theory buy an equivalent set of bonds for her next 5 years and start the process all over again. The $428,280 in the growth portion of her portfolio would need to earn a total return of about 10 percent per year to reach $759,151 in 6 years.

16. This assumes interest rates on bonds will be the same then as now. She could in theory buy an equivalent set of bonds for her next 5 years and start the process all over again.

17. For the technically inclined, the standard deviation of returns, the most common measure of volatility in academic research, also declines as the horizon gets longer.

18. Inflation is not factored into this 10-year span. If inflation were factored in, it would take an average of 14 years to make the portfolio equivalent in real terms.

19. These conclusions ignore the impact of inflation. They relate only to preserving the corpus of the starting portfolio, not its purchasing power.

4

Asset Dedication versus Asset Allocation: Historical Comparisons from 1926

To know the road ahead, ask those coming back.
—CHINESE PROVERB

Asset dedication fills the XYZ gap in asset allocation theory. It also provides an easily understood solution to a problem facing many investors: It protects the income they need to withdraw, nullifying risk where it counts by simply holding U.S. Treasury bonds (or similar high-grade corporate or muni bonds) to maturity. It reduces risk in the growth portion of their portfolio by using stock index funds and holding them for long periods so that short-term fluctuations have a chance to even out. Even more importantly from a practical point of view, it reduces the intangible risk of uninformed, vulnerable investors succumbing to the latest sales pitch or investment scam that comes their way, thereby avoiding the scandals that have wracked mainstream brokers and mutual funds in recent years. These scandals have done much to erode investors' trust in the financial community, and rightly so. Asset dedication represents a new approach to a conservative investment strategy that provides safety for those who need it. It reduces the risks that can hurt personal investors the most.

ASSET DEDICATION RETURNS BEAT ASSET ALLOCATION RETURNS: SIX TESTS COVERING 1926 TO 2003[1]

How about returns? How well does such a conservative portfolio that focuses on reducing risks actually perform in the real world when it comes to growth? Clearly, it cannot provide a higher average return than a 100 percent investment in a stock index fund because some of the portfolio—the minimum needed—must be used to buy the bonds needed to provide the income stream. How well does the asset dedication strategy do against the classic XYZ asset allocation models in the real world?

To answer this question, asset dedication was compared to asset allocation in six separate tests covering increasing spans of time back to 1926.[2] The first four included only large-company stocks and intermediate-term U.S. Treasury bonds (the same mix used for Ms. Smith in Chapter 3). The last two tests consisted of large-company stocks with other types of bonds (corporate bonds, long-term U.S. Treasuries, and Treasury bills), and then this test was repeated using small-company stocks.

> Test 1: 1990–2000 (from the Dorfman study)
>
> Test 2: 1976–2003 (large-company stocks, intermediate-term U.S. Treasuries)
>
> Test 3: 1947–2003 (same as above)
>
> Test 4: 1926–2003 (same as above)
>
> Test 5: 1926–2003 (large-company stocks with other types of bonds)
>
> Test 6: 1926–2003 (small-company stocks with other types of bonds)

The tests are discussed in excruciating detail later in the chapter, but the bottom line is that asset dedication did better than all asset allocation strategies with 70 percent or less in stocks with the remainder in bonds. Results are presented for portfolios consisting of 30 to 70 percent stocks, the range recommended by the model portfolios promoted by most major brokerage houses. Following the details may be somewhat tedious, but evidence from the historical record appears to be the best way to demonstrate the superiority of asset dedication. The primary conclusions will be italicized for those who have a low tolerance for the tedium of following quantitative explanations.

The first test covers the data developed by Dorfman in his 1990–2000 study (first presented in Chapter 2). Though the Dorfman study covered only a single 10-year period, it nevertheless captures the actual recommendations of actual brokers in the real world during the late 1990s, the most recent and greatest bull run in stock market history. This makes an interesting head-to-head comparison between the two approaches. The rest of the tests involved much longer spans based on actual market performance using the same data sets presented in Chapter 1, Table 1.1.[3] The spans were examined separately to provide a thorough range of time periods over which the strategy could be tested.

Test 1: 1990–2000

ASSET DEDICATION BEATS THE BROKERS IN THE *WALL STREET JOURNAL*

Recall that in Chapter 2, the *Wall Street Journal* study by John Dorfman from 1990 to 2000 was based on a case with no cash withdrawals from an initial portfolio of $10,000. The brokers' results were compared to the "optimal" portfolio, which invested with perfect foresight; a pure (100 percent) stock portfolio; a pure bond portfolio; and a pure cash portfolio.[4]

For the first test, the Dorfman study was repeated using the Ms. Smith scenario in Chapter 3: an initial portfolio of $600,000 and an annual withdrawal of $30,000 spread evenly throughout the year ($7500 at that start of each quarter) plus 4 percent inflation ($31,200 the next year, or $7800 each quarter, and so on). A fixed 10-year horizon was selected to match the data span.

Had she followed an asset dedication plan, the estimated cost of the bonds for Ms. Smith's 10-year asset dedication strategy would have been $233,809, based on the actual prevailing 1990 prices for U.S. Treasury bonds. The balance, $358,691, would then be invested in stocks. For test purposes, she was assumed to invest this growth portion entirely in an S&P 500 index fund with all dividends automatically reinvested to achieve total return over the ensuing 10 years. For the brokers, the funds were invested according to the XYZ formulas recommended by the brokers each quarter, as detailed in Chapter 2.

In the case of asset dedication, the cash withdrawals are funded as one bond matures and the others pay interest (the growth portion was left untouched over the entire 10-year period with all dividends automatically reinvested in the same stocks). In the case of the broker asset allocation models, it was assumed that she would sell off whichever investment had grown the fastest over the preceding quarter. All portfolios remained fully invested except for the withdrawals. Since the cash was withdrawn in quarterly payments but assumed to be spent monthly, the funds were assumed to earn a small amount of interest, namely whatever money market rates were prevailing at the time.

Table 4.1 presents a series of resulting scores for asset dedication and each of the brokers for both return and ending value. Scores 1 and 2 show that *asset dedication overwhelmed the broker-recommended asset allocation portfolios, with an internal rate of return of 16.0 percent compared to 14.4 percent for the best broker, 13.3 percent for the average of all brokers, and 10.9 percent for the worst broker.* The internal rate of return (IRR) factors in the amount and timing of the withdrawals as well as the starting and ending values.[5] Asset dedication cannot match the optimal or 100 percent stock portfolio returns, of course, though it comes closest, with 61 percent of the optimal and 92 percent of the 100 percent stock return. Figure 4.1 provides a graphical illustration of the return results.

Scores 3 and 4 relate to the actual ending value of Ms. Smith's portfolio after it has funded her income stream over the prior 10 years. Figure 4.2 plots the value of the portfolio over time. The value of the asset dedication portfolio at the end of the 10-year period amounts to $1,838,206, or 38 percent of the optimal (Score 3) and 87 percent of the pure stock (Score 4). The best of the brokers were Goldman Sachs ($1,567,250) and Lehman Brothers ($1,563,949), but they achieved only 32 percent of the optimal and 74 percent of the pure stock portfolio.

The superior performance of asset dedication stems from the fact that it keeps each portion of the portfolio focused on what it does best: supplying steady income or earning the highest growth. Neither portion (income or growth) gets in the way of the other portion's purpose.

The other advantage of asset dedication is the rationality it brings to asset allocation. Ms. Smith initially has 39 percent invested in bonds (included a small reserve for cash). Ask her why she chose 39 percent, and she will tell you that it is just enough to generate the

Table 4.1

Asset Dedication versus Brokers, 1990–2000 Dorfman Study—Results of Comparisons for Ms. Smith
$600,000 Initial Investment, $30,000 Annual Withdrawal, 4 Percent Inflation

Portfolio Design	Internal Rate of Return*	Score 1 = % of Optimal	Score 2 = % of 100% Stocks	Ending Value†	Score 3 = % of Optimal	Score 4 = % of 100% Stocks
Optimal	26.3%	100%		$4,827,192	100%	
100% stocks	17.3%	66%	100%	$2,104,461	44%	100%
Asset dedication	16.0%	61%	92%	$1,843,827	38%	88%
Goldman Sachs	14.4%	55%	83%	$1,567,250	32%	74%
Lehman Brothers	14.4%	55%	83%	$1,563,949	32%	74%
Morgan Stanley D.W.	14.1%	54%	82%	$1,521,070	32%	72%
Prudential Securities5	13.9%	53%	80%	$1,485,704	31%	71%
PaineWebber	13.9%	53%	80%	$1,481,722	31%	70%
A.G. Edwards	13.4%	51%	78%	$1,412,192	29%	67%
Robot Blend	13.2%	50%	76%	$1,373,574	28%	65%
Salomon Smith Barney	12.9%	49%	74%	$1,329,185	28%	63%
Merrill Lynch	11.8%	45%	68%	$1,187,266	25%	56%
Raymond James	10.9%	42%	63%	$1,073,741	22%	51%
100% bonds	8.1%	31%	47%	$774,790	16%	37%
100% cash	5.1%	19%	29%	$522,899	11%	25%
Average—All brokers	13.3%	50.6%	76.8%	$1,402,453	29.1%	66.6%

*Internal rate of return factors in the cash flows that are withdrawn from the portfolio.
†The ending value includes the final cash flow payment made for the fortieth quarter.
Source: See Table 2.1.

Figure 4.1

Asset Dedication versus Broker Returns, 1990–2000 Dorfman Study—
Comparisons for Ms. Smith

$600,000 Initial Investment, $30,000 Annual Withdrawal, 4 Percent Inflation

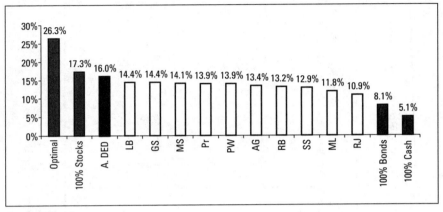

Source: Table 4.1.

Figure 4.2

Asset Dedication versus Broker Portfolios, 1990–2000 Dorfman Study—
Comparisons for Ms. Smith

$600,000 Initial Investment, $30,000 Annual Withdrawal, 4 Percent Inflation

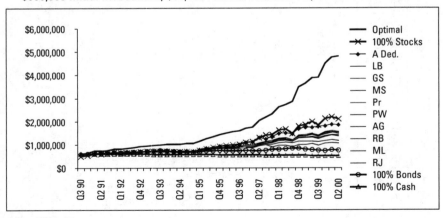

Source: Table 4.1.

money she needs to live on for the next 3 months plus buy the bonds needed to fund her over the next 9 years and 9 months. Ask her why she has 61 percent in stocks, and she will tell you that she does not need it for income and has put it where it promises to grow the fastest.[6] In other words, she understands the rationale for why she has invested the way she has. She does not need to ask her broker.

Test 2: 1976–2003

ASSET DEDICATION WINS MOST OVER RECENT YEARS

The Dorfman study used for Test 1 examined a single 10-year period, 1990–2000.[7] Clearly asset dedication provided better returns than the asset allocation models recommended by Dorfman's group of mainstream brokers, while simultaneously reducing or eliminating many of the risks commonly associated with investing. But what sort of returns could be expected over many 10-year periods? Was 1990–2000 just a fluke?

To answer these questions, spans of increasing length were examined. Test 2 repeats the Ms. Smith scenario using the data sets from Table 1.1 but covers a longer span, from 1976–2003, divided into 19 ten-year rolling spans: 1976–1985, 1977–1986, . . ., 1994–2003. For each of these 19 decades, asset dedication was compared against the investment results for six different stock/bond asset allocation models: 70/30, 60/40, 50/50, 40/60, and 30/70 (the first two digits indicate the percentage allocated to stocks, the second, the percentage allocated to bonds). To make the comparisons valid, all parameters were maintained at identical values except for the differences in the strategies. Returns on stocks for all models were based on a large-company stock index, which mirrors the S&P 500. Returns on bonds for the asset allocation models were based on the returns on intermediate government bonds (a common benchmark for measuring bond returns). The data for these returns came from two sources: the Center for Research in Security Prices (CRSP) and Global Financial Data, Inc. Returns on bonds for the asset dedication strategy were based on the actual prices and coupon interest rates quoted in the *Wall Street Journal* for the U.S. Treasuries needed to fund the income portion of the initial portfolio. All portfolios remained entirely invested in either stocks or bonds 100 percent of the time. Stock dividends were assumed to be immediately reinvested to achieve total return. There was no designated allocation to cash.[8]

Very aggressive portfolios with 80/20, 90/10, or 100/0 (pure stocks) allocations were not included because Ms. Smith is a retiree and few brokers would recommend such aggressive portfolios for someone her age. Neither would they be likely recommend the other extreme, 20/80, 10/90, or 0/100 (pure bonds) portfolios, for someone like Ms. Smith, who is 65 years old and has many years ahead of her. For the record, the very aggressive portfolios produced slightly higher returns than asset dedication. They also beat the six tested asset allocations models by an even greater margin. The reverse is true for the very conservative portfolios. On average, the very aggressive portfolios outperformed all portfolios during this period, and the very conservative portfolios underperformed all portfolios. For anyone who can stomach the volatility, 100 percent stocks (especially in small company value stocks) is the way to maximize overall long-run returns.

Ms. Smith was assumed to withdraw $2500 at the start of each month ($30,000 annually) from her $600,000 portfolio the first year, with the amount growing to keep up with 4 percent inflation, adjusted once a year. In the asset dedication model, the income portion generated the cash needed for withdrawals. Any excess over her withdrawals was invested in Treasury bills until withdrawn. In the six asset allocation models, withdrawals were made by selling off whichever asset had the highest trailing 12-month return.

The asset allocation models were evaluated and rebalanced once a year. The asset dedication model was evaluated using actual prices of U.S. Treasury bonds with maturities of 1 through 10 years as reported in the *Wall Street Journal* to get as precise an estimate as possible. (Bond price data from the *Journal* became sporadic for earlier periods, so the cost of the portfolio had to be estimated from bond data in the data sets). For the six asset allocation models, the bond portion of the portfolio was valued based on the intermediate government bond index for each month. By maintaining full investment at all times and using only indexes, timing and selection were completely removed from the analysis.

No fees, transaction costs, taxes, or other such external costs were factored in. This was actually unfair to the asset dedication approach, since the asset allocation approaches would theoretically incur more transaction costs at least because of rebalancing. Furthermore, the asset allocation models would incur additional transaction costs from selling bonds or stocks to replenish cash. If management fees were deducted from Ms. Smith's portfolio each quarter, the performance of the asset allocation models would have been even worse. Nevertheless, most comparisons of this nature in the literature do not factor in such costs, and so they are omitted here also.

Some advisers allocate assets to bonds by simply putting a portion of the funds into actively managed bond funds. But actively managed bond fund results were not used for any tests because such funds do not behave the way bonds themselves do. Bond fund managers who engage in active management typically trade bonds rather than holding them to maturity. They are, in essence, speculating on future interest-rate movements, which actually increases the risk of the portfolio compared to holding bonds to maturity. This would invalidate the comparison with asset dedication. Some brokers also attempt to sell annuities to their clients on the premise that annuities remove the risks associated with volatility just as bonds do. But insiders know that annuities have a lot of disadvantages from an investment standpoint. They often have heavy legal restrictions, lack any benefit for heirs, seldom grow with inflation, pay lower returns, and provide fat commissions for the brokers selling them. They have little to recommend them except for the provision that they will pay until you die. Magazines that cater to brokers and financial planners are full of advertisements by annuity companies trumpeting the high commissions they pay to anyone who can get clients to buy their products. Many people who buy them ultimately regret it when they learn how much commission their broker earned from selling the annuity to them. Asset dedication with a rolling horizon, always keeping 5 or 10 years ahead of you, is a simple way to self-annuitize much more cheaply and retain full control over your funds.

Table 4.2 lists the ending values for Ms. Smith's portfolio for all cases. This is the amount of money she will still have at the end of each 10-year period after making all her monthly withdrawals, which grow with inflation. These figures provide a sense of the absolute magnitudes of the amounts involved and give the proper perspective for evaluating the various models. The financial community often fails to provide the perspective that comes from knowing the absolute magnitudes of the dollars involved, which can distort a person's judgment in making informed decisions. This is something we will discuss in Chapter 12.

The bold figures in Table 4.2 represent the winning strategy for that particular time span, the one with the highest ending value. Figures in italics indicate a portfolio that beat asset dedication.

In the 1976–1985 period, for instance, *asset dedication would have had an ending value of $1,192,815, higher than any other*

Table 4.2

Asset Dedication versus Asset Allocation: Ending Portfolio Value Comparisons for Ms. Smith,
19 Ten-Year Spans, 1976–2003
$600,000 Initial Investment, $30,000 Annual Withdrawal, 4 Percent Inflation

		Ending Values for Ms. Smith's Portfolio				
Decade	Dedicated Portfolios	Stk/Bnd 70/30	Stk/Bnd 60/40	Stk/Bnd 50/50	Stk/Bnd 40/60	Stk/Bnd 30/70
1976 to 1985	$1,192,815	$1,147,178	$1,109,977	$1,072,283	$1,034,172	$995,720
1977 to 1986	$1,499,727	$1,427,442	$1,351,958	$1,277,929	$1,205,446	$1,134,592
1978 to 1987	$1,627,775	$1,635,197	$1,530,310	$1,428,891	$1,330,934	$1,236,430
1979 to 1988	$1,714,205	$1,669,202	$1,565,689	$1,465,830	$1,369,611	$1,277,014
1980 to 1989	$1,767,661	$1,666,850	$1,595,952	$1,526,398	$1,458,225	$1,391,467
1981 to 1990	$1,605,504	$1,574,529	$1,537,475	$1,500,094	$1,462,424	$1,424,507
1982 to 1991	$2,049,589	$1,975,758	$1,888,806	$1,804,050	$1,721,485	$1,641,102
1983 to 1992	$1,643,743	$1,653,057	$1,579,049	$1,506,759	$1,436,191	$1,367,347
1984 to 1993	$1,603,060	$1,591,053	$1,528,759	$1,467,558	$1,407,466	$1,348,495
1985 to 1994	$1,380,091	$1,379,309	$1,317,608	$1,257,329	$1,198,473	$1,141,040
1986 to 1995	$1,462,720	$1,447,878	$1,360,720	$1,276,826	$1,196,149	$1,118,641
1987 to 1996	$1,335,905	$1,253,260	$1,171,801	$1,093,735	$1,019,006	$947,556
1988 to 1997	$1,804,213	$1,641,316	$1,491,354	$1,351,868	$1,222,302	$1,102,116
1989 to 1998	$2,069,957	$1,778,602	$1,612,489	$1,458,407	$1,315,687	$1,183,687
1990 to 1999	$1,971,873	$1,688,647	$1,512,137	$1,350,100	$1,201,593	$1,065,718
1991 to 2000	$1,774,385	$1,639,569	$1,478,742	$1,328,793	$1,189,260	$1,059,679
1992 to 2001	$1,179,411	$1,209,580	$1,127,104	$1,045,664	$965,549	$887,022
1993 to 2002	$766,927	$936,958	$911,646	$880,880	$845,070	$804,640
1994 to 2003	$934,898	$1,061,525	$1,002,424	$939,775	$874,335	$806,842

Average return	**$1,546,550**	$1,493,522	$1,403,895	$1,317,535	$1,234,388	$1,154,401
Best return	**$2,069,957**	$1,975,758	$1,888,806	$1,804,050	$1,721,485	$1,641,102
Lowest return	$766,927	*$936,958*	*$911,646*	*$880,880*	*$845,070*	*$804,640*
Capture ratio	**98.2%**	96.0%	90.5%	85.1%	79.9%	74.8%
Decades won	14	5	0	0	0	0

Boldface font indicates winning model for that decade or measure.

Source: Based on analysis of data sets that support Table 1.1 (see text for details).

strategy. In 1978–1987, the 70/30 asset allocation portfolio had the highest ending value ($1,635,197), with asset dedication a close second ($1,627,775). The ending value "capture ratio" of asset dedication in this case would be 99.5 percent, indicating how close it was to the winner ($1,627,775/$1,635,197 = 99.5 percent).

The general superiority of the asset dedication approach since 1976 is obvious in these figures. *Asset dedication won 14 of the 19 decades, had the highest average ending value ($1,546,550), the highest maximum ($2,069,557 for 1989–1998, and the highest average capture ratio (98.2 percent).* The 98.2 percent capture ratio means asset dedication was within 1.8 percent of the winner. The most aggressive portfolio (70/30) took second place on the various measures for which asset dedication took first place, and the 70/30 also won the five cases that asset dedication lost. In three of those five decades, however, asset dedication came in a close second to the 70/30 portfolio, and even at its worst, its ending value was still about 82 percent of the best. For the record, its worst decade, which was also the worst for all other portfolios, was 1993–2002. It had an ending value of $766,927, a capture ratio of about 82 percent of the winning $936,958 for the 70/30 portfolio. The major decline beginning in 2000 hurt all portfolios.

Asset dedication performs so well because it maximizes the portion of the portfolio devoted to equities to capture the long-term advantage that they offer over bonds. This means that in the few periods in history in which a great bear market has caused stocks to temporarily underperform bonds, asset dedication will not perform quite as well as portfolios that are more heavily laden with bonds. But, statistically speaking, it does not make sense to ignore the strategy that produces the winner most of the time for other strategies that lose most of the time.

Table 4.3 converts Ms. Smith's monthly withdrawals over the 10-year periods and the ending values in Table 4.2 into internal rates of total return. Not surprisingly, the same conclusions regarding the superiority of the asset dedication approach for this time span are evident here, as they were in Table 4.2. The summary results are printed at the bottom of the table. *As can be seen, the asset dedication strategy achieves the highest IRR, averaging 12.6 percent per year including all 19 decades, with a high of 15.4 percent (1989–1998) and a low of 7.2 percent (1993–2002).* The fact that performance in 1993–2002 was the worst for all the portfolios demonstrates the severity of the decline after the market bubble burst in 2000.

Table 4.3

Asset Dedication versus Asset Allocation: Total Returns (IRR) for Ms. Smith, 19 Ten-Year Spans, 1976–2003
$600,000 Initial Investment, $30,000 Annual Withdrawal, 4 Percent Inflation

	Internal Rate of Return for Ms. Smith's Portfolio*					
Decade	Dedicated Portfolios	Stk/Bnd 70/30	Stk/Bnd 60/40	Stk/Bnd 50/50	Stk/Bnd 40/60	Stk/Bnd 30/70
1976 to 1985	10.7%	10.3%	10.1%	9.8%	9.5%	9.2%
1977 to 1986	12.6%	12.1%	11.7%	11.2%	10.7%	10.3%
1978 to 1987	13.3%	13.3%	12.7%	12.1%	11.6%	10.9%
1979 to 1988	13.7%	13.5%	12.9%	12.4%	11.8%	11.2%
1980 to 1989	14.0%	13.5%	13.1%	12.7%	12.3%	11.9%
1981 to 1990	13.1%	13.0%	12.8%	12.6%	12.3%	12.1%
1982 to 1991	15.3%	15.0%	14.6%	14.1%	13.7%	13.3%
1983 to 1992	13.3%	13.4%	13.0%	12.6%	12.2%	11.8%
1984 to 1993	13.1%	13.1%	12.7%	12.4%	12.0%	11.7%
1985 to 1994	11.9%	11.8%	11.5%	11.1%	10.7%	10.3%
1986 to 1995	12.3%	12.3%	11.7%	11.2%	10.7%	10.1%
1987 to 1996	11.6%	11.1%	10.5%	10.0%	9.4%	8.8%
1988 to 1997	14.1%	13.3%	12.5%	11.7%	10.9%	10.0%
1989 to 1998	15.4%	14.0%	13.2%	12.3%	11.5%	10.6%
1990 to 1999	14.9%	13.6%	12.6%	11.7%	10.7%	9.8%
1991 to 2000	14.0%	13.3%	12.4%	11.5%	10.6%	9.7%
1992 to 2001	10.6%	10.8%	10.2%	9.6%	9.0%	8.3%
1993 to 2002	7.2%	8.7%	8.5%	8.3%	8.0%	7.6%
1994 to 2003	8.7%	9.7%	9.3%	8.8%	8.2%	7.6%
Average return	12.6%	12.4%	11.9%	11.4%	10.8%	10.3%
Best return	15.4%	15.0%	14.6%	14.1%	13.7%	13.3%
Lowest return	7.2%	8.7%	8.5%	8.3%	8.0%	7.6%

*Internal rate of total return, including cash withdrawals and ending value of portfolio.
Source: Table 4.2.

Figure 4.3 charts the average IRR for each of the models tested. The good news for anyone like Ms. Smith who retired at the start of any of these decades from 1976 to 1993 was that the ending values of her portfolio would have been higher than the starting value of $600,000 (in current and real dollars). This stems from the fact that this entire span was good to investors almost no matter when they entered the market or which strategy they used. All portfolios were good; it's just that some were better than others. This remarkable performance of the U.S. stock market is probably partly responsible

Figure 4.3

Asset Dedication versus Asset Allocation: Returns for Ms. Smith,
19 Ten-Year Spans, 1976–2003

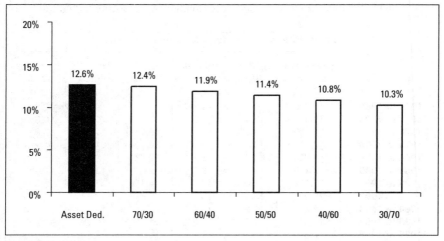

Source: Table 4.3.

for the increasingly positive attitude toward investing that people acquired, which culminated in the excesses of the late 1990s before the bubble burst in 2000. Unfortunately, it also unleashed corporate greed and corruption on a scale larger than ever before, as the recent scandals have made evident.

Test 3: 1947–2003

ASSET DEDICATION WINS MOST OVER THE POSTWAR ERA

Test 3 covered a longer period, a total of 48 decades (1947–1956, 1948–1957, . . .,1994–2003). Its final 19 decades overlap the span covered in Test 2. Because the market in general did not do as well in the first 29 decades as in the final 19, the results in absolute terms are not as impressive for any of the portfolios. However, the primary conclusion about the relative performance remains: Asset dedication tends to dominate all asset allocation models tested.

The results for all 48 individual decades become quite voluminous, but the first 29 can be found in Appendix 3. The same measures and procedures were used for this span as were used for the

1976–2003 span. Table 4.4 summarizes the results. *Again, the historical record demonstrates the superior performance of asset dedication compared to the asset allocation models. It wins 26 of the 48 decades in terms of return, has the highest capture ratio (96.8 percent), and has the highest average return (9.9 percent) and maximum return (15.4 percent).*

Test 4: 1926–2003

ASSET DEDICATION WINS MOST OVER THE TWENTIETH CENTURY

This period is the most comprehensive, covering 69 decades (78 years inclusive) beginning in 1926–35. Accurate information on returns prior to 1926 is difficult to obtain on a monthly basis, as they begin to reach the back edge of trustworthy data. Dedicated scholars have been able to reconstruct a few series for periods prior to 1926, but some researchers began to question the relevancy of observations from such a distant past anyway. In the science of statistics, there is no theoretical line of demarcation as to how far back data should be included in attempting to understand current market behavior. Usually the line is drawn by a lack of reliable data, which simply become unavailable at some point in the past. Even when reliable data are available, however, there is no objective way to decide where to stop, and subjective judgments must be made. We will discuss this and other issues related to forecasting in Part 3 of this book.

But starting in 1926 means that Test 4 includes the Great Depression of the 1930s, the worst time period that financial markets in the United States have ever known. Returns on many financial investments were negative in these years, default rates on bonds approached 10 percent (see Appendix 2), and the economy was in about as bad a shape as it ever has been. The dampening effect on the performance of all the portfolios was evident. One argument many researchers make is that it is better to start at 1947, after the distortions and aberrations stemming from the cataclysmic events of the Great Depression and World War II were presumably over.

Table 4.5 suggests that over the 78 year span, asset dedication continued to be superior, although it does not dominate to the same extent as over more recent periods. *Asset dedication won in 34 of the 69 decades and had the highest average return, 8.7 percent, and the highest capture ratio, 93.8 percent.* The worst decade for all portfolios was 1929–1938, coinciding with the Great Depression. Asset dedication lost 0.4 percent per year over this decade (the most

Table 4.4

Asset Dedication versus Asset Allocation: Summary Comparisons for Ms. Smith, 48 Ten-Year Spans, 1947–2003

$600,000 Initial Investment, $30,000 Annual Withdrawal, 4 Percent Inflation

Results for 1947–2003 (48 Decades)	Asset Dedication	Stk/Bnd 70/30	Stk/Bnd 60/40	Stk/Bnd 50/50	Stk/Bnd 40/60	Stk/Bnd 30/70
Average ending value	$1,162,394	$1,136,265	$1,052,872	$974,945	$902,104	$833,994
Maximum ending value	$2,069,957	$1,975,758	$1,888,806	$1,804,050	$1,721,485	$1,641,102
Minimum ending value	$386,662	$429,421	$443,109	$456,164	$468,534	$480,170
Average return	9.9%	9.8%	9.2%	8.7%	8.1%	7.5%
Highest return	15.4%	15.0%	14.6%	14.1%	13.7%	13.3%
Lowest return	2.7%	3.3%	3.5%	3.7%	3.8%	4.0%
Capture ratio	96.8%	95.9%	90.0%	84.4%	79.2%	74.2%
Decades won	26	16	0	1	0	5

Source: Analysis of results displayed in Appendix 3 for 1947 to 1975 combined with results from Table 4.2 for 1976 to 2003.

Table 4.5

Asset Dedication versus Asset Allocation: Summary Comparisons for Ms. Smith, 69 Ten-Year Spans, 1926–2003
$600,000 Initial Investment, $30,000 Annual Withdrawal, 4 Percent Inflation

Results for 1926–2003 (69 Decades)	Asset Dedication	Stk/Bnd 70/30	Stk/Bnd 60/40	Stk/Bnd 50/50	Stk/Bnd 40/60	Stk/Bnd 30/70
Average ending value	$1,026,165	$1,009,695	$936,813	$867,982	$802,835	$741,043
Maximum ending value	$2,069,957	$1,975,758	$1,888,806	$1,804,050	$1,721,485	$1,641,102
Minimum ending value	$220,460	$147,260	$212,319	$275,017	$333,515	$386,016
Average return	8.7%	8.6%	8.2%	7.7%	7.2%	6.6%
Highest return	15.4%	15.0%	14.6%	14.1%	13.7%	13.3%
Lowest return	-0.4%	-2.2%	-0.6%	0.7%	1.8%	2.6%
Capture ratio	93.8%	93.6%	88.6%	83.8%	79.1%	74.5%
Decades won	34	23	1	2	0	9

Source: Analysis of results displayed in Appendix 4 for 1926 to 1946 combined with results from Table 4.3 for 1947 to 2003.

aggressive asset allocation portfolio suffered the greatest loss at 2.2 percent per year). Bonds were clearly the place to be during that time, with the most conservative portfolio (30/70) returning 2.6 percent per year. Appendix 4 contains the results for the early decades.

Figures 4.4, 4.5, and 4.6 display the results shown in Table 4.5 graphically. They all point to the same conclusion: Asset dedication appears to be a superior strategy that not only is easy to understand, inexpensive to implement, and favorable in reducing risk, but also provides higher returns than most asset allocation strategies, at least based on these historical comparisons. It should be apparent why Ms. Smith, and millions more like her, will benefit from asset dedication.

WHAT ABOUT OTHER STOCK AND BOND CHOICES?

Asset Dedication Wins in Nearly Every Category, 1926–2003

All of the tests discussed so far in this chapter assumed that the growth portion of the portfolio was invested in large-company stocks (the S&P 500), and the income portion in intermediate-term government bonds.

Figure 4.4

Average Annual Total Rate of Return, 69 Ten-Year Periods, 1926–2003

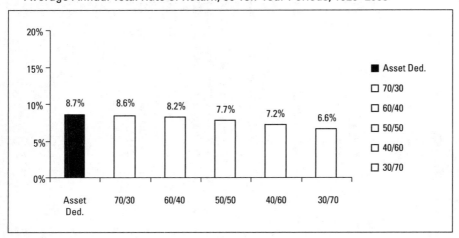

Source: Table 4.5.

Figure 4.5

Asset Dedication versus Asset Allocation Portfolio Returns by 10-Year Period, 1926–2003

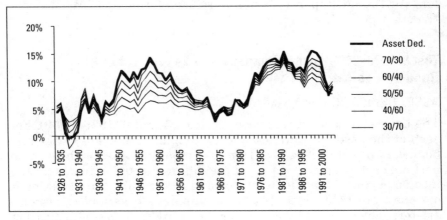

Source: Table 4.5.

Figure 4.6

Asset Dedication versus Asset Allocation: Number of 10-Year Periods with Highest Total Return, 1926–2003

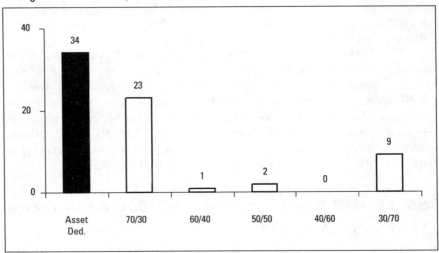

Source: Table 4.5.

It is logical to wonder how well asset dedication compares to the asset allocation models when other choices are used for stocks and bonds. For example, what if small-company stocks were used for growth and corporate bonds were used for income? What about the other possible combinations?

Test 5: 1926–2003, Large-Company Stocks with Other Bond Categories

ASSET DEDICATION WINS AGAIN

The longest time span was used for Tests 5 and 6 (1926–2003). For each of the asset allocation models, six combinations of stocks and bonds are possible: large- and small-company stocks for the growth portion, each coupled with the three different types of bonds for the income portion.[9] For the asset dedication portfolio, the investment options were held constant (large-company stocks and intermediate-term government bonds). Over the entire span, asset dedication averaged a total return of 8.7 percent. To beat asset dedication, an asset allocation portfolio would have to provide a higher return than 8.7 percent.

The results become quite voluminous for such a long span, but decade-by-decade comparisons back to 1926 can be found at www.assetdedication.com under the "Research" link. Table 4.6 summarizes the results for large-company stocks with each of the three possible choices for bonds. The asset allocation portfolios are labeled as Portfolio 1, 2, and 3. Portfolio 2 is the same as the portfolio used in Test 4 in the prior section.

The bottom line from Table 4.6 is that asset dedication again proves to be superior to asset allocation models regardless of the choice of bonds. The one exception was the most aggressive allocation, 70/30, using corporate bonds, which beat asset dedication by a hair (averaging 8.8 percent versus 8.7 percent) Recall that asset dedication used intermediate Treasury bonds, however, while the 70/30 allocation used corporate bonds, which traditionally pay higher interest and carry slightly higher risk. Figure 4.7 charts these results.

Test 6: 1926–2003, Small-Company Stocks with Other Bond Categories

ASSET DEDICATION WINS AGAIN

Recall from Table 1.1 that small-company stocks have grown faster than large-company stocks over the long term (12.1 percent versus

Table 4.6

Asset Dedication versus Asset Allocation: Comparisons of Average Annual Rates of Return for Combinations of *Large*-Company Stocks and Various Bond Classes, 1926–2003

Portfolio	Stocks	Bonds	Asset Ded.*	Stk/Bnd 70/30	Stk/Bnd 60/40	Stk/Bnd 50/50	Stk/Bnd 40/60	Stk/Bnd 30/70
1	Large Co.	Corp	8.7%	8.8%	8.5%	8.0%	7.6%	6.8%
2	Large Co.	Int Gov	8.7%	8.6%	8.2%	7.7%	7.2%	6.6%
3	Large Co.	LT Gov	8.7%	8.6%	8.1%	7.6%	7.0%	6.4%
	Mean		8.7%	8.6%	8.1%	7.6%	7.0%	6.4%

*Asset dedication used only intermediate-term government bonds in all comparisons.

Source: Decade-by-decade results available at www.assetdedication.com, (see "Research" link).

Figure 4.7

Asset Dedication versus Asset Allocation: Comparisons of Average Annual Rates of Return for Combinations of *Large*-Company Stocks and Various Bond Classes, 1926–2003

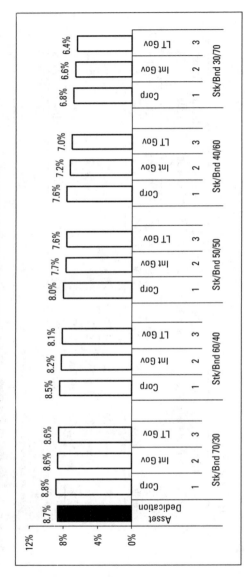

Source: Table 4.6.

10.1 percent per year). What if Ms. Smith, realizing that her income would be protected over the next 10 years, had chosen to invest in small-company stocks rather than large-company stocks? How would asset dedication compare to the asset allocation portfolios using small-company stocks for growth? Clearly, the overall returns should all be higher, but does asset dedication continue to dominate?

Table 4.7 shows that asset dedication continues to dominate. Its total return now averages 10.6 percent, and the only asset allocation portfolio that can beat it is 70/30, and then only by a hair (at 10.7 percent) if it uses corporate bonds. Recall again that corporate bonds traditionally have higher yields than the government bonds that asset dedication was constrained to use in order to protect Ms. Smith's income stream as much as possible. No other asset allocation model beats asset dedication (the 60/40 allocation model ties it using corporate bonds). Figure 4.8 provides a chart of the comparisons. Note that it tells the same story for small-company stocks as Figure 4.7 told for large-company stocks: Asset dedication works better than asset allocation in nearly all cases. As before, decade-by-decade comparisons back to 1926 can be found at www.assetdedication.com under the "Research" link.

WHAT ABOUT RISK?

Measuring Volatility and Risk

Asset allocation is the darling of the brokerage houses, and one of the first issues that brokers are likely to raise about asset dedication is risk. Does asset dedication put the investor at higher risk than the asset allocation strategies?

We will discuss risk and how it is measured by the financial community in greater detail in Chapter 12, but a few of the fundamentals about the true meaning of risk need to be considered now. First, it is important to understand that the most common measure of risk, the standard deviation, really measures volatility, including both up and down fluctuations in the market, either on a quarterly or an annual basis. It is calculated (sort of) by computing the average amount by which the portfolio's return differs each quarter (or year) from its own overall average return.[10]

Is volatility the same as risk? The answer is no. The two are related, but they are not identical. Fluctuations are meaningless unless the stocks have to be sold at a time when the market is lower

Table 4.7

Asset Dedication versus Asset Allocation: Comparisons of Average Annual Rates of Return for Combinations of *Small*-Company Stocks and Various Bond Classes, 1926–2003

Portfolio	Stocks	Bonds	Asset Ded.*	Stk/Bnd 70/30	Stk/Bnd 60/40	Stk/Bnd 50/50	Stk/Bnd 40/60	Stk/Bnd 30/70
4	Small Co.	Corp	10.6%	10.7%	10.3%	9.8%	9.1%	8.3%
5	Small Co.	Int Gov	10.6%	10.6%	10.1%	9.5%	8.8%	7.9%
6	Small Co.	LT Gov	10.6%	10.5%	10.0%	9.3%	8.6%	7.7%
		Mean	10.6%	10.6%	10.1%	9.5%	8.8%	8.0%

*Asset dedication used only intermediate-term government bonds in all comparisons.

Source: Decade-by-decade results available at www.assetdedication.com (see "Research" link).

Figure 4.8

Asset Dedication versus Asset Allocation: Comparisons of Average Annual Rates of Return for Combinations of *Small*-Company Stocks and Various Bond Classes, 1926–2003

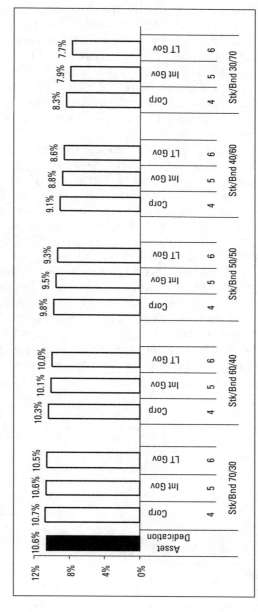

Source: Table 4.7.

than some target value. Consider first an example in which the rates of return are different (meaning that the ending values are different). In Figure 4.9, two investors both have starting portfolios worth $600,000. Portfolio 1 is very stable and has a constant 10 percent return per year. Portfolio 2 provides a higher return (about 16 percent per year) but has more volatility. By the measures of risk most commonly used in the financial community, Portfolio 2 is a riskier portfolio because it fluctuates more than Portfolio 1, which appears to have no volatility at all.

But is Portfolio 2 really riskier? Notice that it always has a higher value than Portfolio 1. Even when it drops in value, its lowest point is never below the value of Portfolio 1. How can Portfolio 2 be considered riskier than Portfolio 1 if its value is always greater? Clearly, any risk measure like the standard deviation that would cause a person to reach such a silly conclusion should be judged as misleading at best and dangerous at worst. Standard deviation must be used with full knowledge of its disadvantages as a yardstick.

The actual historical record closely represents this sort of situation. Consider Figure 4.5 again. Note how the rates of return for the decades move up and down for all the portfolios tested, including asset dedication and all the asset allocation portfolios. The most conservative asset allocation portfolio (30 percent stocks, 70 percent bonds) lies at the bottom of the chart and has the least amount of fluctuation. It would thus be considered the least risky as meas-

Figure 4.9

Portfolio 1 versus Portfolio 2—Which Is Riskier?

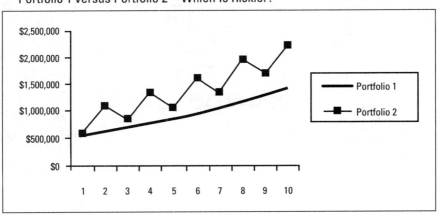

ured by the standard deviation and other measures based on the standard deviation. Asset dedication has more volatility, but, like Portfolio 2 in Figure 4.9, it nearly always stays above the 30/70 portfolio. How can it be judged riskier?

Now consider an example in which the returns are identical. In Figure 4.10, both portfolios start at $600,000, earn an average return of 10 percent per year, and end at $1,414,769. Portfolio 1 follows a smooth line, and Portfolio 3 fluctuates in value up and down. Portfolio 3 has higher volatility and would therefore be considered riskier.

But how much riskier is it really? By definition, risk means that something bad may happen. It is true that the investor with Portfolio 3 would suffer if she had to sell when the portfolio was below the line that represents her target return. But if she sold when it was above that line, she would actually be ahead of her target. It is really only the downward ticks that represent risk. But if the portfolio does not have to be sold, there is no risk to a downward tick in its value. For someone like Ms. Smith who is investing for a 10-year period, the fluctuations of the stocks in her portfolio do not matter. They have no impact. So long as she reaches her target by the end of 10 years, volatility means nothing.

Unfortunately, the standard deviation treats both upticks and downticks as equally bad, whereas common sense correctly assesses upticks as favorable. Furthermore, both portfolios have the same ending value (and thus the same average return). Fluctuations before

Figure 4.10

Portfolio 1 versus Portfolio 3—Which Is Riskier?

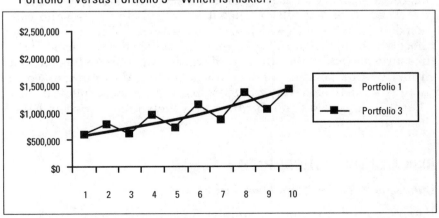

the ending date are irrelevant. The bottom line is that it may be correct that Portfolio 3 is more volatile, but how this may or may not translate into risk needs to be clearly understood by any investor in order to make the appropriate judgment.

But if you ask your broker how he or she believes risk should be measured mathematically, the knee-jerk response you are likely to receive is "the standard deviation," without equivocation and without explanation. How many investors make the wrong investment decisions because these fundamental concepts are not explained to them? How many brokers understand these fundamental concepts well enough to explain them? Nobody knows, but it is easy to fear the worst.

One final note on risk and asset dedication: The income portion holds all bonds to maturity, so that portion of the portfolio is taken off the table, so to speak, in terms of risk. Only the portion invested in growth is subject to risk as it is typically measured. Therefore, asset dedication automatically reduces risk because fewer dollars are subject to the fluctuations. Unfortunately, risk is usually measured as the fluctuations in the rate of return rather than the magnitude of the dollars invested. But with asset allocation, brokers often put clients into bond funds that treat bonds like sluggish stocks, trading them based on what they think will happen to the prices of the bonds in the future. This puts the entire portfolio at risk, rather than just the growth portion.

The many different ways to measure portfolio performance with various combinations of risk and return present an almost overwhelming menu of choices. For extremely large portfolios, such an embarrassment of riches may be a good thing. But for personal investing, the complexity leads more to confusion than to enlightenment.

The ultimate reality is that it is difficult to find a valid common denominator with which to compare asset dedication and asset allocation in terms of risk. Comparing standard deviations or any measures based on the standard deviation appears to be deficient. From the standpoint of personal investors like Ms. Smith, however, there is a fairly easy way to determine if a financial plan is doing what it is supposed to do. It utilizes a widely known concept called the *critical path*.

RISK AND THE CRITICAL PATH

Checking If the Portfolio Is on Target

For individual investors, a simpler and clearer way to track performance is the *critical path* method: Compare where your portfolio actually is right now with where it should be in absolute dollar terms. It is a simple comparison of two numbers: What your investments ought to be worth if you are on target and what they are actually worth at any point in time.

The term *critical path* comes from project management techniques first developed in the 1950s known as PERT (Program Evaluation and Review Technique) and CPM (Critical Path Method). Complex projects are broken down into a series of separate tasks, each requiring a different amount of time and resources to complete. Examples of such projects would be constructing a house, developing a new product, or even making a movie. Some tasks can be done simultaneously (such as wiring and plumbing) but some must be done in a prescribed sequence (wall supports must go up before the roof does). The critical path is the longest sequence of tasks that must be done one after another and represents the minimum total elapsed time to complete the overall project.

The same concept applies to portfolio management. Assume that you need to earn an average of 10 percent per year to reach your goal in 5 years. By simple projection, for each $100 you start with, you should be at or above $110 at the end of the first year, $121 at the end of the second year, and so on. These values trace the critical path that your portfolio must follow if you are to reach your goal. Fluctuations in your portfolio do not matter so long as your portfolio stays at or above this critical path. This concept will be discussed in greater detail in Chapter 6.

CONCLUSION

Asset dedication provides returns that are superior to those on all asset allocation portfolios tested. The test portfolios encompass the range commonly recommended by brokers. The time frame examined included 10-year periods spanning most of the twentieth century for which reliable data are available. Not only does asset dedication make sense theoretically, but it also appears to provide superior performance by most measures, including returns, capture ratio, and so on.

Past performance is no guarantee of future success, of course, but the evidence suggests that asset dedication is a certainly a worthy contender that all financial advisers and investors should consider. It may represent the start of a paradigm shift in personal investing strategies. Asset allocation should no longer be considered the only game in town. The rest of this book embellishes these arguments and shows how they relate to the critical path of retirement saving. But the basic ideas presented in these chapters will not change.

NOTES

1. The majority of this book was written before year-end figures for 2003 were available, so all tables and figures in other chapters end with 2002 data. However, year-end data for 2003 became available shortly before the book went to press, so the tables in this chapter were updated to reflect 2003 results. Other chapters remained as they were.
2. 1926 is a common stopping point for historical comparisons in investment analysis.
3. Data for analyses came from the Center for Research in Security Prices (CRSP) of the University of Chicago (www.crsp.uchicago.edu) and from Global Financial Data (www.globalfindata.com) as noted in Table 1.1.
4. Returns on stocks, bonds, and cash respectively were based on the CRSP and GFD databases of large-company stocks as measured by the value-weighted S&P 500 Index, intermediate U.S. Treasury bond index, and 30-day U.S. Treasury bills.
5. As will be explained in Chapter 12, the internal rate of return (IRR) is the appropriate return calculation to use for situations that involve periodic cash flows.
6. Although the scenario tested used the S&P 500 index funds to keep the comparisons valid and simple to explain, she might well have invested in a small-cap index fund or some other investment that she or her adviser felt would grow even faster.
7. The 40 quarters actually used started with the third quarter of 1990 and ended with the second quarter of 2000.
8. Proponents of asset allocation may claim that cash is needed in order to take advantage of market timing, but, as has been already pointed out, attribution studies tend to refute the claim that brokers succeed at timing, at least for the average broker.
9. Results for Treasury bills are not shown here because they are considered the equivalent of cash rather than bonds. Trial tests demonstrated that the results were slightly below the worst returns reported here.
10. The mathematical formula for the standard deviation is $\sigma = \sqrt{[\sum (X - \mu)^2/n]}$, where σ = standard deviation, X = individual value, μ = the mean of the population, and n = number of observations. The value of the mean must usually be estimated from a sample, so an approximation of σ must be made by dividing by n-1 instead of n.

PART 2

Dedicating Assets before and after Retirement

Most financial planners split life into three phases: accumulation, distribution, and transfer. Each phase represents a completely different investing environment, and no book related to financial planning would be complete if it did not address the issues involved. Part 1 of this book introduced asset dedication and demonstrated how well it did against the traditional asset allocation approach to personal investing. In Chapter 3 we sketched out the basic ideas of how asset dedication was set up for the mythical Ms. Smith, aged 65 and just beginning her retirement.

This part demonstrates asset dedication in real life. These chapters use data on stock and bond returns since 1993 to describe how asset dedication fits into the accumulation and distribution phases for Mr. and Mrs. Brown, a couple in their mid-50s. It highlights the questions they must answer before and after retirement if they are to navigate their financial lifetimes successfully. Summary results for three other personal investors, who are 20, 30, and 40 years from retirement, are also presented, along with other applications, including legal settlements, investment policies for foundations, irregular cash flow patterns, and so on.

Chapter 5 begins with the Browns. Bob and Helen, both age 56, must answer some hard policy questions in order to figure out how much they will need in order to be able to live independently until age 100, a span of 44 years. They will perform the classic "independence calculation" as the starting point in establishing their overall financial plan. Chapter 6 will then set up the critical path that the Browns' portfolio must follow if it is to stay on target. The critical path demarcates the boundary line between the safety zone and the danger zone for their portfolio. Using data from 1993 to 2002, we will show how following the critical path would have allowed them to avoid the major blunder that many people made at the end of the bull market in 2000. Chapter 7 continues with the Browns through the actual dedication process and subsequent planning horizons along their critical path until they reach a little beyond age 100. Chapter 8 shows how anyone can do what the Browns did by going online at www.assetdedication.com. Finally, Chapter 9 will provide more examples of how asset dedication can be used for situations other than retirement, such as structuring settlements for legal cases, meeting the goals of charitable foundations, and matching uneven, irregular cash flows.

5

Calculating Your Financial Independence

One today is worth two tomorrows.

—BENJAMIN FRANKLIN

Life begins with childhood and youth, of course. In this phase, education and training are the dominant activities. Once this phase is finished (is it ever?), financial planners tend to split the rest of a person's financial lifetime into three major investment phases. The goals and environments for each are fundamentally different.

ECONOMIC PHASES IN A PERSON'S LIFE

Accumulation, Distribution, and Transfer—Separate Phases, Environments, and Goals

Figure 5.1 starts with the education phase, then shows the three major phases in a person's life from a financial and economic standpoint:[1]

Figure 5.1

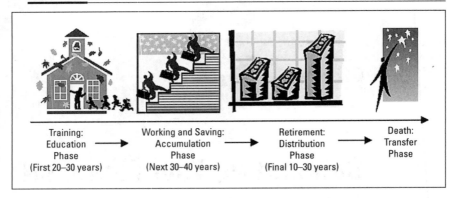

| Training: Education Phase (First 20–30 years) | Working and Saving: Accumulation Phase (Next 30–40 years) | Retirement: Distribution Phase (Final 10–30 years) | Death: Transfer Phase |

1. The accumulation phase—when money is added (the working years)
2. The distribution phase—when money is withdrawn (retirement)
3. The transfer phase—when money is passed on to heirs

Each phase has its own particular investing environment, problems, and goals. Most of this book focuses on the distribution phase. But the issues of the distribution phase must not be confused with the issues that dominate the other phases. Later chapters will discuss each phase in some detail. For now it is best to simply realize that these are the three primary phases of most people's financial lives.

Accumulation phase: Most people spend most of their lives in this phase. They are adding money to their portfolio by not spending everything they earn. The big question here is, "How much should I be saving in order to reach my investment goals for supporting myself and family when (or if) I retire?" A second, equally important question is, "How should I invest my money in order to reach my goals?" This chapter and Chapter 6 will help answer these questions.

Distribution phase: This begins at retirement, when people begin to withdraw money from their portfolio to replace their paychecks. Most people would like to maintain the same lifestyle that they had before without working. Common questions in this phase are: "How long will my money last? How much can I take out? How much does it have to earn?" Legal restrictions and tax issues become important in this phase, especially with regard to 401(k) and similar "qualified" accounts. These issues will be discussed in Chapter 7.

Transfer phase: No one likes to contemplate death, but as the old joke goes, none of us is getting out of this alive. Wills, estates, and similar sorts of issues get even more involved here than in the distribution phase. It is imperative that you consult with attorneys or other professionals who specialize in these matters to draw up the proper papers. A slip-up here can undo a lifetime of financial preparation.

FINANCIAL PLANNING IN THE ACCUMULATION PHASE

Figuring Out How Much to Save—It's Not an Easy Job, but We All Have to Do It

The primary issue during the accumulation phase is figuring out how much to save. Regardless of whether asset dedication, asset allocation, or some other investment approach is used, all should be driven by a plan. Financially, life is a big balancing act: balancing what you need to live on today against what you will need to live on in the future. The goal is usually to keep life on an even keel over time. It would not make sense to live like a pauper throughout most of your life just to live like a king when you retire, or vice versa. Psychologists suggest that people who live too much in the future, too much in the present, or too much in the past make poor choices in the inevitable trade-offs among these three in how they live their lives. Healthy, functional people have figured out how to balance all three perspectives.

The calculations needed to create and maintain a financial balance are tedious. They also seem irrelevant to the young. Retirement seems very far off when you are in your twenties and thirties because most of your life lies ahead of you. Establishing a career, paying off student loans, buying a house, and having a family take priority. This is appropriate, especially the purchase of a house, since the tax laws in our country treat home ownership very favorably.

But the calculations must ultimately be confronted. They are not simple because they involve one of the most fundamental economic trade-offs: spend it now or save it for later? Each of us must choose between spending now and spending later, and we all have different time preferences. Setting the retirement goal is one of the critical strategic financial decisions of life. It is no surprise that money is a common source of conflict for couples (how to earn it, spend it, or save it).

There is also a natural resistance to planning that comes from the inherent desire for freedom and spontaneity. Planning tends to invoke the specter of restriction and constraint, a straight and narrow path to be followed that might cramp our "free spirit." Planning also invokes the fear of failure. If we don't make specific plans, if we avoid measuring our progress or outcome, we may be able to make enough excuses along the way to evade the awful realization that we are not perfect. If we keep our goals vague and hazy, no one will ever know if we achieved them or not, including ourselves. If things don't seem to have worked out very well, we can always blame our misfortune on bad luck or unforeseeable events.

But if we get specific and take the time and trouble to plan, then something else is going on. We have now begun to take our responsibility for our situation seriously. We have internalized the situation by planning and executing to the best of our ability. We are no longer allowing external forces to completely determine our fate, and we are making ourselves accountable. If we now fail to achieve our goal, a goal that was clear, specific, and on the record, we will come face to face with our own limitations and imperfections. We will have to acknowledge that we are not perfect. And we know that this will hurt. A natural inclination that many people succumb to, therefore, is to avoid the pain by simply not planning.[2]

Unfortunately, from a financial standpoint, failing to get specific plans in place can be disastrous. We go through the accumulation phase only once. If we mess it up, we could well end our lives in either absolute or relative poverty. The prospect of dying a miserable derelict (or forcing someone we love to do so) ought to be enough to motivate anyone to deal with these issues. Taking advantage of our working years to stash away money for retirement, or in case of disability, is really the only option we have. Anyone who has been through a divorce or similar personal tragedy knows that life does not always go the way we think it will. We cannot expect others to protect us.[3]

This chapter discusses how to approach the problems of planning for retirement while there is still time to do something about it. The case study in this chapter will set up a financial plan for Bob and Helen Brown, 10 years before their retirement. It will introduce the concept of the critical path, and how the Browns can use it to trace their actual progress toward the goal they set for themselves. It will show that by simply knowing what was needed, they could have avoided the major market decline that began in the year 2000.

THE INDEPENDENCE CALCULATION

Saving for Retirement—How Much Is Enough?

The dominant questions faced during the accumulation period are, "Am I saving the right amount? How much should I be saving? Will I have enough?"

These are obvious questions without obvious answers. Financial planners often start the retirement planning process by performing the "independence calculation" or "nest egg calculation." They begin by determining how much money you will need on the day you retire in order to be able to live independently until you die. Estimating this amount, even roughly, requires a number of assumptions and projections that they are trained to deal with. The underlying idea is to get specific in setting a target or goal for your portfolio by performing the independence calculation. This chapter will show you how to do it. Once the goal has been set, you must then find the critical path that leads to it, which is the topic of the next chapter. By tracking your progress along the critical path, you will know whether or not you are "on target."

If you have no goal, you will never know whether you are on track or not. To simply say, "I want as much as I can get!" begs the question. Everyone obviously wants as much as he or she can get. If you are not specific about what you really need, however, you could easily fall into a trap that will cost you a great deal of money needlessly. Or you may be saving too much (this is rarer), making needless sacrifices in your present situation. The question is, realistically, how much do you really need in order to reach the minimum level of living that will satisfy you?

Table 5.1 lists the questions that must be answered in order to set a realistic target. One of the ways in which financial planners provide true value to their clients is by helping them to sort through such calculations.

Other factors become part of the calculation also, such as tax rates, special expenses, or planned gifts. But the questions in Table 5.1 provide the essential information that any financial planner needs to start the process. They can help with some questions, but you must answer most of them pretty much on your own.

Table 5.1

Basic Information Needed to Set the Target Portfolio for Retirement

> *1. How long before you retire?*
> *2. How much income will you need from your portfolio (today's dollars)?*
> *3. How long do you want it to last?*
> *4. How much can you earn on it **after** you retire?*
> *5. How much inflation should you allow for?*
> *6. How much do you want to leave to your heirs?*

Many web sites will make these calculations for you as a free service or to get your business.[4] Financial advisers, banks, brokers, and other financial professionals will also provide a standardized "retirement calculator form" that leads to the answer. Even newspapers and financial magazines print them occasionally. The problem is that you have to know a little about what you are doing in order to interpret the results correctly. That is why many people turn to advisers for help to guide them through the process.

THE HARD PART: BASIC LIFE CHOICES

Six Fundamental Pieces of Information

Acquiring the information you need in order to perform the independence calculation can be a lengthy and soul-searching process if you do it seriously. The next section details the choices made by Mr. and Mrs. Brown to arrive at their numbers. The interested reader can pursue how the Browns arrived at their conclusions for each question. For brevity's sake, the following list simply provides the results without explanation. This is the information that will be carried over to the next chapter to find the critical path to reach the goal.

A summary of the information regarding the Brown's independence calculation is as follows, with details in the rest of this section:

1. How long before you retire?
   Answer: 10 years
2. How much income will you need from your portfolio (today's dollars)?
   Answer: $30,000 annually
3. How long do you want it to last?
   Answer: To age 100

4. How much can you earn on it after you retire?
   Answer: 8 percent
5. How much inflation should you allow for?
   Answer: 4 percent
6. How much do you want to leave to your heirs?
   Answer: Zero

Describing the details of the information-gathering process for Bob and Helen Brown is somewhat lengthy, but it is informative for anyone who has not done it at least once. Results for other people in different life stages will be given later, but for now we will focus on the Browns, who are the closest to retirement.

To keep it simple, we will frame the discussion around Bob (it could be either spouse). Helen worked full time before their children were born and intermittently as the children were growing up, but she devoted most of her life to making their home a warm environment and a comforting refuge for the family. Both she and Bob will reach age 56 this year. Retirement was beginning to show up in their conversations, so they decided to see a financial adviser. The explanations of their answers to the questions in Table 5.1 are listed here.

1. HOW LONG BEFORE YOU RETIRE?

Bob plans to retire at age 66 when his full social security benefits can begin. He has 10 years left to achieve his goal.[5]

2. HOW MUCH INCOME WILL YOU NEED IN TODAY'S DOLLARS?

The Browns' initial desire is to maintain the same type of lifestyle they have now, with no dramatic changes. They will continue to live in the same house and do the same types of things they do currently. They estimate that it will take a gross income of $70,000 per year, or $5833 per month, to do this in today's dollars. From their tax returns, they estimate their average tax rate (not their marginal rate) to be about 20 percent (federal plus local).[6] This will leave them with a net of $56,000 per year or $4667 per month, their best estimate of what their monthly out-of-pocket expenses will be.

Gross income need can also be figured out by working backward from net expenses per month. If their average tax rate is 20 percent, then they will take home an average of 80 percent of each dollar of gross income. This means that they will need 25 percent more (net $= 0.80 \times$ gross, so gross $= (1/0.80) \times$ net $= 1.25 \times$ net). In this case, $1.25 \times \$4667 = \$5833$ gross income needed per month, or $12 \times \$5833 = \$70,000$ per year.[7]

Estimates such as this are good enough for planning. Some people postpone planning because they cannot predict their expenses with precision. But precision is not necessary. Precision is helpful, of course, but the lack of it is not a good reason to postpone planning. Crude estimates are better than none. The important thing is not to drift aimlessly.

Where will the $70,000 come from? A quick check with the online benefits calculator on the Social Security web site shows that Bob can expect about $20,000 in today's dollars. Also, both he and his wife will receive pensions from former employers plus income from other miscellaneous sources in the amount of about $20,000 in today's dollars. This means that they will have to withdraw the equivalent of $30,000 annually from their retirement portfolio.

3. HOW LONG DO YOU WANT IT TO LAST?

The Browns have no idea exactly when they will die, of course. But they realize that they are likely to be gone by age 100. Financial advisers commonly use age 100 because most people find it acceptable. Setting an earlier age tends to arouse morbid feelings that few of us wish to think about, and advisers have learned that clients may not come back if they leave a session feeling depressed.

Assume that the Browns want to take steps to make sure their money lasts until they reach 100. This means that they want enough money in the nest egg on Bob's sixty-sixth birthday to support them for 34 years, through Bob's ninety-ninth year.

Novice financial advisers will sometimes use an investor's life expectancy (or the spouse's, if that is longer) to determine the length of time the portfolio should last. This is a rookie error. There is a 50-50 chance that a person will live beyond her or his life expectancy. This means that half the people who plan in this way will end up in trouble, and the other half will be dead. Clients are hardly winners in either case.

Some planners suggest using life expectancy plus 10 years. Adding 10 years at least recognizes that the life expectancy figure is too short for half the people. But it is entirely arbitrary and does not really address the problem (why not 15 or 20 years?).

A more precise method is to use a 95 percent life expectancy table. This shows the age to which a person has less than a 5 percent chance of surviving. It is age 93 for Bob (or any man under age 60) and 98 for Helen (or any woman between 45 and 74). Table 5.2 provides the equivalent figures for other ages. To be even more conservative, 99 percent life expectancies are also shown in Table 5.2. This would be age 98 for Bob and 103 for Helen. Interestingly, the "age 100" rule of thumb will be correct between 95 and 99 percent of the time.[8]

These figures are based on the 1999 life tables put out by the Department of Health and Human Services. The figures change over time, but only very slowly, by a tenth of a year or so, as public health practices and medicine gradually extend life. Life expectancy tables published by the government also vary by race. Table 5.2 is the average for all races, so the figures should be considered only approximate.[9] But they are likely to be accurate to within a year or two for most practical purposes.

4. HOW MUCH CAN YOU EARN ON IT AFTER YOU RETIRE?

At the beginning of each year, enough income will be withdrawn from the nest egg to pay expenses for that year (or set aside for monthly withdrawals), but the balance will be left to grow. The rate of return will determine how fast it grows, and this is obviously a crucial number because of the compounding effect over long periods. The return depends on how the nest egg is invested and what happens to those investments.

If the Browns use asset dedication, the income portion of their portfolio will be based on prevailing interest rates for bonds of the maturities they dedicate to providing their income. The growth portion will depend on the equities they choose, but if they play it safe and select an index fund, they can at least estimate the probability of various return rates with greater confidence.

The next chapter will explore the return rates that the Browns might achieve. For now, assume that they expect to average at least 8 percent total return per year on their overall portfolio. This tends to be the default return rate that many financial advisers use for conservative investors. From Chapter 1, it is clear that this is below the average for equities, which means that the probability of achieving an 8 percent return is more than 50 percent. Assume that their adviser believes that the most realistic benchmark will be the period since 1947 (this will omit the impact of the Great Depression and World War II). Based on the record since then, it turns out that there is about a 77 percent probability of getting 8 percent or better.

Table 5.2

95 and 99 Percent Life Expectancies for Various Ages
(Age at which there is less than a 5 percent and 1 percent
chance of survival)

*Example 1: Mr. Brown is 56 years old. For any man between 20 and
59, there is a 95 percent probability that he will die by age 93,
and a 99 percent chance that he will die by age 98.*

*Example 2: Mrs. Brown is also 56 years old. For any woman
between 45 and 74, there is a 95 percent probability that she
will die at age 98 or before, and a 99 percent chance that
she will die at age 103 or before.*

Men			Women		
Current Age	95%	99%	Current Age	95%	99%
20–59	93	98	20–44	97	102
60–71	94	99	45–74	98	103
72–77	95	100	75–82	99	103
78–81	96	101	83–87	100	104
82–84	97	101	88–89	101	105
85–87	98	102	90–92	102	106
88–89	99	103	93–94	103	106
90–91	100	104	95–96	104	107
92–93	101	105	97–98	105	108
94–95	102	106	99–100	106	109
96	103	106	100 +	105+	107+
97	104	107			
98	104	107			
99	105	108			
100	106	108			
100+	104+	106+			

Source: Based on data from the U.S. Department of Health and Human Services, 1999 Life Tables.

The next two tables illustrate where this 77 percent comes from. With asset dedication, the majority of their portfolio will be invested in equities. Table 5.3 presents the historical record of average annual total return on the S&P 500 for all 10-year spans from 1947–1956 to 1993–2002, sorted from highest to lowest. If you count, you will see that 36 of the 47 decades had return rates of 8 percent or more. The overall average was 12.4 percent per year, the highest was 20.1 percent (1949–1958), and the lowest was 1.2 percent (1965–1974), with a standard deviation of 5.0 percent.

Table 5.3

Annualized Returns over Each Decade Since 1947,
Sorted Best to Worst

Total Return	Decade	Total Return	Decade
20.1%	1949–1958	13.4%	1953–1962
19.4%	1950–1959	12.9%	1992–2001
19.2%	1989–1998	12.8%	1958–1967
18.4%	1947–1956	12.8%	1955–1964
18.2%	1990–1999	11.1%	1956–1965
18.0%	1988–1997	10.6%	1974–1983
17.6%	1982–1991	10.0%	1959–1968
17.5%	1980–1989	9.9%	1963–1972
17.5%	1991–2000	9.3%	1993– 2002
16.4%	1948–1957	9.2%	1957–1966
16.4%	1952–1961	8.4%	1971–1980
16.3%	1979–1988	8.2%	1961–1970
16.2%	1983–1992	7.8%	1960–1969
16.2%	1951–1960	7.1%	1962–1971
15.9%	1954–1963	6.7%	1973–1982
15.3%	1987–1996	6.6%	1967–1976
15.3%	1978–1987	6.5%	1972–1981
14.9%	1984–1993	6.0%	1964–1973
14.8%	1986–1995	5.9%	1970–1979
14.8%	1975–1984	3.6%	1968–1977
14.4%	1985–1994	3.3%	1966–1975
14.3%	1976–1985	3.2%	1969–1978
13.9%	1981–1990	1.2%	1965–1974
13.8%	1977–1986		
Average	**12.4%**	**Highest**	**20.1%**
Std. Dev.	**5.0%**	**Lowest**	**1.2%**

Table 5.4 summarizes the data from Table 5.3 in a frequency distribution. It counts how often the returns over all 47 decades beat 1 percent, 2 percent, and so on. Assuming that history will repeat itself, the resulting distribution provides an estimate of the probability of achieving or beating any level of return. The probabilities in Table 5.4 are similar to those used for Monte Carlo simulation studies of the stock market (see Chapter 13).

For example, the 77 percent probability of beating 8 percent comes from the far right column in Table 5.4. Similarly, there is a 34/47 = 72 percent chance of beating 9 percent per year, a 31/47 = 66

Table 5.4

Distribution of Average Annual Total Returns over All Decades, 1947–1956 to 1993–2002

Lower Limit	Upper Limit	Decade Ending Dec. 31 in Year:	Number	Number Exceeding Lower Limit	Probability of Exceeding the Lower Limit
1%	2%	1974	1	47	100%
2%	4%	1975 1977 1978	3	46	98%
4%	6%	1979	1	43	91%
6%	7%	1973 1976 1981 1982	4	42	89%
7%	8%	1969 1971	2	38	81%
8%	9%	1970 1980	2	36	77%
9%	10%	1966 1972 2002	3	34	72%
10%	11%	1968 1983	2	31	66%
11%	12%	1965	1	29	62%
12%	13%	1964 1967 2001	3	28	60%
13%	14%	1962 1986 1990	3	25	53%
14%	15%	1984 1985 1993 1994 1995	5	22	47%
15%	16%	1963 1987 1996	3	17	36%
16%	17%	1957 1960 1961 1988 1992	5	14	30%
17%	18%	1989 1991 2000	3	9	19%
18%	19%	1956 1997 1999	3	6	13%
19%	20%	1959 1998	2	3	6%
20%	21%	1958	1	1	2%
		Total:	47		

percent chance of beating 10 percent per year, and so on. If the entire portfolio were invested in equities, these figures could be used as guidelines as to what sort of return to expect. After retirement, however, some portion of the portfolio will be held in bonds, so the total return on the portfolio is likely to be less. Thus, 8 percent is conservative, but not unreasonable.

5. HOW MUCH INFLATION SHOULD YOU ALLOW FOR?

The Browns will need an income starting at $30,000 in today's dollars. This must grow with inflation. Since 1947, inflation has averaged 4.1 percent over all 10-year periods. Assume the Browns decide to allow for 4 percent inflation per year. This means that after 1 year, they will need $31,200 to have the equivalent purchasing power of $30,000 today. The next year the amount they need will climb another 4 percent to $32,448, and so on, up to $44,407 in 10 years. Table 5.5 illustrates this growth over the next 10 years.

Table 5.6 projects the continuing income need for the next 34 years, until age 100. Each year, the withdrawal will increase by 4 percent to match inflation. Of course, if inflation is lower, the Browns can always withdraw less, subject to any minimum distributions they must take. If inflation is higher, they will have to cut back on their spending. One of the interesting things about retired

Table 5.5

Projected Income Need in 10 Years

Year	Becomes Age	Income Plus Inflation	Comments
0	56	$30,000	Current year
1	57	$31,200	
2	58	$32,448	
3	59	$33,746	
4	60	$35,096	
5	61	$36,500	
6	62	$37,960	
7	63	$39,478	
8	64	$41,057	
9	65	$42,699	
10	66	$44,407	First withdrawal

people and inflation is that retirees are generally very good at knowing how to be frugal. When the price of beef goes up, they switch to chicken. When the price of movies goes up, they wait and get the rental. Age tends to nurture adaptability, patience, and, in most cases, wisdom.

If both Mr. and Mrs. Brown beat the odds and live past age 99, they will ultimately receive a total payout from their portfolio of $3,102,203. Their last check would be $162,015 on their ninety-ninth birthday. This sounds like a lot by today's standards, but $30,000 sounded like a lot 34 years ago! This will completely deplete their nest egg account and nothing will be left for their heirs (there will probably be some insurance proceeds, of course, but those are outside this account).

Had Bob and Helen passed away prior to this, their heirs would have received whatever was in the account at the time of their death. If both parents live beyond age 100, the children will inherit nothing and in fact will probably have to contribute to their support unless social security or other income sources are sufficient for their needs. But all of this should have been discussed many years earlier. These are vagaries of life that we all must face and make informed choices about.

Table 5.6

Projected Income Needs after Retirement
(Target Nest Egg Must Support 34 Withdrawals)

Year	Becomes Age	Income plus Inflation	Withdrawals for Income During Retirement
1	66	$44,407	1st withdrawal
2	67	$46,184	2nd withdrawal
3	68	$48,031	3rd withdrawal
4	69	$49,952	4th withdrawal
5	70	$51,950	5th withdrawal
⋮	⋮	⋮	⋮
15	80	$76,899	15th withdrawal
⋮	⋮	⋮	⋮
25	90	$113,829	25th withdrawal
⋮	⋮	⋮	⋮
34	99	$162,015	34th and final withdrawal
		$3,102,203	Total, all 34 withdrawals

Inflation of 4 percent seems high given recent inflationary trends, but not by historical standards. Table 5.7 tabulates inflation over all 10-year periods beginning with 1947–1956. The overall average was 4.1 percent per year, but the highest was 8.7 percent (1973–1982) and the lowest was 1.3 percent (1952–1961 and 1953–1962), with a standard deviation of 2.2 percent. Perhaps government policymakers have finally tamed inflation, but it seems better to err on the side of caution.

Table 5.8 does for inflation what Table 5.4 did for return rates. It summarizes the information in Table 5.7 by tabulating the number of decades that fall into each inflation range. For example,

Table 5.7

Average Annual Inflation over 47 Decades,
1947–1956 to 1993–2002

Inflation Rate	Decade	Inflation Rate	Decade
8.7%	1973–1982	3.4%	1963–1972
8.6%	1972–1981	3.4%	1988–1997
8.2%	1974–1983	3.2%	1962–1971
8.1%	1971–1980	3.1%	1989–1998
7.4%	1970–1979	2.9%	1990–1999
7.3%	1975–1984	2.9%	1961–1970
7.0%	1976–1985	2.7%	1991–2000
6.7%	1969–1978	2.5%	1947–1956
6.6%	1977–1986	2.5%	1960–1969
6.4%	1978–1987	2.5%	1992–2001
6.2%	1968–1977	2.5%	1993–2002
5.9%	1979–1988	2.2%	1950–1959
5.9%	1967–1976	2.1%	1959–1968
5.7%	1966–1975	2.0%	1948–1957
5.2%	1965–1974	1.9%	1949–1958
5.1%	1980–1989	1.8%	1957–1966
4.5%	1981–1990	1.8%	1958–1967
4.1%	1964–1973	1.8%	1951–1960
3.9%	1982–1991	1.7%	1956–1965
3.8%	1983–1992	1.6%	1955–1964
3.7%	1984–1993	1.4%	1954–1963
3.7%	1987–1996	1.3%	1953–1962
3.6%	1985–1994	1.3%	1952–1961
3.5%	1986–1995		
Average	**4.1%**	**Highest**	**8.7%**
Std. Dev.	**2.2%**	**Lowest**	**1.3%**

Table 5.8

Distribution of Inflation over All 47 Decades Beginning 1947–1956 and Ending 1993–2002

Lower Limit	Upper Limit	Which Decade? Decade Ending Dec. 31 in Year:	Number of Decades	Number Staying below Upper Limit	Probability of Staying below Upper Limit
1%	2%	1957 1958 1960 1961 1962 1963 1964 1965 1966 1967	10	10	21%
2%	3%	1956 1959 1968 1969 1970 1999 2000 2001 2002	9	19	40%
3%	4%	1971 1972 1991 1992 1993 1994 1995 1996 1997 1998	10	29	62%
4%	5%	1973 1990	2	31	66%
5%	6%	1974 1975 1976 1988 1989	5	36	77%
6%	7%	1977 1978 1986 1987	4	40	85%
7%	8%	1979 1984 1985	3	43	91%
8%	9%	1980 1981 1982 1983	4	47	100%

10 decades had average inflation rates of between 1 and 2 percent per year, 9 had rates of between 2 and 3 percent, and so on.

The average (mean) inflation rates stayed below 4 percent per year for 29 of the 47 decades, or 62 percent of the time. It might seem that this value should be closer to 50 percent, but the distribution is skewed, which pulls the mean up. It might be better from a statistical point of view to use the median, which is closer to 3 percent, instead of the mean as the average, but for demonstration purposes, we will be conservative.

6. HOW MUCH DO YOU WANT TO LEAVE TO YOUR HEIRS?

Assume that the Browns have a functional family and were able to talk these matters over with their children. Everyone has agreed that the kids are welcome to whatever is left over after both Bob and Helen are gone, but Bob and Helen will not make any significant sacrifices now to leave them a bigger inheritance. Clearly, they raised their kids right. They will do what they can to be able to live independently without becoming a burden on the rest of the family.

Table 5.9 summarizes all of the assembled information and repeats the information given earlier. This is the raw material that will enable Bob and Helen to determine how much money they will need to meet their goals and live out the retirement they are planning. It will allow them to set the appropriate target for the size of the nest egg, and the critical path that leads to it can now be determined.

THE RETIREMENT GOAL

Setting the Target from the Independence Calculation

Once the information in Table 5.9 has been established, it must be converted into a final number, the nest egg target that will provide the money needed to sustain the Browns. It turns out that for Bob and Helen Brown, the required nest egg is $866,687. They need to have this amount sitting in their retirement account on Bob's sixty-sixth birthday. On that day, he will withdraw $44,407, which is $30,000 in today's dollars plus 4 percent inflation over 10 years. If their actual expenses have not risen that much every year, and they feel that they really do not need that much, they can always reinvest it. Nothing says that they have to spend it. Every year thereafter for

Table 5.9

Mr. and Mrs. Bob Brown—Summary

Life Choice Question	Life Choice Decision
1. *How long before you retire?*	10 years
2. *How much income will you need from your portfolio (in today's dollars)?*	$30,000
3. *How long do you want it to last?*	To age 100
4. *How much can you earn on it **after** you retire?*	8 percent
5. *How much inflation should you allow for?*	4 percent
6. *How much do you want to leave to your heirs?*	Zero

the next 34 years, Bob will receive a check on his birthday for 4 percent more than he received the previous year (see Table 5.6).

The calculations to derive the actual figure of $866,687 are tedious, but if you are a do-it-yourselfer and comfortable with number crunching, you can use the calculators on the web sites listed in the notes at the end of this chapter. Though they do not give exactly the same answer, they are close enough.

The general idea of the calculations need to arrive at the specific value is fairly straightforward. Step A is to add inflation to the income needed to cover expenses in today's dollars. This amount will have to be withdrawn from the portfolio each year for the next 34 years (from ages 66 or 67 to age 99 or 100). Step B is to estimate the present value of these 34 years of withdrawals at the date of retirement, using the projected rate of return on the retirement portfolio. Step C is to sum these present values. I have my college students perform a crude version of this exercise on a spreadsheet every semester.[10] The result tends to be a real eye-opener for them. Most financial advisers are trained to perform this calculation.

The important thing here is that the target amount of $866,687 is the strategic centerpiece of the Browns' retirement plan. It becomes the central guide for their saving and investment decisions. Decision making becomes clearer, plans become precise, and blunders become avoidable. Without a specific target like this, financial planning is done in an environment of tension, apprehension, and confusion that may lead to oblivion. One of the few things all financial advisers agree upon is the need to set specific, realistic goals. The Cheshire Cat stated it quite succinctly:

"Would you tell me, please, which way I ought to walk from here?"
"That depends a good deal on where you want to get to," said
the Cat.
    "I don't much care where—," said Alice.
    "Then it doesn't matter which way you go," said the Cat.

—LEWIS CARROLL,
ALICE'S ADVENTURES IN WONDERLAND

CONCLUSION

Once the target has been set, the Browns must now implement the plan. They have made their retirement decisions and performed the independence calculation. They must now take the steps that will implement their decisions. They must invest the money they have already saved and add the correct amount to it each month. They must also monitor their progress to make certain that their money is growing at the correct rate. This will be covered in the next chapter.

NOTES

1. Some writers suggest a more refined breakdown with more phases. In his book, *Facing Financial Dysfunction: Why Smart People Do Stupid Things with Money!* (West Conshohocken, PA: Infinity Publishing, 2002). Bert Whitehead, a psychologist who also holds degrees in business and law) suggests the following phases: (1) infancy, (2) early childhood, (3) teen years, (4) early accumulation (net worth 1–3 times annual income), (5) rapid accumulation (net worth 3–7 times annual income), (6) financial independence (net worth 7–10 times annual living expenses), and (7) conservation (net worth 10–15 times annual living expenses).
2. There may be an element of selfishness here also—we will be dead anyway, so let someone else worry about it.
3. One of the disadvantages that the children of wealthy people have is that they may fail to deal with the hard choices that must be made about the trade-offs between the present and the future. In the back of their mind is the thought that they will someday inherit the wealth, and so they don't really need to worry about the future. Hard choices build character, so these people are, in a way, handicapped. They may lead shallow, aimless lives, focused on the present, never thinking about tomorrow and never quite getting their act together.
4. Web sites that perform these calculations include www.assetdedication.com, www.aarp.org, www.asec.com, and www.fidelity.com. Almost all major brokerage houses also have calculators on their web sites.
5. Anyone born in 1960 or later currently will have to wait until age 67 before becoming eligible for full social security benefits. (The eligible retirement age can always be changed by an act of Congress, of course). To keep the calculations simple we will avoid the mathematical complications of fractional years and assume that the Browns are exactly 10 years from retirement.

6. The tax rate to apply here is the average tax rate, not the marginal tax rate. The average tax rate is the total tax paid as a percentage of the total income earned. It is reported as the effective tax rate in government statistics. One major problem is that it is difficult to know how tax laws and social security will have changed by the time Bob and Helen retire. For the Browns, assume no changes from current law.

7. All figures have been rounded off to the nearest dollar starting with the annual sums, so the calculations needed to replicate the exact sums shown here would need to be carried out to the penny.

8. Annuity specialists will quickly point out that they can remove all doubt by guaranteeing coverage until death whenever it occurs. But annuities carry a lot of restrictions and traditionally offer very low rates of return.

9. Although life expectancies are sometimes broken out by race, it is doubtful that race itself causes different life expectancies. A more likely explanation is the sad commentary that minorities usually lead riskier and therefore shorter lives because of their economic circumstances. They drive older, less safe cars, have less access to medical care, and may spend more time working to make ends meet (two full-time jobs are not uncommon). They eat fast food on the run, get too little sleep, and may develop bad habits to ease their stress. All of these add up to a shorter life span. I seriously doubt that skin color has much to do with shorter life spans.

10. This spreadsheet exercise may be found on the web site www.assetdedication.com on the "Research" link.

CHAPTER 6

Finding Your Critical Path

When there is no wind, row.

—Latin Proverb

Financial planning for retirement starts with the independence calculation. The first step in almost any type of planning is to specify as clearly and specifically as possible the goal to be reached. The next step in the planning process is to develop a path that will lead to the goal and a way to check our progress along that path to make sure that we are headed in the right direction at the right speed.

As mentioned in Chapter 4, the critical path concept was developed in the early 1950s for the project management techniques PERT (Program Evaluation and Review Technique) and CPM (Critical Path Method).[1] The idea was to determine how best to manage large projects that involved hundreds or thousands of interlinking tasks for their completion.

The critical path concept becomes useful in financial planning as an easy way to see whether the portfolio is on target toward reaching the goal set by the independence calculation. Only two numbers need to be compared: the value of the portfolio today and where it should be today if progress is on target. The critical path itself is not the final destination, but it serves as a road map to make sure we reach the goal we want. Bob and Helen Brown from the last chapter made the tough choices to arrive at a specific goal for their retirement portfolio: $866,687 on Bob's sixty-sixth birthday, 10 years hence. The critical path will lead them to it.

Most people get scared when they see such large numbers. Their goal is close a million dollars—a lot of money for most of us. Where will it come from? How much needs to be saved each month in order to reach such lofty heights? How should they dedicate their assets at this point in time in order to reach their goal? Knowing the critical path will help them answer these sorts of questions.

THE CRITICAL PATH LEADING TO FINANCIAL INDEPENDENCE

Projecting the Required Growth Rate Makes It Easier to Stay on Target

Once the retirement target is in place, it is important to find the critical path that the existing portfolio must follow and make sure that the portfolio stays on or above that path as it grows each year toward the retirement goal.

Finding the critical path is the final step in formulating the overall retirement plan. Once they have implemented the plan, the Browns can then get on with other aspects of their lives, comfortable in the thought that the great unknown about their future retirement has been addressed. They know where they are headed.

To find and follow the critical path, four basic questions must be answered:

1. How much has already been saved?
2. What total return can be expected between today and retirement?
3. How much must be saved each month?
4. Does the portfolio's year-end value match what it should be?

Answering the first three of these questions will allow the Browns to plot the critical path that their portfolio should follow if it is on target. Armed with the knowledge of where their portfolio should be at the end of each year (or each quarter) will allow them to answer the fourth question easily. By knowing where they should be at each point in time, they will know whether or not they are on target and can make informed decisions to take corrective action if needed.

1. HOW MUCH HAS ALREADY BEEN SAVED?

Most people who are looking into their finances have probably already started saving for their retirement. They need to project how much their current portfolio will grow between now and their retirement and make up the difference by saving the appropriate amount each month until then. Assume that the Browns have $275,000 in their retirement account right now. This is the current value of their portfolio. How fast it will grow is the next question.

2. WHAT TOTAL RETURN CAN BE EXPECTED ON THE EXISTING PORTFOLIO BETWEEN TODAY AND RETIREMENT?

The Browns have 10 years to close the gap between their current $275,000 and the target $866,687. They will not have to worry about selling any stocks during this time and risking a loss. Knowing that they have a 10-year window for their planning horizon helps make their plan more specific.

First, it reduces concern about fluctuations in the market between now and then. The only fluctuations they need to worry about are those that cause the portfolio to dip below the path it must follow in order to reach the retirement target. Second, volatility over 10-year periods is lower than volatility over shorter periods. Third, they may be able to earn a higher return by investing in mutual funds (or stocks) that have higher average growth rates because the annual volatility of such funds no longer matters for retirement purposes.[2]

For demonstration purposes, assume that they intend to keep the account fully invested in an S&P 500 index fund. Assume that they wish to be conservative and use a return of 11 percent. Table 5.4 showed that this gives them a 62 percent chance of meeting the goal for the next 10 years. Remember that the 8 percent return discussed earlier will apply after they retire, when they will have some of their money invested in bonds, which have a lower expected return rate. Right now, they can and should put all their money in the stock index fund.[3]

Advisers who have a knee-jerk allegiance to asset allocation will balk at the idea of a 100 percent allocation to stocks, even with an index fund. They are used to thinking that asset allocation must be followed at all costs. They will needlessly recommend putting some money into bonds because that is what they are used to doing. Inertia is a strong force in the mental realm as well as the physical realm. They have accepted that it is "too risky" to have 100 percent in stocks without really understanding why.

For someone who must withdraw funds from a portfolio at unpredictable points in time, perhaps it is too risky. But for someone who is committing funds to a retirement portfolio that will not be touched until the end of the planning horizon, what purpose do the low returns on bonds serve? Accepting the low returns on bonds over long periods of time is like paying for a very expensive insurance policy in a very clumsy way. As we shall see, it is far more important to find the critical path that the portfolio must follow and make sure that it stays on or above that path than to blindly obey an arbitrary fixed formula for asset allocation. We shall return to this question again.

Notice that the rate of return *before* retirement determines the critical path but not the ending target itself. This is somewhat nonintuitive. The explanation is that the time available to accumulate the target amount determines how fast it needs to grow from contributions and earnings. But the target itself does not depend directly on how quickly the nest egg needs to grow in order to reach it. Instead, the target depends on the factors listed in the section "Setting the Target" in the prior chapter (desired standard of living, how long the nest egg should last, how much it earns after retirement, and so on). The preretirement annual return represents the speed needed in order to reach the target, but it does not directly influence the size of the target itself.

Indirectly, however, preretirement returns set limits on what can realistically be attained. If the portfolio would have to earn 50 percent per year (or any unreasonably high rate of return) or if you have to save 99 percent of your current paycheck, the target will have to be reduced. This means lowering your expected lifestyle, retiring later, or choosing one or more of the options explained later.

3. HOW MUCH MUST BE SAVED EACH MONTH?

The calculations to determine required savings are tedious by hand but straightforward on a spreadsheet.[4] The web sites mentioned in Chapter 5 can do this, and so can most financial planners. The Browns will need savings of $407.64 per month. At 11 percent per year compounded annually, saving $407.64 each month will accumulate to $85,846 at the end of 10 years, and the $275,000 will grow to $780,841, for a combined total of $866,687.

Will the Browns be able to save $407.64 per month? That depends on what they currently earn, their current spending patterns, their tax rate, and so on. If their gross annual income is $70,000 and their average or effective tax rate is 20 percent, then $408 represents 7.1 percent of their gross income and 8.8 percent of their net. This payment will remain fixed from the day they begin saving until the day they retire, but as a percentage of their wages, it will decrease over the next 10 years as their wages increase.

If they cannot quite save the needed $408 per month to start with, another option would be a graduated savings schedule. With graduated payments into their retirement funds, they could start by saving a slightly lower amount and then increase it over time with inflation. Graduated payments help a little, but not much. In this case, for the Browns, the initial payment would be about $368 and the payments would increase by 4 percent each year thereafter, reaching a monthly savings of $524 in the final year. The difference in the beginning is only about $40 a month, barely more than a dollar a day.

Furthermore, the graduated payments become higher than $408 after only three years. Graduated payments start a little lower, but even with a 40-year horizon, the saving in the initial month is only about 30 percent less than the amount required with level saving. The bad news is that they surpass the corresponding level payments about a third of the way into the horizon. Table 6.4 will give the required monthly savings for both level and graduated savings plans for the Browns, with 10 years to retirement, and three other people who are 20, 30, and 40 years from retirement, respectively.

4. DOES THE PORTFOLIO'S YEAR-END VALUE MATCH WHAT IT SHOULD BE?

In the lexicon of post-modern portfolio theory, the Browns' 11 percent target return rate on their nest egg as it builds is referred to as the *minimum acceptable return (MAR)*, a very apt term to describe what is needed to achieve the goal set by their independence calculation.[5] It is a fairly straightforward mathematical exercise to project an 11 percent growth rate and lay out the critical path that their accumulated portfolio ought to follow at each point in time to reach the target. If we begin adding $407.64 each month to $275,000 and the total return averages 11 percent per year, then the portfolio should be worth $310,384 at the end of the first year, $349,660 at the end of the second year, and so on.

Table 6.1 tabulates the critical path values for each year. In a perfect world with no uncertainty, the portfolio would track exactly along this path, culminating in the final target value of $866,687 after 10 years. No portfolio would actually grow like this, of course, because of market fluctuations, but the figures provide a useful and enlightening road map.

Figure 6.1 charts the critical path. Note that the critical path divides the area into two zones, the Safety Zone and the Danger Zone. If the value of the Browns' portfolio stays within the Safety Zone, they will meet or beat their retirement target. Fluctuations and volatility above the critical path in the Safety Zone are not very relevant to the Browns. In fact, they should welcome volatility above the critical path because greater volatility usually provides greater return. Fluctuations are dangerous only if they cause the portfolio's value to dip below the critical path and stay there.

How will they know if their portfolio dips below the critical path? If their financial adviser traced it out for them and gave them Table 6.1, all they need to do is compare two figures: the portfolio values shown on their year-end account statements and the critical path values.[6] For instance, if their ending statement after 5 years

Table 6.1

Critical Path for the Browns' Retirement Portfolio

Year	Becomes Age	Savings per Month	Accumulated	Initial Portfolio	Total Portfolio = Critical Path
0	56	$408	0	$275,000	$275,000
1	57	$408	$5,134	$305,250	$310,384
2	58	$408	$10,832	$338,828	$349,660
3	59	$408	$17,157	$376,099	$393,256
4	60	$408	$24,179	$417,469	$441,648
5	61	$408	$31,972	$463,391	$495,363
6	62	$408	$40,623	$514,364	$554,987
7	63	$408	$50,225	$570,944	$621,169
8	64	$408	$60,883	$633,748	$694,631
9	65	$408	$72,714	$703,460	$776,174
10	66	$408	$85,846	$780,841	$866,687

Figure 6.1

Critical Path Chart of Accumulated Savings over 10 Years

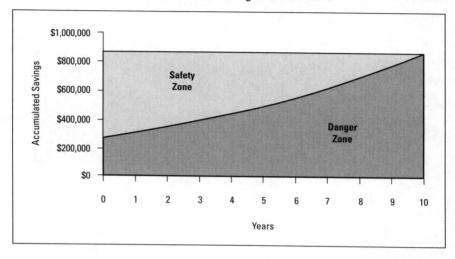

shows that their portfolio is less than $495,363, they may need to begin saving more, investing differently, or postponing retirement (or switching advisers).

On the other hand, if the fluctuations do not lead the portfolio to dip below the critical path, they can rest easy that their portfolio is on target and that they will reach their goal. Such a simple comparison is inherently easier to understand and interpret than a comparison of rates of return. If the Browns have invested mostly in one of the main index funds, such as the S&P 500, they can track the progress of their portfolio almost daily by simply listening to the reports on the stock market that are given on every news broadcast.[7]

THE CRITICAL PATH AS THE ROAD MAP TO RETIREMENT

Why Some Fluctuations Are Harmless and Some Are Dangerous

Figure 6.2 illustrates why fluctuations will mean little to the Browns as long as their portfolio stays above the critical path. Assume that the wiggly line represents the actual value of their portfolio. It oscillates up and down but never drops below the critical path. Therefore, the Browns need not worry about these fluctuations. So long as their portfolio stays at or above the critical path,

Figure 6.2

High Volatility above the Critical Path Is Still Safe

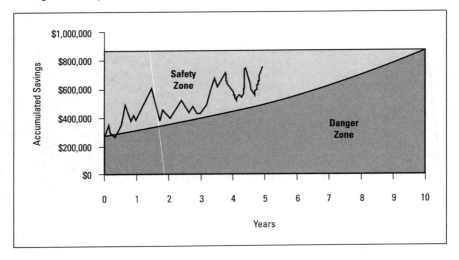

fluctuations mean little. They may be a little irritating, but they are harmless so long as even the lowest fluctuations stay above the critical path.

By contrast, Figure 6.3 illustrates a bad situation. In this case, the volatility of the portfolio has caused it to drop below the critical path. It rose above the critical path a few times, but it appears to be stuck in the Danger Zone most of the time. In this case, the Browns have every right to be concerned about their retirement plans. Will their portfolio bounce back enough to reach the target by the time they retire? Should they sit tight and hope for the best? Or should they take steps to rectify the situation now—redesign their portfolio, save more, or postpone their retirement? At least they are aware of the situation and can make informed decisions based on a correct perspective on their situation.

Figure 6.4 illustrates yet another possibility. In this case, the volatility of the portfolio's value is much less, but there is still a problem because the portfolio is meandering almost entirely in the Danger Zone. If this continues, there is very little probability that the target will be reached. Again, the Browns need to make changes in order to get back into the Safety Zone above the critical path. High volatility above the critical path is obviously much better than low volatility below the critical path.

Figure 6.3

High Volatility and Dropping below the Critical Path Means Danger

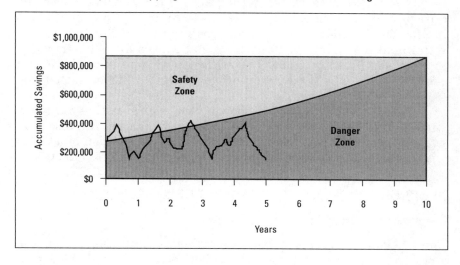

Figure 6.4

Low Volatility below the Critical Path Means Danger

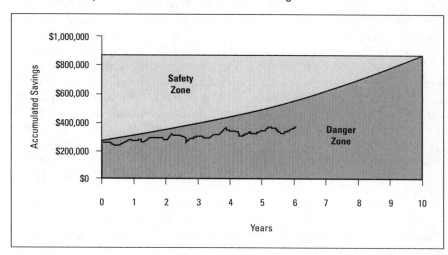

What these charts should make clear is that volatility is not the real problem. The real problem is making sure that the average return is high enough to keep the value of the portfolio above the critical path. The value may go up or down, but as long as it stays in the Safety Zone, these fluctuations cause no damage to the retirement plan. However, anything that causes the portfolio value to drop significantly below the critical path and stay there will cause damage. The target will not be achieved, at least in the time frame that was planned.

This is the advantage of knowing the critical path—you know when to be legitimately nervous. Knowing your target can also help you make critical investment decisions, as the next section illustrates with a real example based on the bear market that started in 2000.

AVOIDING A BLUNDER—THE MARKET DECLINE OF 2000

Clear Selling Signals Ahead of Time

The examples just given were hypothetical situations. But the stock market's actual performance between 1993 and 2002 provided a perfect example that demonstrates the importance of setting the target and tracking the portfolio's progress along the critical path under real-world circumstances.

Assume that the Browns had formulated their plans and started in 1993.[8] They made all the same decisions as in the previous example in terms of setting their target. They put 100 percent of their initial portfolio plus all monthly savings into an S&P 500 index fund and simply tracked it against the critical path. Table 6.2 and Figure 6.5 plot the actual path that their portfolio would have followed over the 120 months from January 1993 to December 2002.

Note that the portfolio began to rise rapidly with the bull market in 1995. It stayed above the critical path, widening the gap as the bull market gained steam. By the end of June 1998, the portfolio had actually achieved the target, more than four years ahead of schedule! It did so again five months later, in November 1998. Because they had set their target and tracked their portfolio, the Browns (or their financial adviser) could have sold and locked up their retirement at that point. Imagine the freedom they would have felt from doing this!

Table 6.2 gives the actual values at the end of each year and at the end of each month in 1998. On June 30, 1998, Column D shows that the portfolio stood at $868,976, slightly above their target of $866,687 and well above the critical path value of $524,397. If they

Table 6.2

Portfolio Values Based on Actual S&P 500 Total
Returns, 1993–2002

A	B	C	D	E
Year	Month	Critical Path	Actual Portfolio Value	Potential Portfolio Value
1992	Dec	$275,000	$275,000	$275,000
1993	Dec	$310,384	$307,573	$307,573
1994	Dec	$349,660	$316,541	$316,541
1995	Dec	$393,256	$440,632	$440,632
1996	Dec	$441,648	$547,750	$547,750
1997	Dec	$495,363	$735,999	$735,999
1998	Jan	$500,097	$744,576	$744,576
	Feb	$504,873	$798,682	$798,682
	Mar	$509,690	$839,991	$839,991
	Apr	$514,550	$848,849	$848,849
	May	$519,452	$834,664	$834,664
	Jun	$524,397	$868,976	$868,976
	Jul	$529,385	$860,129	$872,487
	Aug	$534,416	$736,179	$876,236
	Sep	$539,492	$783,747	$880,223
	Oct	$544,612	$847,904	$883,080
	Nov	$549,777	$899,704	$885,817
	Dec	$554,986	$951,952	$889,149
1999	Dec	$621,168	$1,157,731	$930,744
2000	Dec	$694,631	$1,056,896	$985,610
2001	Dec	$776,174	$936,080	$1,023,337
2002	Dec	$866,687	$733,606	$1,040,177

had not sold then, the portfolio dropped over the succeeding few months, then rose again to $899,704 at the end of November. This was a second opportunity to sell and lock in their retirement dream.

If they had sold all their equities in June 1998, they could then have reinvested the proceeds in much safer investments, such as Treasury bills or a 4-year bond, that would earn interest until they actually retired 4 years later. If they did this and continued with their established saving plan of $408, they would have built their nest egg up to an even higher value. Column E in Table 6.2 shows what would have happened if they had done this. Their portfolio would have ultimately reached a value of

$1,040,177 by the end of December 2002. This would have been $173,491 above their target. Figure 6.6 illustrates the result. The extra money could have provided more than a few luxuries—ocean cruises, college educations for the grandchildren, home remodeling, a housekeeper, and so on.

Figure 6.5

Portfolio Fluctuations Based on Actual S&P 500 Index, 1993–2002

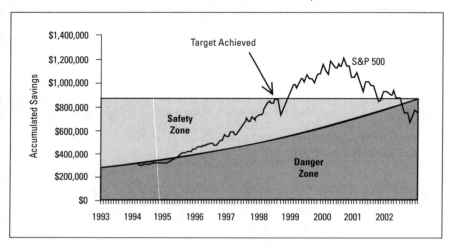

Figure 6.6

Potential Portfolio Values from Avoiding the Decline

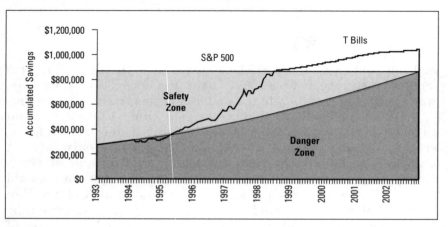

LOCKING IN RETIREMENT EARLY BY FINE-TUNING
Buying Bonds When the Portfolio Is within Striking Distance

Actually, the Browns could have fine-tuned the timing of their sale if they had actively monitored their portfolio and the existing interest rates at each point in time. For example, what if, with 1 year to go, they were within 5 percent of their target? If the interest rate on 1-year bonds were 5 percent, they could have sold their stocks, bought the bonds, and locked in their goal a year early.

In fact, they could actually buy bonds (U.S. Treasuries or equivalent, always) any time when they were within reach of their goal. If they were 4 years away from retirement, but rates on 4-year bonds were high enough to allow them to reach their target, they could simply switch from stocks to bonds. The bonds could provide a final laser-lock on the ultimate goal once they were within striking distance as measured by existing interest rates. Rates on 5-year bonds might allow them to "cash out" of stocks 5 years early and buy bonds ("bond-out" might be a more descriptive term) and still reach their target with no further risk, assuming they were satisfied with their goal. The idea is that by monitoring their portfolio and existing rates, they could shift into an autopilot mode and coast the rest of the way on bonds—right on target, right on time. They would have fully immunized themselves against any further volatility risks.

Other, more sophisticated scenarios involving bonds are also possible. For example, assume that the Browns are in the situation outlined in the previous section, where they reached their goal 4 years early. They could buy an asset dedication income portfolio with bonds timed to generate the desired cash flow beginning when they retired and continuing for the first 5 years of retirement. That is, they could buy bonds maturing in 4, 5, 6, 7, and 8 years. They could deposit the preretirement interest on these bonds into their stock account along with the rest of their growth portfolio until they reached retirement. At that point, they would have already locked in the next 5 years of income using bonds at the far end of the yield curve, which would be likely to have higher yields. This could work for any span.

Another example is a rolling horizon. Assume again that the Browns are within 4 years of retirement and wish to begin dedicating their assets now. They purchase a dedicated portfolio with bonds maturing successively to match the income they expect to need each year over the first 5 years of retirement. At the end of each year, they use the cash flow from the maturing bond to extend the horizon back out to 5 years again and invest any excess in the growth portion of the portfolio. By the time they reach retirement, they will have already funded a 5-year horizon and can continue doing this throughout their retirement, either with the rolling horizon or by converting to a fixed horizon. Chapter 9 will illustrate that an asset dedication strategy with a rolling horizon would have performed very well during the period from 1990 to 2000.

The fine-tuning that these scenarios represent requires some degree of sophistication and vigilance, as most forms of active management do. But that is what advisers are paid to do. As asset dedication begins to proliferate, reputable and progressive advisers within the financial community will no doubt discover other ways to benefit their clients by developing new ways to utilize the basic ideas.

THE BLUNDER OF IGNORANCE AND GREED

The $300,000 Penalty for Ignoring or Being Ignorant of the Selling Signals

What if the Browns had not sold when they hit the target? Column D shows that the market would have taken them up as high as $1,157,731 at the end of 1999.[9] These were giddy times, and everyone was wondering how much longer the bull could run. Skeptics warned that it could not last, but they were drowned out by a chorus exhorting the virtues of the "new economy" and how the Internet had changed everything.

But the skeptics proved right. The bull finally stumbled in 2000. Table 6.3 is similar to Column D in Table 6.2, but it tracks the portfolio on a month-by-month basis. Its value began to fall but was still above the target until September 2001, when it dipped below the target value. It rose above the target again in November 2001 and stayed above it until June 2002, when it dropped below it for good. By the end of 2002, the value of the portfolio had dropped to $733,606. If the Browns had not sold but held on, as a result of ignorance, greed, or bad advice, it would have been a major blunder and would have cost them dearly.

This points out a problem alluded to earlier that all financial advisers face as part of their business. Hindsight is always

Table 6.3

Portfolio Values Month by Month (in $000)

Year	Jan	Feb	Mar	Apr	May	Jun	Jul	Aug	Sep	Oct	Nov	Dec
1993	$277	$282	$288	$281	$289	$291	$290	$301	$299	$306	$303	$308
1994	$318	$310	$297	$301	$307	$299	$310	$323	$315	$323	$312	$317
1995	$325	$338	$349	$359	$374	$383	$396	$398	$415	$414	$432	$441
1996	$456	$461	$466	$473	$486	$488	$467	$477	$504	$519	$558	$548
1997	$582	$587	$563	$597	$634	$663	$716	$677	$714	$691	$723	$736
1998	$745	$799	$840	$849	$835	**$869**	$860	$736	$784	$848	**$900**	**$952**
1999	$992	$962	$1,001	$1,040	$1,016	$1,072	$1,039	$1,035	$1,007	$1,071	$1,093	$1,158
2000	$1,100	$1,080	$1,186	$1,150	$1,127	$1,155	$1,138	$1,209	$1,145	$1,141	$1,051	$1,057
2001	$1,095	$995	$933	$1,006	$1,013	$989	$979	$918	$845	$861	$928	$936
2002	$923	$905	$940	$883	$877	$815	$752	$757	$675	$735	$779	$734

20/20, and some clients will always measure their progress by the "high water mark" of their portfolios. These are the clients who will never be satisfied because their goal is not specific. If they say that their goal is simply to "get as much as I can," they will never reach their goal because they will never know what it is.

If they had a goal and reached it on the way up—which it must do the first time in most cases—they should sell and lock it in. But instead, they change their goal to something higher, then hold on hoping to reach the new goal. If they do reach it, they will set an even higher goal. When the market finally falls back, they then complain about their "losses." They will always groan that their portfolio is not worth as much as it was when it hit its highest level. It is difficult to muster much sympathy for such people. The root cause is not the random movements of the market. The root cause is an unspecified goal and unfettered greed. Such clients are the bane of the financial advisory profession.

In the final analysis, the Browns had at least five opportunities to lock up their dreams when they hit the target. If they had stubbornly ignored every one, they would have ended with a portfolio of $733,606. This is $133,081 below their target. Clearly, the warning signs were there. If they had followed their plan, sold on the initial signal the first time the portfolio reached the target in June 1998, and bought Treasury bills, they would have been worth $1,040,177 at retirement. The total cost of their blunder (or ignorance or greed) amounts to $306,571! Imagine the whining their friends and family will have to endure.

I have read a number of newspaper and magazine articles quoting the laments of people who fell into this trap. Most of them blame the market, the current president, their broker, or anyone else they can think of. They have to postpone their retirement or accept the fact that they will not retire in the fashion that their minds had become accustomed to. The great sadness is that this would have been entirely avoidable if they had simply set their target, tracked their portfolio, and sold when they reached their target.[10]

Performing these sorts of analyses and monitoring portfolio progress is what everyone should do. If someone does not have the skills to do this, that person should find financial advisers who will do it for him. This is how advisers should earn their fees—not by selling products with the highest commissions.

MORE EXAMPLES—A YOUNGER GROUP

Twenty-, Thirty-, and Forty-Somethings Face the Same Problem

The Browns in the previous example were 10 years from their target retirement date. Table 6.4 presents a summary for a younger group, aged 47, 37, and 27, respectively. Their situations differ from those of the Browns because they are younger. They have smaller starting portfolios, lower incomes, and longer planning horizons to retirement compared to Bob. But they all face the same problem and have the same goal as the Browns. The only difference is that Table 6.4 assumes that because of their longer planning horizon, they are willing to invest in small-cap mutual funds that promise higher average rates of return.

WHAT IF I CANNOT SAVE ENOUGH?

Many Solutions, None Painless

Financial advisers often suggest saving 10 percent of one's income as a good rule of thumb for everyone. This requires a modicum of self-discipline when it comes to other spending. Psychologists point out that the pain felt by giving up a few things will be only temporary, and this makes the pain much more tolerable. The permanent peace of mind that emanates from knowing that the long run is taken care of and the realization that financial independence will happen far outweighs the short-lived pain.

But what if one's current circumstances make it simply impossible to achieve the needed savings? There are solutions to this dilemma, but each one has drawbacks:

Solution 1: Cut the income needed from $60,000 to $50,000 or $40,000 or whatever it takes to make it possible.

Solution 2: Find a higher preretirement rate of return.

Solution 3: Retire later.

Solution 4: Don't plan for such a long life after retirement.

SOLUTION 1: CUT THE INCOME NEEDED FROM $60,000 TO $50,000 OR $40,000 OR WHATEVER IT TAKES TO MAKE THE ACCOUNTS BALANCE

Unfortunately, this is the best solution. It gets to the heart of the problem. As discussed earlier, withdrawing more than about 4 per-

Table 6.4

Basic Data for Bob and Helen, Carol, Ted, and Alice

Item	Bob	Carol	Ted	Alice
Current age	56	47	37	27
Age at retirement	66	67	67	67
Gross Income	$70,000	$60,000	$50,000	$40,000
Taxes	20%	20%	20%	20%
Net Income	$56,000	$48,000	$40,000	$32,000
1. How long before you retire?	10	20	30	40
2. How much income will you need in today's dollars from your retirement portfolio?	$30,000	$30,000	$30,000	$30,000
3. How much do you want to leave to your heirs?	Zero	Zero	Zero	Zero
4. How long do you want it to last?	To age 100	To age 100	To age 100	To age 100
5. How much can you earn on it after you retire?	8%	8%	8%	8%
6. How much should you allow for inflation?	4%	4%	4%	4%
7. What total return can be expected on the existing portfolio between today and retirement?	11%	12%	12%	12%
8. How much has already been saved?	$275,000	$85,000	$25,000	$0
9. How much to save each month?	$408	$381	$368	$285
(Graduated savings increasing with inflation):	$368	$302	$273	$205
Required monthly saving as % of Gross	7.0%	6.8%	6.7%	7.1%
Required monthly saving as % of Net	8.7%	8.5%	8.3%	8.8%
Nest egg after 10 years	$866,687	$379,713	$163,871	$68,245
Nest egg after 20 years		$1,263,990	$289,389	$264,673
Nest egg after 30 years			$1,871,013	$874,750
Nest egg after 40 years				$2,769,557

132

cent a year from your nest egg runs the risk of depleting it before you reach 100, depending on what happens to the investments you made with it. But lowering your standard of living by spending less means hard choices. It is always easier said than done. There is an old saying that you are financially secure if you spend less than you earn. The logic is inescapable, whether you're talking about before or after retirement.

Trying to decide how much is enough in retirement may seem tougher than it actually is. Consider what income level it would take to make you feel comfortable. A conventional suggestion is 70 to 80 percent of your final working income. Other studies have suggested that people always want about 10 or 20 percent more than they are already making (though one wonders if satisfying one need brings another to the surface that was hidden before). Here is what it would take to make me feel comfortable when I retire: I would want to have enough income to

- Pay off all debts every month
- Allow me to carry on with my usual leisure activities (movies, plays, monthly trips to new or favorite places, visiting and being a support for the kids and grandkids whenever I want)
- Take an international trip once or twice a year
- Provide nice holiday, birthday, and other gifts for my family and friends
- Support the charities and causes I like
- Have enough insurance covering health, long-term care, property, and life to nullify the economic consequences of these risks
- Have a new computer every 2 or 3 years
- Have a new car whenever my current one gets to 100,000 to 150,000 miles
- Hire someone to do yardwork for me and housework for my wife
- Have cash readily available equal to 6 months of the regular expenses
- And the big one—not work[11]

It should be noted here that Bob's nest egg, $866,687 is much less than the total number of dollars that the account will actually pay out between Bob's sixty-sixth and ninety-ninth birthdays. The total paid out will actually equal $3,102,203. The difference is due to interest earned on whatever portion of the nest egg is left in the account earning interest each year until it is withdrawn.

One of the most common methods of cutting your income needs and providing a source of funds for retirement is to cash in on the equity in your house if you have owned it for a long time. Most people in this day and age realize that because of inflation, their house is probably worth more than they paid for it. They simply sell it and move to a smaller, cheaper location either in the same town or somewhere else. With the continued progress in telecommunications, this trend is likely to accelerate as people find it easier to stay in touch with each other without being physically close. Hopefully, some of the savings in housing costs will fund travel back to the old hometown.

SOLUTION 2: FIND A HIGHER PRERETIREMENT RATE OF RETURN

More revenue will obviously solve the problem, but where can you find it? Growth is the primary objective, and stocks clearly have a better long-term record than bonds or cash. Within stocks, index funds that specialize in small-company stocks do better over the long run.

Unfortunately, some brokers believe in their own clairvoyance. They actually think that they can forecast the future behavior of individual stocks. But this is inherently risky because no broker ever guarantees results,[12] and no insurance company has ever offered a policy that would cover losses from bad stock selection. You are gambling that the risk will pay off and the stock will go up. If it does, everyone is happy.

If it does not, your broker will apologize profusely for losing your money and try to figure out how to pacify you. He or she knows that you will likely find another adviser and will waste as little time with you as possible. If this happens with too many clients, the adviser will probably seek another line of work. That will not solve your problem, of course.

For the reasons outlined in the chapter on asset allocation, I would recommend putting money allocated to stocks into an index fund based on broad market averages. With index funds, you at least have the historical record to provide some guidance as to the rate of return you are likely to achieve over long periods of time, and they cost less to own because the management fees are lower. To be conservative, you can use whatever growth rate the S&P 500 has beaten 60, 70, or even 90 percent of the time over the period you will be investing. Web sites have this sort of information at your fingertips.[13]

SOLUTION 3: RETIRE LATER

This is another obvious and convenient solution unless you are really anxious to retire or are physically unable to continue working. If you work longer, you can save more, and your nest egg will not have to last as long.

SOLUTION 4: DON'T PLAN FOR SUCH A LONG LIFE AFTER RETIREMENT

This gets into an area that most people find depressing: their own mortality. As mentioned earlier, it is very unwise to use simple life expectancy for financial planning. We all have a 50-50 chance of dying before or after this age. If a man reaches age 65, his life expectancy becomes 81. For a woman, it is 84. From a financial planning standpoint, it would be terrible to have a financial plan that reaches no further than your life expectancy. There is a 50 percent chance that you will outlive your nest egg. What do you do then—move in with the kids?

This is why financial planners often plan for living to age 100. Anything less than that may depress their clients, and they won't come back. Recall Table 5.2, which lists the 95 percent and 99 percent life expectancies.

CONCLUSION

To summarize, the accumulation phase is the time during which the retirement nest egg must be built. Deciding on your retirement goals, making your nest egg grow as quickly as possible, and figuring out how much to save to meet your goals with only modest growth in your portfolio are the primary issues. Developing a complete lifetime financial plan requires answering some tough questions and doing some deep soul searching—what do you expect out of the hundred or less years that you will walk around on this planet? But not answering them directly leaves your life to chance and increases the possibility of a blunder that will force you to live in much harsher circumstances than you would otherwise face. You will make your life something to endure rather than something to enjoy.

The next two chapters follow the Browns 10 years later, when they have reached their retirement goal and must implement the asset dedication plan that will see them through the rest of their lives. These chapters will demonstrate how they actually invest their nest egg to implement their plan, much like our mythical Ms. Smith in Chapter 3.

NOTES

1. In project management, all tasks that must be done in order to complete the project are listed. They are then drawn on a network diagram (or "PERT chart") that shows which tasks are independent and which tasks depend on others being done first. Those that are dependent on others must follow a prescribed sequence, while those that are independent can be done simultaneously. For example, in constructing a house, the foundation must be built first, then the walls, then the roof, but plumbing and wiring can proceed simultaneously. Once the network is drawn, the longest pathway through the diagram determines the earliest time that the overall project can be completed. Finishing shorter pathways in any phase means waiting until all the tasks along the longest path are done before the next phase or project can be started. The longest path is, therefore, called the *critical path* because if anything goes wrong along that path, the overall project will be delayed unless the time can somehow be made up by using extra resources or somehow doing later tasks faster. It is difficult to cover the whole idea of project management in one paragraph, since entire books are written on it and college courses are devoted to it. Microsoft Project is a popular software program used by project managers. The critical path method in financial planning that is described here is a very simple application of this basic concept.
2. If some emergency arose that forced them to dip into their retirement funds, then annual volatility would create a risk that the market would be down at the exact time they needed to withdraw the money. But this should not be the guiding motivation for how to invest the preretirement portfolio. Insurance policies are the best weapon against such emergencies.
3. With 10 years to go, they may begin to think about starting to follow the asset dedication approach, but simply reinvesting the proceeds from the interest and the maturing bonds in the stock market instead of spending the money as they will after retirement. This would allow them to get used to the way asset dedication works before relying on it entirely once they retire. But they would probably receive a lower return because of their use of bonds, which usually lower portfolio returns.
4. On an Excel spreadsheet, the PMT worksheet function does the needed calculation for the amount to save each month for 120 months. There is one complicated element to this, however: Yearly compound rates must be converted to their corresponding monthly compound rates if the money is being saved monthly. If the amount is being compounded monthly, it takes only about 10.5 percent to provide the same value at the end of the year as 11.0 percent compounded annually. The formula needed to compute this is monthly rate = $12*((1+\text{annual rate})(1/12-1))$.
5. The issue of measuring risk using only the downward movements in a portfolio is generally traced to Brian Rom and Kathleen Ferguson, "Post Modern Portfolio Theory Comes of Age," *Journal of Investing*, Winter 1993. Additional articles on the topic appeared in the Fall 1994 issue.

6. They may wish to do this with their monthly or quarterly statements instead of just the annual statement. It depends on how closely they want to monitor their progress.

7. Recall, however, that the index levels reported in the news media exclude dividends. So long as they are aware of this, the daily stock reports could prove beneficial.

8. To keep the example simple, we will assume they start their plan at the beginning of 1993 for this chapter and track the Brown's portfolio over each calendar year.

9. Their portfolio would have reached its highest end-of-month value in August 2000, at \$1,208,726.

10. To be fair, some people may have wanted to sell but their company's retirement plan would not allow them to sell their investments. Enron was a classic example, where employees could not sell the stocks the company had contributed in their 401(k) retirement plans even though the stock was falling rapidly. It is not uncommon for companies to contribute their own stocks to employee retirement plans but restrict the employees from selling those stocks. In the wake of the Enron scandal, recent legislation has alleviated some of these problems.

11. A professor's life may seem idyllic, but some aspects of higher education are wearying—grade-grubbing students, dithering committees, carping colleagues, and so on. Teaching itself it great, but every profession has its darker side.

12. I once knew of a real estate broker who guaranteed that he would sell your house within 6 months at the agreed-upon price or else he would buy it. When the real estate market was doing well, he attracted a lot of clients and made a lot of money. When the market tanked, however, he ended up going bankrupt.

13. The asset dedication web site, www.assetdedication.com, automatically indicates the probability of achieving a given rate of return based on the historical record.

CHAPTER 7

The Distribution Phase: Dedicating Assets to Do Their Job

Defer no time, delays have dangerous ends.
                    —WILLIAM SHAKESPEARE, I HENRY IV

The distribution phase begins the day you draw your last paycheck. You are now officially retired. Distributions from the savings in your portfolio must now begin to provide you with income to supplement whatever you are receiving from social security or other sources. Accordingly, income generation must now replace growth as the primary goal of your portfolio strategy. Some financial advisers call this the "retention" or "conservation" phase, meaning that the goal becomes to make the your nest egg last as long as needed.

Often, retirement is not an abrupt, dramatic break in life. A gradual shifting of activities might be a better description for many people (workaholics excepted). It may simply mean that your job is no longer your primary focus. You may still work in some capacity, either part-time or as a consultant, or pursue another income-earning activity. Many people find their early retirement years busier than their preretirement years (health permitting) because they volunteer for more activities or do things that they had always wanted to do but never felt they had the time to spare for. Interestingly, people sometimes end up making higher incomes in retirement because they begin to do things they like, which unlocks their creative juices. When this is coupled with their insights from a lifetime of experience in dealing with the human race, they become very productive at doing things that really turn them on professionally and reap the rewards.

This chapter describes the actual asset dedication process in detail. It traces how the Browns put their retirement plan into action to minimize their costs and worry and maximize the efficiency of their portfolio. In the very early stages of their retirement, the Browns have a large sum of money (and are probably on every broker's hit list). But as we saw in the prior two chapters, each dollar is already earmarked to supply income in some future year. The success of the plan is predicated on their promptly dedicating the assets and getting them working as soon as possible so that they can do the job they were designed to do. If the Browns do not realize this, they will be vulnerable to every adviser who calls them, mails them, or bumps into them with promises to show them how to "live the carefree life you've always wanted" or similar enticing, honeyed words.

For most people, retirement begins at age 66 or 67, when full Social Security payments begin (see Table 10.1). Social Security now ratchets up with inflation. Congress can always change the laws regarding Social Security, of course, and the program will certainly evolve as the political climate evolves. But it is doubtful that Social Security will ever fold entirely, as some people fear.

THE THREE CLASSIC RETIREMENT QUESTIONS
Building the Foundation for Asset Dedication

The three most common questions asked of financial advisers by those beginning their retirement are

1. How much can I spend?
2. How long will my money last?
3. How much does my portfolio have to earn?

There are some obvious trade-offs here. The more you spend, the quicker the money will run out for a given level of return on its earnings. A higher return means that it will last longer. Interestingly, there is a withdrawal rate at which the money will never run out. This happens if you withdraw less than what the portfolio is earning each year. A number of researchers have investigated these questions. The answers depend, of course, on the rate of return on the portfolio, which in turn depends on how it is invested and the length of the investment period. It also depends on whether or not inflation is to be included in the amount withdrawn. In very rough terms, these researchers were able to construct portfolios that, based on the historical returns to the stock market, could earn a sufficient return so that the portfolio would last forever if no more than about 4 percent should be withdrawn from a portfolio and inflation is ignored. The best work appears to have been done in what has been called the Trinity study; this is discussed in Chapter 10.[1]

Note that these are actually the first three questions that Bob and Helen Brown had to answer when their situation was covered in detail in Chapter 6. They are also the questions that Ms. Smith had to answer in Chapter 3. Therefore, these questions have already been answered as part of the preretirement planning. The Browns have saved enough money and their nest egg portfolio has grown to approximately the size needed to last until after they reach their ninety-ninth birthdays. The Browns began the process when they were 10 years away from retirement. They calculated what their nest egg target would have to be and how much they had to save, and they pinpointed the critical path that their portfolio would have to follow if they were to reach their target. Now they need to harness (hatch?) their nest egg to generate the cash flows they need. It will have its own critical path.

Most of us who are older probably did not follow a critical path when we were younger. Based on surveys of saving and retirement planning in America, we were not all that different from younger people today.[2] We were busy with other issues: finding a job, paying off educational debts, buying a house, having kids, and generally making a life for ourselves. It may also be that no one ever guided us in these issues or that we ignored them. Retirement and pensions were far beyond our planning horizon. Like most young people, we figured, consciously or subconsciously, that we would have plenty of time to deal with these matters in the future. Perhaps we would become rich and never have to worry about it anyway.

There comes a time, however, when retirement no longer seems like such a distant place. It may be a gradual realization, or it may come suddenly. In conventional wisdom, the thirties are the old age of youth, and the forties are the youth of old age. Perhaps it is one of these landmark birthdays (or kids growing up, or the death of a parent, or whatever) that forces us to accept the fact that time is moving on. Eventually, most people come to the realization that sooner or later they are going to have to deal with these matters. The old joke is that inside every old person is a young person saying, "What the hell happened?"

My own first brush with this decision came at the University of San Francisco (USF), where I began my teaching career in 1973 at age 30. The fellow in the personnel department asked me how much I wanted to set aside out of my paycheck for retirement. He explained to me that whatever I put in would grow tax free and that USF would match whatever I put in up to a maximum of 2 percent. I realized at the time that doubling my money in a year was a good deal, so I saved the maximum, meaning that I was saving 4 percent of my salary every year. I did not do the independence calculation, plot a critical path, or consider any of the factors outlined in the previous chapter. I had never heard of them. Actually, I was just thankful to have the job. I would cross the retirement bridge when I came to it. First things first—focus on doing a good job and getting tenure!

A "DO-IT-YOURSELF" RETIREMENT PORTFOLIO

Implementing the Retirement Plan

Recall the questions that Bob and Helen Brown had to answer in Chapter 5 to make the life choice decision for their independence calculation. These are repeated in Table 7.1.

Based on these specifications, the Browns had set the target for their retirement portfolio at $866,687. This required them to save $407.64 each month, assuming that they started with $275,000 and earned 11 percent per year over the 10 years prior to retirement. The historical record on the rate of return from equities (S&P 500 Index) suggested they would achieve this about 60 percent of the time. Recall from Chapter 6 that if they had followed the critical path and implemented their plan, they would have been able to achieve their goal easily.[3]

For purposes of our example, let us assume that things worked out just as they had expected, and they ended up right on target with $866,687. Assume that today is October 8, 2003, the day after Bob's sixty-sixth birthday.[4] That means that today is the first day of his official retirement. It also means that today is the day when he and Helen must implement their postretirement plan and put their nest egg to work immediately. Income will now arrive from three sources: (1) this portfolio, (2) social security, and (3) their other pensions.

Table 7.1

Life Choice Decisions Made by Mr. and Mrs. Brown

Life Choice Question	Life Choice Decision
1. *How long before you retire?*	10 years
2. *How much income will you need from your portfolio (in today's dollars)?*	$30,000
3. *How long do you want it to last?*	To age 100
4. *How much can you earn on it **after** you retire?*	8 percent
5. *How much inflation should you allow for?*	4 percent
6. *How much do you want to leave to your heirs?*	Zero

If they had eased into retirement by setting up a rolling horizon 5 or so years before retirement, as described in Chapter 6, the transition would already have taken place. The bonds purchased before retirement would ready to mature in the right amounts at the right times to provide their income. But we will assume that they chose not to set it up in advance and will do the dedication now.

Ten years earlier, they believed that they would need the equivalent of $30,000 from their portfolio. If inflation did in fact raise prices on the items they purchase by 4 percent per year, $30,000 then equates to $44,407 now. Their first transaction will be to withdraw $44,407 from the portfolio for their first year plus their emergency reserves. This will leave $822,280 available for investment.

In order to supply their needs until age 100, they will have to earn at least 8 percent per year on this portfolio over the next 34 years. They should dedicate their assets by following the step-by-step process outlined in Chapter 3 for Ms. Smith. They have several options for implementing their plan. They can follow a "do-it-for-me" approach by hiring a financial adviser to handle everything. A second option would be for them to do it entirely for themselves in order to save the fees that the adviser will charge. A compromise between the "do-it-for-me" and "do-it-myself" extremes is also possible. The Browns could get their legal and life planning advice from an adviser (and/or an attorney) by paying an hourly fee but construct the income and growth portions of their portfolio on their own, using an online broker.[5] Sometimes financial advisers may be quite knowledgeable about taxes and the rules associated with different types of retirement accounts, but not very good at knowing how to invest the funds in those accounts.

THE MATHEMATICS BEHIND ASSET DEDICATION

Precision-Guided Bonds to Hit the Exact Target Income Stream

This section describes the mathematical models that underlie asset dedication. If you have no interest in this or you do not have sufficient training to follow the technicalities of why asset dedication works, you may want to skip this section and go on the next, which describes the critical path that the Browns' portfolio must follow after they retire if it is to last until they reach age 100. Chapter 8 will provide a step-by-step description of how to use the web site that supports this book (www.assetdedication.com). Those who prefer the do-it-yourself approach can use the web site to find the specific bonds that will make up the income portion of their portfolio. The web site requires no mathematical training and is self-explanatory. It is really a matter of filling in the blanks and letting the site do the work.

The mathematical algorithms that underlie asset dedication are based on a technique called *mathematical programming*. Discovered in 1947 by a mathematician working for the U.S. Air Force during World War II, it is a tool that has been used by airlines, oil refineries, and shipping companies to save billions of dollars.[6] Its applications grow every year, and it has become an established component of all college curriculums that include a course in quantitative methods.

In the vernacular of mathematical modelers, the problem faced by the Browns is a scheduling problem. They must schedule the maturities of their bonds to match the cash flow needs related to their living expenses over the planning horizon they choose. In finance books, it is referred to as the *cash-matching* problem.

This problem was at one time considered intractable. Recall the quote from Chapter 3 by William Sharpe, 1990 Nobel Prize winner in Economic Sciences, in his recent text:

> *Cash matching is not so easily accomplished. This is because the promised cash outflows may involve an uneven stream of payments for which no zero coupon bonds exist. Indeed, it can be difficult (if not impossible) and expensive to exactly match cash inflows with promised outflows.*[7]

Sharpe is correct when he says that cash matching is difficult, but it is no longer impossible. High-end money managers that control large pension funds with millions or billions of dollars have access to the technology that can deal with this problem. But until now, no one had made it available to individual investors except in a crude, manual way.

If only zero-coupon bonds are used to fund the income portion of the portfolio, higher-level mathematics is not required. Zero-coupon bonds pay no interest until they mature. At that point, they pay all the interest due in one lump sum that is added to the principal. (Zeros also have some tax disadvantages, which are described shortly). To match an income stream, you simply buy the number of zeros required to match the amount needed each year. Table 7.2 demonstrates the simple mathematics with zeros for Ms. Smith from Chapter 3. Recall that she wanted to withdraw $30,000 plus 4 percent inflation from her portfolio. Her target income stream is shown in the middle column of Table 7.2. Divide the cash flow needed by $1000 and round off. You must round off because zeros, like nearly all bonds, come only in denominations of $1000. The target income stream comes to $168,990 excluding the $30,000 needed for the current year. The face value of the zeros is $169,000. They will cost less than $169,000, of course, reflecting the interest they will earn until they mature plus a lower purchase price if current interest rates are higher than the coupon rates the bonds pay.

The practical problem with this is that even though the interest is not received, Ms. Smith must still pay taxes as if it were if the

Table 7.2

Zero-Coupon Bonds to Buy for
$30,000 plus 4 Percent Inflation

Year	Target Income	Zeros to Buy
1	$31,200	$31,000
2	$32,448	$32,000
3	$33,746	$34,000
4	$35,096	$35,000
5	$36,500	$37,000
Total	$168,990	$169,000

funds are in a taxable account. For example, assume that the $37,000 in zero-coupon bonds purchased to fund the fifth year in Table 7.2 cost $30,000 at today's interest rates. One year from now, the same zeros are selling for $31,000. As far as the IRS is concerned, Ms. Smith earned the equivalent of $1000 on her investment and must pay taxes on that $1000.

But, you may think, "She did not actually receive the money. It is only 'phantom' interest. Why should she pay taxes on it?" Too bad—she will have to pay those taxes with money from somewhere else. Zero-coupon bonds hold a somewhat unique position in the tax code, as taxes must be paid regardless of the fact that the bonds did not actually pay interest. Once this phantom interest tax issue is factored in, zero-coupon bonds are not quite the convenient solution that they appear to be. Also, they sometimes pay less interest than coupon bonds. If the money is held in a tax-free account like an IRA, the tax problem does not apply, and zero-coupon bonds can be used if they pay the highest interest. They certainly make the calculations easy—you just buy what you need for each year in the future after factoring in inflation.

Coupon bonds, on the other hand, are more common among corporate and municipal bonds.[8] They also complicate the mathematics. For a 10-year target income stream, the appropriate number of coupon bonds would be used in precisely the same way to build a portfolio that provides the same income stream as the zero-coupon bonds discussed in Table 7.2. But a coupon bond maturing in 10 years actually pays the interest every year between now and then. If $20,000 is invested in a bond with a 5 percent coupon, it will generate $1,000 interest every year for the next 10 years (in fact, probably $500 every 6 months). It therefore supplies $1,000 cash flow each year. The same is true of a similar bond that matures in 9 years, 8 years, 7 years, and so on. The cash flows provided by these interest payments must be factored in when estimating how many additional bonds must mature each year in order to match the needed withdrawal exactly. The number to buy for any given year depends on how much interest is already being generated for that year by all the bonds maturing in later years.

Piecing together the right coupon bonds in the right way to generate the right income stream in a precise manner is difficult. The simultaneity introduced by the interrelationships of bonds with different maturities makes the problem mathematically challenging, especially when the income need is "lumpy," or irregular. If the Browns want to take a cruise every other year, for example, and need $10,000 more than normal to pay for it, the extra withdrawals represent lumps in the otherwise smooth payment stream.

Fortunately, mathematical programming can solve this sort of problem. Unfortunately, like many high-level mathematical techniques, it is not easily understood. The formulations and solution algorithms are admittedly complex. It is a little like playing the violin: It only looks easy by someone who knows how to do it. Anyone who has had a course that includes mathematical programming can testify to its complexity (unfortunately, I am convinced that some of my MBA students never really catch on). So the actual calculations are best left to a computer, which is exactly what Chapter 8 describes how to do.

THE CRITICAL PATH AFTER RETIREMENT

Tracing a Portfolio That Is Reloaded Every 5 Years to Age 100 and Beyond

Recall that 10 years earlier, the Browns had made the decisions that led to a target nest egg of $866,687 on the day of retirement when Bob Brown turned age 66 (see Table 7.1). Assume that these choices have not changed. The Browns had wanted the equivalent of $30,000 in annual income plus 4 percent inflation, or $44,407 for the first year of retirement. This withdrawal would continue to grow by 4 percent annually to allow for inflation until they reached age 100.

Assume that today is the day after their retirement. To make the asset dedication approach work, they need to implement their plan as soon as possible.[9] Therefore, they withdraw $44,407 (rounded off to $44,400, or $3700 per month) to cover their first year and dedicate the rest to income or growth. Assume the Browns decide to construct their income portion from U.S. Treasuries, using a combination of coupon and zero-coupon ("strips") bonds, whatever does the job for the least cost.

Assume that they feel comfortable with a 5-year planning horizon. Table 7.3 lists their projected withdrawals over the first 5 years; these total $250,104. At the time of this writing (late 2003), the estimated cost of this income stream would be $228,230, or 26.3 percent of their original $866,687. Assume that they invest the balance of their funds, $594,050, in an S&P 500 index fund.

That is it. They have now implemented the plan that will take care of them for this year plus the next 5 years. Theoretically, they could now sit back and not worry about their portfolio, focusing instead on their grandchildren, their golf swing, their volunteer

Table 7.3

The Browns' First 5 Years of
Withdrawals after Retirement

Age	Year	Income Withdrawals with Inflation
66	0	$44,400
67	1	$46,176
68	2	$48,023
69	3	$49,944
70	4	$51,942
71	5	$54,019
Total, Years 1–5:		$250,104

activities, or whatever else turns them on. Volatility should no longer bother them, nor should the puzzling prognostications of the market pundits. By dedicating their assets, they have locked in a plan that will automatically take care of them for the next 5 years. Sometime in the fifth year, they will need to withdraw $56,180 to support their sixth year of retirement and reload the portfolio for the next 5 years.

They have answered the three classic retirement questions:

1. How much can I spend?

Answer: Recall from Chapter 5 that 10 years earlier, the Browns estimated that they would need the equivalent of about $70,000 gross annual income when they retired. Under their plan, that income would be supplied from three sources: $30,000 from their retirement portfolio, $20,000 from Social Security, and $20,000 from other pensions. Adjusting for 4 percent inflation increases this $70,000 gross to $103,617.[10] After taxes, this would leave them a net spending budget of $82,894 per year, or $6908 per month. They do not have to spend every penny, of course, and they could always plow any leftover money back into the growth portion of their portfolio. But this is what they had planned for.

2. How long will my money last?

Answer: If all their projections and assumptions hold true, their income should last until they reach their hundredth birthdays.

3. How much does my portfolio have to earn?

     Answer: The growth portion will have to earn a total return of 11 percent per year, and the overall portfolio, 8 percent.

By monitoring their portfolio as they withdraw funds from it, the Browns can follow the critical path that their portfolio has to trace out if it is to remain on target. Table 7.4 shows what their portfolio ought to be worth every 5 years of their retirement.

     Figure 7.1 charts the critical path from age 56 through age 102. The left-hand portion represents the preretirement critical path from age 56 to 66 and is the same as Figure 6.1. Note that it began at $275,000 and, with their additional savings and growth, grew to $866,687 on the day of their retirement. It then continues to grow because the initial withdrawals are less than the annual growth. By the time the Browns reach age 86, the portfolio reaches the maximum estimated value shown, $1,264,942. At this point, they are probably feeling very comfortable.

     But their portfolio begins to decline after they reach age 86, as the income withdrawals (including inflation) begin to outpace growth. The decline is not a surprise. Recall that they deliberately chose to withdraw more than the recommended 4 percent necessary for a self-sustaining portfolio that would probably never run

Table 7.4

Critical Path of Nest Egg Balance
after Retirement

Age	Income Withdrawals	Critical Path = Nest Egg Balance before Withdrawals
66	$44,400	$866,687
72	$56,180	$1,025,634
77	$68,352	$1,146,459
82	$83,160	$1,238,306
87	$101,177	$1,264,942
92	$123,098	$1,162,785
97	$149,767	$828,388
102	$94,918	$94,918

Figure 7.1

The Critical Path before and after Retirement

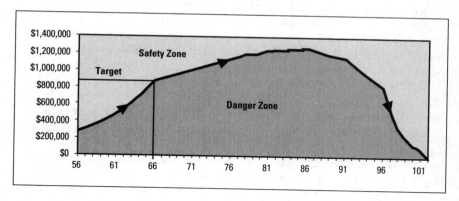

out. They planned for their portfolio to last until they were age 100. That is, they had planned their last withdrawal for their ninety-ninth birthday. At that point, they expected the account to be completely liquidated.

It may be exhausted a little sooner or a little later. Projections can be made assuming that market conditions remain the same over time. For example, the Browns can assume that the yield curve on interest rates will remain exactly the same in the future as it was on the day they started their retirement, that the 11 percent total return on the growth portion remains the same, and that inflation remains the same at 4 percent. They can plug the ending values of their growth portfolio after each planning horizon into the input screen, and also plug in what their withdrawals will be in future dollars. Chapter 8 will project their retirement experience if these assumptions hold and they survive beyond the 99th percentile life expectancy. It turns out that under these assumptions, their portfolio will last a little beyond age 100. At about that time, their funds will become exhausted and they will be broke. But the portfolio did the job it was designed to do: It supported them to age 100 and actually a little bit beyond.

There is no way to know what interest rates or rates of return will be in the future, of course, so the portfolio may or may not last exactly to their ninety-ninth birthdays. These projections are only estimates, of course. Because future interest rates and rates of return cannot be predicted with accuracy, there is no way to know exactly what each successive 5-year income bridge will cost. Market conditions will differ at each point in time. During 2003, bond yields dropped to near historic lows as the Fed cut its lowest lending rate to 1 percent, a rate that had not been seen since the 1940s. This low spot appeared to end the long, slow decline of interest rates that occurred during the 1990s and continued until 2004. But who knows what the future holds? The further out you go, the hazier it gets.

The important thing for the Browns is for their portfolio to stay above this critical path. It will then continue to supply the needed income over their lifetimes. They need not worry about financial problems so long as their portfolio stays in the Safety Zone shown in Figure 7.1.

If they have not yet done so, they must arrange their wills, trusts, and other legal documents to legally transfer their assets to their heirs. This is one of those life tasks that must be taken care of to make sure the transfer phase goes smoothly. If they have not done this by now, they need to do it because time is beginning to run out for the Browns.

MAINTAINING AND RELOADING THE INCOME PORTION

Fixed versus Rolling Horizons, Extending Horizons Manually or Automatically

Table 7.4 and Figure 7.1 assume that the Browns will continue to renew their income portfolio every 5 years. No active management is needed until the end of 5 years. At that point, the assets are rededicated to set up the next 5-year plan. The Browns will determine the list of bonds to buy for the next 5-year horizon and sell a sufficient amount of the growth portion of the portfolio to buy the bonds.

There is always the risk, however, that just when the Browns need to sell their equities, the market may be momentarily down. So long as it is not below their critical path, it will not really hurt them. But if the market decline happens to be severe enough that it falls below the critical path, they may legitimately worry about whether their portfolio will last as long as they want it to.

They can reduce this potential worry, as indicated in Chapter 3, by choosing other rededication plans. Instead of the "once every 5 years, fixed-horizon plan," which is the simplest and easiest to understand, they may wish to choose an alternative rededication plan:

1. *Yearly automatic reloading.* Instead of waiting 5 years before reloading, the Browns could start out with a 5-year horizon, then update the portfolio at the end of the first year to extend it out to the full 5 years again. This may simply require them to buy a new 5-year bond. Or, if interest rates have dropped significantly, they may wish to sell the complete 5-year set of bonds and purchase a new set at a lower price.[11] If they do this every year, they will keep a perennial 5-year horizon in front of them at all times. They will have protected themselves with a 5-year buffer. A nice benefit is that each year the portfolio is recalculated, buying bonds with 5-year maturities usually means that they will be getting higher interest rates. This happens because the yield curve is usually positively sloped, meaning that 5-year bonds generally have higher yields than 1-year bonds.

2. *Yearly discretionary reloading.* At the end of each year, the Browns can make a discretionary decision based on their evaluation of market conditions: Reload now or wait. If their growth portion has done well and bond prices are right, they can sell enough of their growth assets to extend the horizon. If these conditions are not met, they can wait another year or so, then review the situation again to see how the market looks. For example, assume that the return on their growth portfolio has been good enough after the first year to allow them to extend the horizon to 6 years and still stay above the critical path. They would then protect their income for the next 6 years. Prudence may suggest locking in their gains by doing this.

3. *Continuous discretionary reloading.* With this option, the assessment is continuous. Gains in the growth portfolio are constantly balanced against the cost of reloading and/or extending the income portion. Extension of the horizon can become automatic, with an arrangement that more assets are dedicated to income by purchasing bonds whenever returns in the growth portion permit stocks to be sold to extend the horizon without dropping the growth portion below the critical path. This is active management of the portfolio based on what is happening now rather than on forecasts of what may happen in the

future. This approach will be more expensive than the passive management afforded by the simplest fixed-horizon approach because conditions will have to be monitored constantly and transactions costs may be slightly higher, but for conservative investors, locking up their gains may provide a greater sense of security.

4. *Tax swapping*. Tax swapping is an active management strategy that takes advantage of losses within the income portion to offset gains in the growth portion and thus negate any capital gains tax. For example, assume that interest rates were to rise at the end of the second year of the Browns' first 5-year horizon. Assume further that stocks have risen rapidly, and they want to sell some of their growth portfolio to buy bonds and extend their income protection. Their last 3 years of bonds will have decreased in market value temporarily, although this has no effect on the cash flow from interest that they generate. It may be that if the Browns sold bonds out of the income portfolio, they would create a capital loss. They could then use this loss to offset the gains from their stock sale, thereby reducing their overall capital gains tax liability. They might be able then to buy similar bonds with the proceeds and reconstruct their income portfolio with essentially the same characteristics.[12] It is best to consult a tax expert before implementing tax-related strategies such as these, but the opportunities may be well worth pursuing.

CONCLUSION

Figure 7.1 represents the culmination of the asset dedication process. It traces the projected value of the Browns' portfolio from age 56, when they set their target retirement portfolio, to age 102, when it finally reaches a zero balance. The portfolio has done its job: It supported them to age 100.[13] The asset dedication strategy covered them for as long as they wanted to be covered. They took responsibility for their situation when they were 10 years from retirement by looking ahead and setting reasonable targets based on reasonable goals. By knowing the critical path that their portfolio should follow, they will be able to monitor their progress at each point along the way. The essential lifetime balancing act for financial independence will have been accomplished.

The next chapter provides a detailed description of how the Asset Dedication web site (www.assetdedication.com) performs the asset dedication process. By answering nine simple questions (which include the six questions in Table 7.1), it will allow anyone to purchase the correct bonds to initiate an asset dedication strategy. Private individuals who prefer the "do-it-myself" approach should find this web site easy to use after reading this book through Chapter 8. Those who prefer the "do-it-for-me" approach can refer their financial adviser to this book or to the site.

Before leaving this chapter, we should say a word about the transfer phase, the final investment phase of life. This falls under the name *estate planning*. Planning what will happen to your money after you die requires legal counsel. Without proper guidance, taxes can devour the results of brilliant investing and make the government the primary beneficiary of your estate rather than your true heirs. Setting up your affairs correctly requires the help of attorneys who specialize in wills and trusts. If you fail to do this, you will have made a strategic blunder that will penalize your beneficiaries by far more than the cost of the attorney.

NOTES

1. The authors of the study were professors at Trinity University in Texas.
2. The Employee Benefits Research Institute compiles an annual Retirement Confidence Survey that tracks the public's attitudes and actions regarding retirement planning (www.ebri.org).
3. Actually, recall from Chapter 6 that if the 10 years had been 1993 to 2002, they would have reached their target 4 years ahead of schedule because the 1990s averaged a higher rate of return than 11 percent. By following their critical path and knowing their target, they actually had multiple opportunities to sell and lock in their retirement. If they had obeyed the first signal, they could have purchased Treasury bills in 1998 and actually had $1,040,177 in the portfolio on the day Bob retired in 2002. If they had held on, however, as a result of ignorance or greed, they would have lost. The market decline of 2000 would have ultimately dropped their portfolio to $733,606 by the end of 2002, well below their target.
4. For this example, we assume a 2003 retirement date to make use of the prices of bonds at the time this section was written rather than the 2002 retirement date used in Chapter 6.
5. The most efficient portfolio of precision-guided bonds for asset dedication can be found at www.assetdedication.com.
6. The mathematician Dr. George Dantzig conducted research on how mathematics could be applied to help with the logistical problems of the war. His particular research unit dealt with linear equations, which were referred to as the "linear program." The optimizing algorithm that he discovered became known as *linear programming*. Later scholars extended his work to nonlinear and other forms of

equations and variables, calling it generically *mathematical programming*. It continues to be one of the most widely applied branches of mathematics because of its ability to find the optimal solution for problems that have trillions of possible solutions.

7. William F. Sharpe, Gordon J. Alexander, and Jeffery V. Baily, *Investments*, 5th ed. (Englewood Cliffs, N.J.: Prentice-Hall, 1995), p. 478.

8. In fact, zero-coupon bonds with the right maturities, ratings, and denominations are sometimes hard to find.

9. Most experienced financial planners report that procrastination is the biggest enemy of sound financial planning. A lot of energy may be expended on formulating a plan, but unless the plan is implemented promptly and correctly, it will become stale and represent little more than a waste of time.

10. To keep the calculations simple, this assumes that the other pensions also adjust for inflation like social security. If they do not, then a slightly higher inflation rate may need to be factored into the withdrawals.

11. Selling the bonds may create a taxable event and the tax code forbids certain types of security swapping to generate taxable losses, so it is necessary to consult with a tax expert before taking action.

12. See note 11 above on the need to consult with a tax expert before doing this.

13. Actually, it supported them slightly past age 102, but this is merely an artifact of the prevailing interest rates at the time the example was constructed. This is an idealized version, of course, but it serves as a guide to what people can expect.

CHAPTER 8

Building an Asset Dedicated Portfolio: Doing It Yourself on the Internet

As soon as you trust yourself, you know how to live.
—GOETHE

The previous chapter described some of the mathematics behind asset dedication. It also plotted the critical path for the Browns' portfolio, extending the critical path from the 10 years prior to their retirement to age 102, a total of 46 years. This is about as close to lifetime financial planning as you can get.

This chapter describes in detail how to use the asset dedication web site (www.assetdedication.com) to carry out the dedication process and implement a retirement plan. Recall that asset dedication splits the portfolio into three portions: cash, income, and growth. The web site focuses on the income portion, which is the most difficult to construct from coupon bonds. It is difficult if not impossible to build a dedicated portfolio with coupon bonds without the help of such technology.

The example used here was developed directly from the web site. The web site may look slightly different or contain additional information by the time you read this. The bonds will certainly be different, and the cost of the portfolio will probably be less, since interest rates were low when this sample analysis was run (October 2003). But the mechanics of the inputs and outputs should allow anyone to understand just how simple constructing the portfolio can be. You can test different scenarios until you find the one that works best for you. You can then print out the list of bonds and take it to an adviser to purchase for you (or buy the bonds yourself online). Whatever amount is not needed for the bonds can then be invested in an index fund or in any other investment that you believe promises better growth. Then sit back and relax. You will have dedicated the assets to run the income portion of your portfolio according to your specifications, and that portion of the portfolio will continue to do its job quietly, automatically, and cheaply. If you choose the fixed-horizon approach with a planning horizon of 5 or 10 years, you do not need to worry about the income portion until the end of that time.

The web site requires only three screens to dedicate assets: the Inputs screen (Table 8.1), the Scenarios screen (Table 8.2), and the Details screen (Table 8.5). Each of these is described line by line, using the Browns at the point of their retirement as an example.

MAKING THE CHOICES AND ENTERING THE DECISIONS AS INPUTS

The Data Entry Input Screen

Assume that the Browns or their adviser visit the asset dedication web site and begin filling in the nine blanks. Note that the questions are similar to those that the Browns answered in making their life choices (see Table 7.1). Once the input screen is completed (Table 8.1), they can implement their decisions in order to dedicate their assets and guarantee that their income needs will be met for the next 3 to 10 years. It is possible to custom-build portfolios longer than 10 years, but most people prefer to stay within this range. It is a good idea to test several different possible horizons for comparison purposes. A half-hour of testing various options will provide a good feel for the consequences of different choices.

In Table 8.1, Lines 1 and 2 are self-explanatory. Line 3 assumes that their initial cash allocation is $44,407. This seems like a rather large allocation to cash, but it is set aside to cover their income needs from the date of the analysis to February 15 of the following year plus emergency reserves. In this case, 4 months must

Table 8.1

Input Screen for Mr. and Mrs. Brown, 5-Year Horizon (www.assetdedication.com)

#			
1	Client Name(s):	Browns	
2	Total available for investment:	$ 866,687	e.g., 600,000
	Cash and Income Needed for 2003:		
3	2003 cash plus income BEFORE taxes from today to 2/15/2004:	$ 44,407	e.g., 30,000
4	Interest earned on 2003 cash:	0	% e.g., 1
	Future Income Needs - 2004 and Beyond:		
5	Planning horizon - 2003 plus an additional:	5 more years	
6	Select inflation rate to apply to future income:	4%	
7	Monthly BEFORE-tax income needed in today's dollars:	$ 3,700	e.g., 2,500
8	Class of Fixed Income security to consider:	US Gov't	
	Future Growth - from Today to End of Planning Horizon:		
9	Projected Total Rate of Return on Growth portfolio:	11	% e.g., 10

157

be covered (October 8 through February 15) plus 8 months emergency reserves. The Browns can input whatever amount they wish. Line 4 will take into consideration whatever interest the cash may earn if it is placed in a money market account, which in this case is assumed to be zero.

Lines 5 through 8 deal with what will happen over the Browns' planning horizon. In Line 5, they choose a 5-year horizon. In Line 6, they choose inflation protection of 4 percent starting with monthly withdrawals before taxes of $3700 (Line 7). In Line 8, they choose U.S. government securities, meaning U.S. Treasury or agency bonds. Finally, Line 9 allows them to input the total return they expect to attain on the growth portion of their portfolio. Assume that they use the same return that they used before, namely 11 percent, the average for the S&P 500.

This is the only information that the web site needs in order to perform its analysis. When you click on the "Analyze" button, the software that backs up the web site will project the anticipated results from this scenario as described in the next section. It will also list the precise bonds to purchase in the precise quantities needed to satisfy the Browns' income withdrawals for the next 5 years. Note that the web site deals only with the fixed-horizon approach. Rolling horizons would require visiting the web site at the end of each year.

SCENARIOS: TESTING THE CONSEQUENCES OF VARIOUS CHOICES

The Output Screen

Once the "Analyze" button has been clicked on, the web site runs the calculations and sets up the bonds needed for the income portion of the portfolio. Table 8.2 displays the results completed on October 8, 2003.

Each line of the output is interpreted here. Many of the output items are simply reprints from the input screen for verification purposes.

Scenario for Oct 8, 2003

1	*(Input)* Client Name(s):	The Browns
2	*(Input)* Total available for investment:	$866,687

Lines 1 and 2 are reprints of input information.

Table 8.2

Output Screen for Mr. and Mrs. Brown

Scenario for Oct 8, 2003	
1 *(Input)* Client Name(s):	The Browns
2 *(Input)* Total available for investment:	$866,687
Cash and Income Needed for 2003:	
3 *(Input)* 2003 cash plus income BEFORE taxes from today to 2/15/2004:	$44,407
4 *(Input)* Interest earned on 2003 cash:	0%
5 Initial amount needed in cash BEFORE taxes:	$44,407
6 As Percent of Initial Amount:	5.10%
7 Balance remaining for future growth and income:	$822,280
Future Income Needs - 2004 and Beyond:	
8 *(Input)* Planning horizon - 2003 plus an additional:	5 yrs
9 *(Input)* Select inflation rate to apply to future income:	4%
10 *(Input)* Monthly BEFORE-tax income needed in today's dollars:	$3,700
11 Annual BEFORE-tax income needed in today's dollars:	$44,400
12 Annual BEFORE-tax income needed as a percent of total portfolio:	5.10%
13 Annual BEFORE-tax income needed in next year's dollars:	$46,176
14 *(Input)* Class of Fixed Income security to consider:	US Gov't
15 ESTIMATED amount needed for income in 2004 and beyond	$228,230
16 As Percent of Initial Amount:	26.30%
Future Growth - from Today to End of Planning Horizon:	
17 Estimated balance remaining for future growth investment:	$594,050
18 As Percent of Initial Amount:	68.50%
19 *(Input)* Projected Total Rate of Return on Growth portfolio:	11%
20 Percent of the time the S&P 500 achieved this return over similar spans since 1947:	66%
21 Estimated value of growth portfolio at end in future dollars:	$1,025,634
22 Estimated value of growth portfolio at end in today's dollars:	$835,332
23 Overall Portfolio - Annualized Internal Rate of Return to 2/15/2004:	8.10%

Cash and Income Needed for 2003:

3 *(Input)* 2003 cash plus income BEFORE taxes from today to 2/15/2004:	$44,407
4 *(Input)* Interest earned on 2003 cash:	0%

Lines 3 and 4 focus on emergency and immediate cash needs for the current year. Every figure is in pretax dollars. Again, these are simply reprints of the input information and allow verification of the original data so that there is no question as to what data were used to derive the results. In this example, the total of $44,407 happens to coincide with one full year of income needs, but remember that we assume that the Browns will use it for 4 months of expenses (October 15, 2003, to February 15, 2004) plus another 8 months of cash for emergency reserves. If they did not wish to set aside so much for emergencies, this figure would be less.

5 Initial amount needed in cash BEFORE taxes: $44,407

Line 5 remains at the initial input amount, namely $44,407, since there is zero interest on cash in this example. The Browns withdraw this from their portfolio immediately. If interest rates on cash had been higher between the day of the analysis and Feb. 15, 2004, the amount equal to the interest that could be earned between then and Feb. 15, 2004, would have reduced this figure. The date February 15 is used as the center of the first quarter of the next year. Asset dedication buys only bonds that will mature sometime during the first quarter of each year beginning with the next year. This is designed to keep the cash flows as predictable as possible, a feature that most individual investors prefer.

6 As Percent of Initial Amount: 5.10%

Line 6 gives cash as a percentage of the total portfolio ($44,407/$866,687 = 0.051).

7 Balance remaining for future growth and income: $822,280

Line 7 gives the amount left over after allowing for cash reserves ($866,687 − $44,407 = $822,280).

Future Income Needs - 2004 and Beyond:

8   *(Input)* Planning horizon - 2003 plus an additional: 5 yrs
9   *(Input)* Select inflation rate to apply to future income: 4%
10 *(Input)* Monthly BEFORE-tax income needed in today's dollars: $3,700

Lines 8 through 10 are reprints of input information. This 5-year horizon begins with 2004. The current year at the time of the analysis, 2003, is considered Year 0, 2004 is considered Year 1, 2005 is Year 2, and so on. By the time you read this, these figures will probably have been moved forward (at least) 1 year. Inflation is set at 4 percent, and monthly income needs (before taxes) were rounded off to $3700 per month or $44,400 per year. Table 8.4 (pp. 168-169) will provide the results of all planning horizons from 3 to 10 years.

11	Annual BEFORE-tax income needed in today's dollars:	$44,400
12	Annual BEFORE-tax income needed as a percent of total portfolio:	5.10%

Lines 11 and 12 convert the monthly withdrawals to their annual equivalent in dollars and as a percent of the total portfolio. The Browns' Year 1 withdrawal of $44,400 in today's dollars (representing 5.1 percent of their total portfolio) will become $46,176 to allow for 4 percent inflation.

Because they are withdrawing more than 4 percent, the portfolio may not last indefinitely. But remember that the Browns did not want an indefinitely self-sustaining portfolio. They wanted a portfolio that would last until they reached age 100 because they figured that they would be with their Creator (or Tormentor) by then. Had they wanted their portfolio to last indefinitely, they would have set a different target portfolio 10 years earlier and charted a different critical path. As we shall see, this portfolio will actually support them to a little past age 100 if interest rates remain the same as in 2003, but it will not last forever under the assumptions made.

It needs to be pointed out that preservation of principal is a sacred goal for some people. This is not what most financial planners recommend. They consider maximizing return to be the proper goal. But they also realize that many clients will accept a lower rate of return or survive at a lower standard of living in order to preserve their capital. This may be due to an inner desire to leave something to their heirs, to make absolutely sure that they will have enough to last until their death, or to some other motive. Companies that sell annuities trade on the fear of running out of money and earn handsome profits from that fear.

If the Browns had wanted to preserve their capital, then the historical record on returns and inflation suggests that withdrawal rates should be no more than about 4 percent if the portfolio is to be self-sustaining. It depends on the rate of return the portfolio can earn, of course, but 4 percent seems to work in nearly all situations. This has been supported by a body of research known as the Trinity study, as will be discussed later.[1]

If the Browns had decided 10 years earlier that a self-sustaining portfolio was their goal, they would have needed to build a larger nest egg. Specifically, they would have needed to set a higher target, high enough so that their $44,407 would represent only 4 percent of it. This turns out to be $1,110,175. Alternatively, they could cut their standard of living back to 4 percent of their current nest egg of $866,687, which is $34,667 per year ($2889 per month) instead of their current $44,400 (or $3700 per month).

However, they consciously decided against this. In Chapters 5, 6, and 7, it was assumed that they would not change their lifestyle just so that the kids (or other heirs) would have a larger inheritance. Many financial planners consider preservation of capital at all costs to be wrong for most people. It causes them to lower their standard of living. Everyone is different, of course, and financial planners will follow their clients' wishes once they are convinced that the clients understand the consequences.

We will trace the consequences of the Browns' decisions later to find out that their portfolio would, indeed, run out after they reach 100. But the input screen allows them to test other scenarios (Lines 21 and 22 on the output screen will need to be reviewed to draw the proper interpretation, as described later).

13 Annual BEFORE-tax income needed in next year's dollars: $46,176

Line 13: Line 9 indicated that an annual inflation rate of 4 percent was to be included in future income, so $44,407 (rounded off to $44,400) will need to increase by 4 percent, to $46,176, for 2004. The Browns will withdraw this amount from their portfolio on February 15, 2004. This plus their income from social security and other sources is what they will need to pay their expenses and taxes during 2004.

The income stream over the 5-year planning horizon including inflation adds up to $250,104, as shown in Table 8.3.

14 *(Input)* Class of Fixed Income security to consider: US Gov't

Line 14 is a reprint of input information. Three types of fixed-income securities can be used:

- U.S. government–issued bonds (by the U.S. Treasury or agencies),
- AA- or AAA-rated corporate bonds
- AA- or AAA-rated municipal bonds

(AA and AAA are the highest ratings for safety that corporate bonds can receive. A more detailed discussion of bonds will be given in Chapter 11, and Table 14.1 will demonstrate the near certainty that high-quality bonds will work smoothly, without default.)

Each type of bond has its own advantages and disadvantages. U.S. government bonds are the safest, but have slightly lower rates

Table 8.3

Target Income Stream over the
Planning Horizon

	Becomes Age	Year	Income
1	67	2004	$46,176
2	68	2005	$48,023
3	68	2006	$49,944
4	70	2007	$51,942
5	71	2008	$54,019
		Sum	$250,104

of return. Corporate bonds pay slightly more but are slightly riskier. Munis pay less but are free of federal taxes (and sometimes state taxes as well). Munis are often best for taxable accounts, and the others for nontaxable accounts.

15 ESTIMATED amount needed for income in 2004 and beyond $228,230

Line 15 gives the cost of the actual bonds (shown in Table 8.5) that will be dedicated to supplying the precise 5-year income stream from 2004 through 2008, which, based on market quotes at the time this example was run (October 8, 2003), was $228,230. Quotes are updated regularly on the web site, and the overall cost of the income portion of the portfolio will depend on current market conditions. In times of high interest rates, bonds will cost less, and vice versa. The bonds listed on the site will produce the amount of cash flow that is to be withdrawn for income each year. The cash flow in each year consists of both interest and principal.

Because of the interest the bonds earn, only $228,230 would have been needed to supply the 5-year stream of income, $250,104. The specific bonds selected by the Asset Dedication Portfolio Tool are shown in the "Details" link below the Scenarios page. The price of the bonds changes every day, of course. Furthermore, the actual bonds listed may no longer be available at the prices shown, or at all if all inventories are depleted by the time the decision is made. But alternative bonds that will be close in price to those shown are nearly always available.

The nice thing about the asset dedication approach is that no further active management of the income portion of the portfolio is necessary until the end of the planning horizon. There is no rebalancing to maintain some arbitrary asset allocation formula. Once the bonds are purchased, they will mature on schedule and provide the income needed over the next 5 years. The same would be true for any horizon between 3 and 10 years. This portion of the portfolio will take care of itself and run as if on autopilot.

If the Browns invest the rest of their nest egg in an index fund that automatically reinvests any dividends, the growth portion will also take care of itself. The asset-dedicated portfolio is the ideal example of an efficient, low-cost, passively managed portfolio. The funds will be directly deposited to the Browns' account. The Browns do not need to take any further actions. Recall that asset dedication can be designed as a single-stroke, "set it and forget it" type of portfolio.

In an emergency, of course, the bonds can be sold before they mature because they are owned outright as individual, negotiable securities. They are not part of a bond fund, an annuity, a unit trust, or any other agglomeration. There will be no tax surprises at the end of the year, as there may be with bond funds or mutual funds as a result of capital gains generated by money managers' trades. The Browns have total ownership of and control over the bonds.

Whether the bonds will be worth more or less than what the Browns paid for them at any point in time prior to maturity will depend on the market at the time they want to sell. If interest rates go up after they buy the bonds, the market value of the bonds will be less than what the Browns paid for them. If interest rates go down, the bonds will be worth more. But as long as the Browns do not sell the bonds, there will be no surprises in terms of taxes owed on capital gains or distributions that are beyond the control of the Browns. There is also no fear of scandalous behavior by fund managers because the bonds are not part of a fund.

The prices of the bonds change continuously, of course, so costs may vary from those shown. Also, transaction fees and tax considerations are excluded from this cost. If an adviser handles this for the Browns and charges them 1 percent, then $2,282.30 of this year's annual fee will stem from these bonds.

16 As Percent of Initial Amount: 26.30%

Line 16 merely shows the bonds as a percentage of the portfolio ($228,230/$866,687 = 26.30%). In the classic fixed-formula approach to asset allocation, this represents the initial allocation to bonds. Unlike the asset allocation approach, however, this percentage will change over time as the bonds mature and the proceeds are withdrawn to supply income. Furthermore, there is no rebalancing to achieve this percentage or any other arbitrary percentage. It simply reflects the Browns' real-world needs.

Future Growth - from Today to End of Planning Horizon:

17 Estimated balance remaining for future growth investment: $594,050

Line 17 indicates the balance that remains in the portfolio after the bond and cash allocations: $866,687 – $228,230 – $44,407 = $594,050. This will be dedicated entirely to growth. As pointed out in Chapter 4, passive investing with index funds is difficult to beat. However, those who prefer active management may choose other investments, such as special mutual funds, real estate, or international stocks. Growth is the primary goal for this portion of the portfolio, and the goal is to maximize return because volatility is no longer an issue.

Those who prefer the complete "do-it-myself" approach may wish to handle both the income and the growth portions of their portfolio. Those who prefer the complete "do-it-for-me" approach may pay an adviser to manage everything. A compromise would be to use the web site to buy the bonds for the income portion, then take the rest of the money to an adviser to manage the growth portion. If you do this, at least you will be charged only for the growth portion of the portfolio. If the Browns do this, and if their adviser charges 1 percent but is able to earn 12 percent, their net total return will still be 11 percent, and they will have accomplished their goals.

18 As Percent of Initial Amount: 68.50%

Line 18 calculates the growth portion as a percentage of the portfolio ($594,050/$866,687 = 68.50%).

In the language of classic asset allocation vernacular, the "asset allocation" for this example during the first year (only) would be

Immediate needs (cash):	$44,407	5%
Income (bonds):	$228,230	26%
Growth (stocks?):	$594,050	69%
	$866,687	100%

But there is a fundamental difference between asset allocation and asset dedication. With asset dedication, the allocations are based on the personal goals and individual circumstances of the Browns themselves, not on some arbitrary, one-size-fits-all XYZ formula that has no underlying rationale.

With asset dedication, the question, "Why do you have 26 percent in bonds?" has a clear answer: It will provide 5 years of totally protected income in the precise amount that the Browns need after allowing for inflation. If you ask the same question of a financial adviser who blindly follows asset allocation without really thinking about it, the answer will likely be some vague reference to "our research shows" it is best for the "risk-tolerance level" of "conservative investors," or some other generalized, prerehearsed blurb.

Asset dedication completely reverses the process. The percentage allocations become the by-product of the choices made by the Browns to meet their needs. Allocations are goal-driven rather than formula-driven and are customized uniquely to the Browns, not to a generic "conservative investor."

19 *(Input)* Projected Total Rate of Return on Growth portfolio: 11%

Line 19 is a reprint of input information. This is the total return (appreciation plus dividend yield in the case of stocks) that the growth portfolio is expected to achieve. In this case, the Browns are simply using a return that is close to the long-term average for stocks.

20 Percent of the time the S&P 500 achieved this return over similar   66%
       spans since 1947:

Line 20 indicates how often the S&P 500 Index (of large-company stocks) has achieved the specified total return (11.0 percent) over all 5-year spans since 1947. This probability comes from comprehensive tables similar to Table 5.4. Recall that Table 5.4 tallied how many 10-year spans had achieved various total return rates since 1947. In that case, 62 percent of all 10-year periods had achieved 11 percent or better. In this case, 66 percent of all 5-year periods had achieved 11 percent or better.[2]

Total return is used because all dividends in the growth portfolio are automatically reinvested and no funds are withdrawn until the end of the planning horizon. More conservative investors may wish to use a lower projected growth rate that has a higher chance of occurring.

This assumes, of course, that the pattern of past returns is indicative of future patterns, which can never be guaranteed. Nevertheless, this probability incorporates a Monte Carlo element into the analysis to give some perspective on how likely it is that the Browns' growth portfolio will achieve its goal of 11 percent growth. If the overall average rate is simply plugged into the calculation, as it often is, the corresponding probability would be 50 percent. But this is seldom revealed by the financial adviser, even if she is aware of it.[3]

21 Estimated value of growth portfolio at end in future dollars: $1,025,634

Line 21 projects the value of the growth portfolio at the end of the planning horizon. It is a simple projection of what the result will be if the starting value of the growth portfolio grows at the return rate input by the adviser. It represents the ending value of the critical path if the portfolio does in fact grow steadily at the rate entered in Line 19. There can be no guarantees that it will grow at this rate, of course, but if $594,050 does grow at an annual compound rate of 11 percent per year and is untouched for 5 years, it will reach $1,025,634. This is more than the entire portfolio was worth when the Browns started, but it represents future or "nominal" dollars rather than current dollars. Line 22 will show what the ending value is worth in real terms, after removing inflation.

Nevertheless, if the growth portion does grow at 11 percent per year or better, as the S&P 500 has done about 66 percent of the time over all 5-year horizons since 1947, the Browns will have $1,025,634 with which to start all over again for the next 5 years if they wish to do so. In Chapter 7 we traced what would happen over each successive 5-year period until the Browns reached age 100, when their portfolio would no longer sustain another 5-year period to age 105.

22 Estimated value of growth portfolio at end in today's dollars: $835,332

Line 22 adjusts the ending value to current dollars based on the inflation rate that was input (4 percent in this case). The future value of the portfolio will be greater in future dollars than when the Browns started ($1,025,634 versus $866,687). But it will not be worth more after factoring in inflation. It will worth $31,355 less ($866,687 − $835,332 = $31,355).

These are merely projections, of course. They are based entirely on the assumption that the inflation rate will be 4 percent

Table 8.4

Scenario Results for Planning Horizons of 3 to 10 Years

Scenarios for Oct 8, 2003	8	7
1 (Input) Client Name(s):	The Browns	The Browns
2 (Input) Total available for investment:	$866,687	$866,687
Cash and Income Needed for 2003:		
3 (Input) 2003 cash plus income BEFORE taxes from today to 2/15/2004:	$44,407	$44,407
4 (Input) Interest earned on 2003 cash:	0%	0%
5 Initial amount needed in cash BEFORE taxes:	$44,407	$44,407
6 As Percent of Initial Amount:	5.10%	5.10%
7 Balance remaining for future growth and income:	$822,280	$822,280
Future Income Needs - 2004 and Beyond:		
8 (Input) Planning horizon - 2003 plus an additional:	10 yrs	9 yrs
9 (Input Select inflation rate to apply to future income:	4%	4%
10 (Input) Monthly BEFORE-tax income needed in today's dollars:	$3,700	$3,700
11 Annual BEFORE-tax income needed in today's dollars:	$44,400	$44,400
12 Annual BEFORE-tax income needed as a percent of total portfolio:	5.10%	5.10%
13 Annual BEFORE-tax income needed in next year's dollars:	$46,176	$46,176
14 (Input) Class of Fixed Income security to consider:	US Gov't	US Gov't
15 ESTIMATED amount needed for income in 2004 and beyond	$436,949	$395,953
16 As Percent of Initial Amount:	50.40%	45.70%
Future Growth – from Today to End of Planning Horizon:		
17 Estimated balance remaining for future growth investment:	$385,331	$426,327
18 As Percent of Initial Amount:	44.50%	49.20%
19 (Input) Projected Total Rate of Return on Growth portfolio:	11%	11%
20 Percent of the time the S&P 500 achieved this return over similar spans since 1947:	62%	63%
21 Estimated value of growth portfolio at end in future dollars:	$1,120,712	$1,117,068
22 Estimated value of growth portfolio at end in today's dollars:	$750,310	$777,785
23 Overall Portfolio - Annualized Internal Rate of Return to 2/15/2004:	7.90%	8.00%

6	5	4	3	2	1
The Browns $866,687	The Browns $866,687	The Browns $866,687	The Browns $866,687	The Browns $866,687	The Browns $866,687
$44,407	$44,407	$44,407	$44,407	$44,407	$44,407
0%	0%	0%	0%	0%	0%
$44,407	$44,407	$44,407	$44,407	$44,407	$44,407
5.10%	5.10%	5.10%	5.10%	5.10%	5.10%
$822,280	$822,280	$822,280	$822,280	$822,280	$822,280
8 yrs	7 yrs	6 yrs	5 yrs	4 yrs	3 yrs
4%	4%	4%	4%	4%	4%
$3,700	$3,700	$3,700	$3,700	$3,700	$3,700
$44,400	$44,400	$44,400	$44,400	$44,400	$44,400
5.10%	5.10%	5.10%	5.10%	5.10%	5.10%
$46,176	$46,176	$46,176	$46,176	$46,176	$46,176
US Gov't	US Gov't	US Gov't	US Gov't	US Gov't	US Gov't
$356,611	$314,492	$270,599	$228,230	$182,796	$136,228
41.10%	36.30%	31.20%	26.30%	21.10%	15.70%
$465,669	$507,788	$551,681	$594,050	$639,484	$686,052
53.70%	58.60%	63.70%	68.50%	73.80%	79.20%
11%	11%	11%	11%	11%	11%
64%	67%	67%	66%	65%	62%
$1,099,237	$1,079,875	$1,056,955	$1,025,634	$994,379	$961,073
$795,985	$813,243	$827,821	$835,332	$842,361	$846,714
8.00%	8.10%	8.20%	8.10%	8.00%	7.80%

and the total return rate on the growth portion will be 11 percent. If these figures are different, then the ending value in nominal and real dollars will be different. Without prescience, all we can do is project the consequences of reasonable assumptions.

23 Overall Portfolio - Annualized Internal Rate of Return to 2/15/2004:   8.10%

Line 23 calculates the portfolio's overall internal rate of return, including the income and growth portions.[4] This is based on the cash flows that the portfolio will produce, including income over the planning horizon plus the ending value of the portfolio. The present value date used is February 15, 2004. Note that 8.1 percent is slightly above the 8 percent that the Browns had hoped to achieve. It is predicated, however, on achieving the 11 percent total return on the growth portion and no extra withdrawals.

This completes the Scenario screen of the web site for the first set of inputs. Any of the nine inputs can be changed and the analysis repeated in a few seconds. Testing various projected total return rates, withdrawals, or planning horizon lengths can provide insights into the situation the Browns face. They need to find the combination that most suits their plans at the time they retire in case anything has changed. Advisers can provide real added value for a client by testing various scenarios to discover what feels best to the client given the trade-offs that must be made among current spending, inflation and growth rates, estate values, and other factors.

For example, Table 8.4 illustrates the results from testing different planning horizons between 3 and 10 years in length but keeping all other assumptions the same. The inflation-adjusted ending values in Line 22 or the internal rate of return in Line 23 may provide a useful perspective on the consequences of using different planning horizons. The Browns can choose whatever horizon they wish. They may want to choose a horizon of 3 years because at the time of this analysis (October 2003), market conditions were such that a horizon of 3 years produced the highest ending value in real terms ($846,714). Or they may feel that the difference between 3 years and 5 years ($846,714 − $835,332 = $11,382) is not worth the 2 years of worry. A 6-year horizon, on the other hand, produces the highest internal rate of return (8.20 versus 7.80 percent). It is entirely a matter of choice for the Browns. These are simply estimates based on projections and will most likely change over time.

DETAILS: THE LIST OF BONDS TO BUY

The Right Bonds in the Right Quantities to Do the Trick

Once a decision has been made regarding the planning horizon and other assumptions, the "Details" link at the bottom of the page will list the particular set of bonds to purchase. Table 8.5 provides a list of bonds for the Browns' 5-year example. This is a set of "precision-guided" bonds that will provide the exact income stream needed. This sounds like the sort of bond ladder that is old hat among brokers, but bond ladders are not precision guided. Because these bonds are designed to bridge the volatility of stocks in the growth portion of the portfolio, *bond bridge* might be a more apt description. Most brokers continue to blindly follow the old XYZ formula and allocate Y percent of a portfolio to bonds. They may spread out the maturities, but they have no particular reason in mind when they do so. They may simply use bond funds. Even worse, they may suggest trading bonds based on their precognitive powers (or, "research") concerning future movements in bond prices. All of this plays havoc with the whole reason why bonds were invented in the first place, of course, and loses the primary advantage that they offer. One of the primary advantages of the asset dedication approach is that it uses each financial instrument for the purpose it was designed to serve.

The Details screen not only identifies a list of bonds in the correct quantities that will provide the income, but also illustrates how they meet the target income stream. Each column in Table 8.5 is described in greater detail in the following section.

> *Year:* The year whose income will be supported by the bond listed
>
> *Rating:* The rating for the bond. U.S. Treasuries and strips are one step higher than anything else, so the bond rating services (Moody's and Standard & Poor's) do not rate them. If they did, they would get AAA+. Sometimes, the simple designation "Gov" is used. Corporate and municipal bonds do have safety ratings awarded by bond rating services. Only double- or triple-A-rated bonds are listed on the web site because only the safest investments are eligible.
>
> *CUSIP:* The identification number of the bond.
>
> *Name:* The name of the bond followed by a brief description.
>
> *Matures:* The date on which the bond matures.

Table 8.5

Details Screen: Bonds for the Income Portion of the Browns' 5-Year Plan

Year	Rating	CUSIP	Name	Matures	Coupon	YTM	Price	Quantity	Principal	Interest	Total	Target
2004	Aaa/AAA	31359MEM1	Federal Natl Mtg Assn	2/13/2004	5.125	0.757	$101.82	36	$36,000	$10,581	$46,581	$46,176
2005	Aaa/AAA	3133M3KB0	Federal Home Ln Bks	2/18/2005	5.82	1.519	$106.07	39	$39,000	$8,736	$47,736	$48,023
2006	Aaa/AAA	31359CCD5	Federal Natl Mtg Assn	2/2/2006	5.875	2.281	$108.31	44	$44,000	$6,466	$50,466	$49,944
2007	Aaa/NR	31331Q3M7	Federal Farm Cr Bks									
			Cons Systemwide Bds	1/16/2007	1.875	2.657	$97.51	48	$48,000	$3,881	$51,881	$51,942
2008	Aaa/AAA	3133M2M20	Federal Home Ln Bks	1/22/2008	5.845	3.524	$109.30	51	$51,000	$2,981	$53,981	$54,019
							Total	$228,230	$218,000	$32,644	$250,644	$250,104

Security prices listed are estimates only—actual prices may vary at time of purchase. Also, these particular securities may not be available at any given time depending on market conditions. Other bonds with similar maturities, coupons, and yield to maturity (YTM) may be substituted for those shown. Contact Asset Dedication for assistance if needed.

Coupon: The annual interest rate that the bond pays, usually semiannually.

YTM: The yield to maturity based on the price shown.

Price: The price on the date the information was downloaded to the web site. These prices vary depending on the source of the bond, prevailing interest rates, and continual fluctuations in the market, similar to the fluctuations in the prices of stocks.

Quantity: How many of each bond to purchase. (Bonds must be purchased in $1000 or $5000 units; some brokers require minimum quantities of $10,000 or $25,000.)

Principal: Cash inflows resulting from redemption of the bonds

Interest: Cash inflows resulting from interest payments from bonds that have not yet matured.

Total: Principal plus interest.

Target: The original specified target income stream over the horizon.

Table 8.6 summarizes the resulting income stream from these bonds and compares it to the target income stream. As can be seen, the results are remarkably close. Based on the R squared measure, the correlation between the target income stream and the actual income stream is 99.42 percent. Over the 5-year period, the cumulative difference amounts to $540, or 22 basis points (0.0022).

Table 8.6

Comparison of Target versus Total Actual Income Stream

Target Income	Total Actual Income	Total Minus Target	Absolute Value	As Percent	Absolute Value as Percent
$46,176	$46,581	$405	$405	0.87%	0.87%
$48,023	$47,736	($287)	$287	−0.60%	0.60%
$49,944	$50,466	$522	$522	1.03%	1.03%
$51,942	$51,881	($61)	$61	−0.12%	0.12%
$54,019	$53,981	($38)	$38	−0.07%	0.07%
$250,104	$250,644	$540	$1,313	0.22%	0.54%
	Per year:	$108	$263		
R Squared	99.42%				

The Browns may wish to purchase a different set of bonds, which is perfectly acceptable so long as the bonds have the same characteristics as these do in terms of coupon, yield, price, and rating. In fact, it is unlikely that the particular set of bonds shown on the web site will be available at the moment the Browns decide to proceed. Bond inventories are finite. U.S. government bonds (Treasuries and agencies) are usually available at all times, but corporate and muni bonds may not be. Once they are sold, they are no longer available unless someone who owns them puts them up for sale. Substituting equivalent bonds for those shown should present no problem. The more similar they are to those listed, the closer the results will be to the total dollar figures shown. Minor deviations in the bond characteristics should produce only insignificant differences in results.

CONCLUSION

Once they are comfortable with their plan and have tested as many scenarios as they wish, the Browns can then implement that plan. They have done their homework and set their plan in motion. If they follow the passive approach and use index funds, they can forget about trying to time the market or attempting to be clairvoyant in selecting the next hot stock. The volatility of the market will no longer matter to them. They can turn to other activities, knowing that their portfolio will now provide for their needs, much like a ship entering a safe harbor. Their accumulated assets have been dedicated to the purpose for which they were designed.

NOTES

1. It is called the Trinity study after the three authors, who were professors at Trinity University in San Antonio, Texas. Software that utilizes their methodology is now available from Zunna Corporation (www.zunna.com).
2. If the base period begins in 1926 instead of 1947, the corresponding probabilities are within 1 or 2 percent of these probabilities, which are updated with each passing year. The point is they have about a 60 to 65 percent chance of achieving this return.
3. Theoretically, the 50 percent probability would apply to the median rather than the mean.
4. In Excel, the $=IRR(\cdots)$ worksheet function performs this calculation.

CHAPTER 9

Using Asset Dedication for More than Steady Retirement Income

The important thing is not to stop questioning.
—ALBERT EINSTEIN

In the two previous chapters, we gave detailed examples of how asset dedication worked for the Browns' retirement. In this chapter, we will explore other scenarios in which asset dedication can be applied. Any investment situation that has an initial sum to be invested and predictable withdrawals from that sum over time would qualify. The easiest scenario to understand is the classic retirement situation. But other cases in which asset dedication can be applied are not hard to find.

AN IRREGULAR "LUMPY" WITHDRAWAL STREAM

Sophie Takes Her Grandchildren on Cruises Every Other Year

Sophie has just turned 70 and has always liked traveling, especially cruises. Her husband left her with $1,000,000, and she wants to take advantage of her current good health to take major cruises every other year for the next several years. She is blessed with four grandchildren, including a set of twins, and she plans to take them along on several of these trips. She will start with the oldest one first, followed by the others in turn as they get a little older and can enjoy the experience at a more mature level.

For living expenses, she needs $50,000 per year, of which $36,000 will come from her portfolio. The cruises, which will include her oldest grandchild the first time, will represent extra withdrawals of $8,000 per person. Table 9.1 shows her projected income stream, and Figure 9.1 plots her planned withdrawals to

Table 9.1

Withdrawals for Living plus Cruise Expenses

Year	Becomes Age	Inflation	Monthly	Annual	Cruise	Passengers	Cost	Target
2003	70	4%	$3,000	$36,000				$36,000
2004	71	4%	$3,120	$37,440	$8,000	2	$16,000	**$53,440**
2005	72	4%	$3,245	$38,938				**$38,938**
2006	73	4%	$3,375	$40,495	$8,320	1	$8,320	**$48,815**
2007	74	4%	$3,510	$42,115				**$42,115**
2008	75	4%	$3,650	$43,800	$8,653	3	$25,958	**$69,758**
2009	76	4%	$3,796	$45,551				**$45,551**
2010	77	4%	$3,948	$47,374	$8,999	2	$17,998	**$65,371**
2011	78	4%	$4,106	$49,268				**$49,268**
2012	79	4%	$4,270	$51,239				**$51,239**
2013	80	4%	$4,441	$53,289				**$53,289**
2014	81	4%	$4,618	$55,420				$55,420
2015	82	4%	$4,803	$57,637				$57,637
2016	83	4%	$4,995	$59,943				$59,943
2017	84	4%	$5,195	$62,340				$62,340
2018	85	4%	$5,403	$64,834				$64,834
2019	86	4%	$5,619	$67,427				$67,427
2020	87	4%	$5,844	$70,124				$70,124
2021	88	4%	$6,077	$72,929				$72,929
2022	89	4%	$6,321	$75,847				$75,847
2023	90	4%	$6,573	$78,880				$78,880
2024	91	4%	$6,836	$82,036				$82,036
2025	92	4%	$7,110	$85,317				$85,317
2026	93	4%	$7,394	$88,730				$88,730
2027	94	4%	$7,690	$92,279				$92,279
2028	95	4%	$7,998	$95,970				$95,970
2029	96	4%	$8,317	$99,809				$99,809
2030	97	4%	$8,650	$103,801				$103,801
2031	98	4%	$8,996	$107,953				$107,953
2032	99	4%	$9,356	$112,271				$112,271
2033	100	4%	$9,730	$116,762				$116,762

Figure 9.1

Projected Withdrawals for Sophie to Age 100

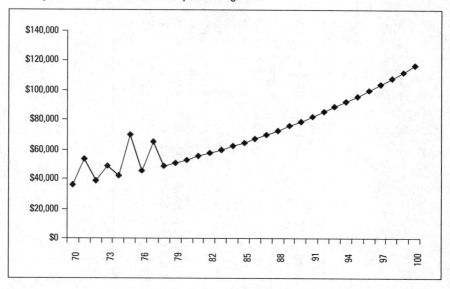

age 100. Note that the extra expenses of the cruises introduce "lumpiness" into the withdrawal pattern between ages 70 and 77.

She asks her financial adviser to set up an initial plan to cover the period until she reaches age 80. She does not wish to worry about these things over the next 10 years. The asset dedication web site cannot be used directly for the period during which she will be making irregular withdrawals. It was designed for a steady stream of cash flows, growing only at whatever rate of inflation is entered.

To accommodate the first 10 years, the technique of mathematical programming must be used to minimize the cost of the bonds needed to supply her irregular withdrawal pattern. Table 9.2 lists the bonds in the quantities needed to supply her first 10 years of lumpy withdrawals. The total cost would be $420,033, or about 42 percent of her overall portfolio. The balance can be invested in an S&P index fund.

Table 9.3 illustrates the interest and principal payments from the bonds listed in Table 9.2. It also shows the difference between the total income generated and the target withdrawals for each year. The average target was $51,778 and the actual total available for withdrawal was $51,872, a difference of a little over $93 or

Table 9.2

Sophie's Bonds: Income Portion of Portfolio for First 10 Years

Year	Rating	CUSIP	Description	Matures	Coupon	YTM	Price
2004	Aaa/AAA	31359MEM1	Federal Natl Mtg Assn	02-13-2004	5.125%	0.785%	$101.525
2005	Aaa/AAA	3133M2K30	Federal Home Ln Bks	01-21-2005	5.810%	1.543%	$105.434
2006	Aaa/AAA	31359CCD5	Federal Natl Mtg Assn	02-02-2006	5.875%	2.284%	$108.073
2007	Aa2/AA–	31359MLU5	Federal Natl Mtg Assn	01-02-2007	4.750%	2.778%	$106.065
2008	Aaa/NR	31331RPX7 MTN	Federal Farm Cr Bks Cons Systemwide Mtn	02-05-2008	5.900%	3.123%	$111.163
2009	Aaa/AAA	3133M7LN4	Federal Home Ln Bks	02-11-2009	5.610%	3.502%	$110.195
2010	Aaa/AAA	3133MATQ2	Federal Home Ln Bks	02-12-2010	7.375%	3.842%	$119.734
2011	Aaa/NR	31331LCX4	Federal Farm Cr Bks Cons Systemwide Bds	03-07-2011	6.000%	4.135%	$111.807
2012	Aaa/AAA	912833DB3	United States Treas Sec Stripped Int Pmt	02-15-2012	0.000%	4.195%	$70.677
2013	Aaa/AAA	31364FPY1 MTN	Federal Natl Mtg Assn Mtn	01-25-2013	5.920%	4.440%	$111.173
						Cost	$420,033

Table 9.3

Interest and Principal from Sophie's Bonds

Year	Interest	Principal	Total	Target	Difference	Cum. Diff.	MAPE[*]
2004	$20,792	$33,000	$53,792	$53,440	$352	$352	0.65%
2005	$19,101	$20,000	$39,101	$38,938	$163	$515	0.42%
2006	$17,939	$31,000	$48,939	$48,815	$124	$638	0.25%
2007	$16,117	$26,000	$42,117	$42,115	$2	$641	0.01%
2008	$14,882	$55,000	$69,882	$69,758	$124	$765	0.18%
2009	$11,637	$34,000	$45,637	$45,551	$86	$851	0.19%
2010	$9,730	$56,000	$65,730	$65,371	$359	$1,210	0.55%
2011	$5,600	$44,000	$49,600	$49,268	$332	$1,542	0.67%
2012	$2,960	$48,000	$50,960	$51,239	−$279	$1,262	−0.55%
2013	$2,960	$50,000	$52,960	$53,289	−$329	$934	−0.62%
		Average	$51,872	$51,778	$93		0.18%

[*]MAPE = mean absolute percentage error.

about 18 basis points. The year-to-year differences never amount to more than $359. If bonds could be purchased in fractional amounts, a perfect fit could be attained, but it is difficult to conceive of greater accuracy being needed for most real-world circumstances.

Assuming that the balance of her portfolio, rounded off to $580,000, is invested in an S&P 500 index fund, it would grow untouched, earning a total return over the 10-year period. At the average of 11 percent, it would reach $1,646,864. With 4 percent inflation, her initial withdrawal of $36,000 would grow to $53,289. This will represent only about 3.2 percent of her portfolio at that time, assuming the 11 percent total return. Because her withdrawal rates are below 4 percent, Sophie's portfolio should be self-sustaining indefinitely. She has achieved what she wanted to do and can easily afford to continue with her cruises every other year if her health permits.

THE LEGAL SETTLEMENT

Generating a Win-Win Compromise

Driving home from his job one night, Tom had the terrible misfortune of being hit by a drunk driver who swerved into his lane and hit him head-on. The other driver was killed, and Tom's injuries left him unable to work at his job as a mechanic. He could no longer stand, bend, or twist for any length of time. At age 52, he still had at least 10 years of worklife left.[1]

There was no question as to legal liability, and the other driver's insurance company made an offer to settle without going to court. As a victim, Tom was entitled under law to compensation for the damage he had suffered. *General damages* is the term used for damages for which there is no objective way to assess dollar values, such as pain, suffering, or grief. *Special damages* are those that can be equated (or at least estimated) directly with dollar values, such as lost wages and earning capacity, the cost of replacing Tom's car, and his medical and rehabilitation costs. The focus here will be on the lost earning capacity to illustrate how asset dedication could play a role, but similar reasoning would apply to the other elements of special damages.

Lost earning capacity is usually estimated as the difference between what someone would have earned over his lifetime had he continued in his current or planned occupation minus whatever he would now be able to earn in an acceptable alternative occupation recommended by a vocational therapist. Under the American judicial system, everyone is assumed to have the responsibility to mitigate the damage from any accident. If you can avoid a car coming at you by getting out of the way, you must do so. The same is true for future damages, meaning that Tom cannot simply retire at age 52 and refuse any further employment at the expense of the other driver's insurance company.

Tom hired an attorney, who would get 30 percent of the award.[2] His attorney thus had an incentive to maximize the award. The other driver's insurance company also hired (or assigned) its own attorney, whose job it would be to minimize the total amount that Tom received. Defense attorneys usually work by the hour. Their incentive to do a good job is the hope of getting future cases from the same or other clients. The standard joke among attorneys is that you will never get rich working the defense side of the street, but the pay is steadier (does this sound sort of like stocks versus bonds?).

The insurance company's offer to settle without going to court would save legal expenses for both sides. It also avoided the risk of either side's ending up a big loser. However, Tom's attorney thought the offer was too low. Tom was an experienced mechanic who had worked at the same automobile dealership for a number of years, and Tom had been earning about $100,000 per year, including wages and benefits. The job recommended by the vocational therapist would pay him only $40,000 per year. The $60,000 per year difference over his expected working lifetime formed the basis for his claim of economic damages.

An intuitive estimate of his loss would be to simply multiply the $60,000 times the 10 years to get $600,000. But this fails to factor in present value or the expected increases in his wages as a result of inflation. Assume both sides agree that 4 percent is a reasonable inflation hedge.

Table 9.4 illustrates Tom's projected wages plus 4 percent inflation, assuming that he would get only cost of living increases. They total $720,366. But these are future values and must be discounted back to present value.

Disputes often arise at this point. What is the appropriate discount rate to use for computing present values? Both sides may hire independent economists to estimate the present value of lost wages.[3] Theoretically, present values should be based on the interest rate, but there is no single interest rate, so the issue often comes down to which interest rate or what combination of rates to use.

Plaintiff's economists tend to argue for low rates in order to maximize the present value of the loss, while defense economists tend to argue the reverse in order to minimize the present value. Both sides can cite historical evidence to support their figures because data for short-term, intermediate-term, or long-term bonds are readily available. Some argue that only interest rates on U.S.

Table 9.4

Estimated Earnings Losses over the Next 10 Years

Year	Loss	Loss plus 4% Inflation
1	$60,000	$60,000
2	$60,000	$62,400
3	$60,000	$64,896
4	$60,000	$67,492
5	$60,000	$70,192
6	$60,000	$72,999
7	$60,000	$75,919
8	$60,000	$78,956
9	$60,000	$82,114
10	$60,000	$85,399
	$600,000	$720,366

Treasuries should be used, and others argue that AAA-rated corporate bonds are appropriate. Occasionally, the expected return on a generic portfolio with a conservative but arbitrary asset allocation including stocks is used. The jury must attempt to cut through the arcane economic arguments to decide what present value to use in reaching its conclusions as to the final award.

Assume that the plaintiff's economist uses 6 percent as the discount rate and the defense's uses 8 percent. Table 9.5 shows that the plaintiff's rate leads to a present value of $551,537, and the defense's, to $509,264. The obvious compromise would be to split it down the middle and use $530,401. The plaintiff would receive $21,137 less than he wanted, and the defense would pay $21,137 more, but the result appears fair.

But better solutions are available with asset dedication, which can play a role in at least two ways. First, a 10-year portfolio consisting of U.S. Treasuries or corporate bonds could be set up, using the web site. It turns out that, because of the low interest rates on bonds as of this writing (late 2003), even the plaintiff's 6 percent is too high for government or corporate bonds. Table 9.6 shows the Scenarios screen from the web site, which indicates that $579,397 would be needed to buy a sufficient portfolio of U.S. Treasury and

Table 9.5

Present Values of Earning Losses
at Two Discount Rates

Year	Loss	Loss plus Inflation 4%	Plaintiff Discount Rate 6%	Defense Discount Rate 8%
1	$60,000	$60,000	$60,000	$60,000
2	$60,000	$62,400	$58,868	$57,778
3	$60,000	$64,896	$57,757	$55,638
4	$60,000	$67,492	$56,667	$53,577
5	$60,000	$70,192	$55,598	$51,593
6	$60,000	$72,999	$54,549	$49,682
7	$60,000	$75,919	$53,520	$47,842
8	$60,000	$78,956	$52,510	$46,070
9	$60,000	$82,114	$51,519	$44,364
10	$60,000	$85,399	$50,547	$42,721
	$600,000	$720,366	$551,537	$509,264

Table 9.6

10-Year Portfolio of Government Bonds for Structured Legal Settlement—
Scenario Screen

Scenarios for Dec 3, 2003	1
1 *(Input)* Client Name(s):	Bob
2 *(Input)* Total available for investment:	$579,397
Cash and Income Needed for 2003:	
3 *(Input)* 2003 cash plus income BEFORE taxes from today to 2/15/2004:	$0
4 *(Input)* Interest earned on 2003 cash:	0%
5 Initial amount needed in cash BEFORE taxes:	$0
6 As Percent of Initial Amount:	0.00%
7 Balance remaining for future growth and income:	$579,397
Future Income Needs - 2004 and Beyond:	
8 *(Input)* Planning horizon - 2003 plus an additional:	10 yrs
9 *(Input)* Select inflation rate to apply to future income:	4%
10 *(Input)* Monthly BEFORE-tax income needed in today's dollars:	$4,808
11 Annual BEFORE-tax income needed in today's dollars:	$57,696
12 Annual BEFORE-tax income needed as a percent of total portfolio:	10.00%
13 Annual BEFORE-tax income needed in next year's dollars:	$60,004
14 *(Input)* Class of Fixed Income security to consider:	US Gov't
15 ESTIMATED amount needed for income in 2004 and beyond	$579,396
16 As Percent of Initial Amount:	100.00%
Future Growth - from Today to End of Planning Horizon:	
17 Estimated balance remaining for future growth investment:	$1
18 As Percent of Initial Amount:	0.00%
19 *(Input)* Projected Total Rate of Return on Growth portfolio:	11%
20 Percent of the time the S&P 500 achieved this return over similar spans since 1947:	62%
21 Estimated value of growth portfolio at end in future dollars:	$4
22 Estimated value of growth portfolio at end in today's dollars:	$3
23 Overall Portfolio - Annualized Internal Rate of Return to 2/15/2004:	3.30%

agency bonds, which are listed in Table 9.7. Tables 9.8 and 9.9 show the equivalent for investment-grade corporate bonds, which would cost almost the same, $571,043. Table 9.7 lists the specific U.S. government bonds that provide the income stream, and Table 9.9 lists the same for the corporate bonds. The plaintiff could present either or both lists in court—or threaten to—because most attorneys believe that nothing beats specificity in front of a jury.

Table 9.7

10-Year Portfolio of Government Bonds for Structured Legal Settlement—Details Screen

Year	Rating	CUSIP	Name	Matures	Coupon	YTM	Price	Quantity	Principal	Interest	Total	Target
2004	Aaa/AAA	3133MD7D9	Federal Home Ln Bks	2/13/2004	5.25	0.835	$101.50	31	$31,000	$29,341	$60,341	$60,000
2005	Aaa/NR	31331	Federal Farm Cr Bks									$62,400
2006	Aaa/AAA	RRQ0 MTN	Cons Sys Mtn	3/11/2005	5.97	1.812	$105.38	35	$35,000	$27,714	$62,714	$64,896
2007	Aaa/AAA	742651CT7	Private Expt Fdg Corp	3/15/2006	5.34	2.202	$107.08	39	$39,000	$25,624	$64,624	$67,492
		3134A1JS0	Federal Home Ln Mtg Corp	1/9/2007	6.704	2.702	$111.98	44	$44,000	$23,542	$67,542	
2008	Aaa/AAA	3134A4TE4	Federal Home Ln Mtg Corp	3/15/2008	2.75	3.114	$98.53	50	$50,000	$20,592	$70,592	$70,192
2009	Aaa/AAA	3133M7UL8	Federal Home Ln Bks	3/2/2009	5.705	3.706	$109.52	54	$54,000	$19,217	$73,217	$72,999
2010	Aaa/AAA	912827SZ1	United States Treas Nts	2/15/2010	6.5	3.482	$116.80	60	$60,000	$16,136	$76,136	$75,919
2011	Aaa/AAA	880591DN9	Tennessee Valley Auth	1/18/2011	5.625	4.362	$107.70	67	$67,000	$12,236	$79,236	$78,956
2012	Aaa/AAA	912827L0	United States Treas Nts	2/15/2012	4.875	3.906	$106.77	74	$74,000	$8,468	$82,468	$82,114
2013	Aaa/AAA	880591CW0	Tennessee Valley Auth	3/15/2013	6	4.47	$111.56	81	$81,000	$4,860	$85,860	$85,399
							Total	$579,396	$535,000	$187,730	$722,730	$720,366

Table 9.8

10-Year Portfolio of Corporate Bonds for Structured Legal Settlement

Scenario for Dec 3, 2003

1	*(Input)* Client Name(s):	Bob
2	*(Input)* Total available for investment:	$571,043

Cash and Income Needed for 2003:

3	*(Input)* 2003 cash plus income BEFORE taxes from today to 2/15/2004:	$0
4	*(Input)* Interest earned on 2003 cash:	0%
5	Initial amount needed in cash BEFORE taxes:	$0
6	As Percent of Initial Amount:	0.00%
7	Balance remaining for future growth and income:	$571,043

Future Income Needs - 2004 and Beyond:

8	*(Input)* Planning horizon - 2003 plus an additional:	10 yrs
9	*(Input)* Select inflation rate to apply to future income:	4%
10	*(Input)* Monthly BEFORE-tax income needed in today's dollars:	$4,808
11	Annual BEFORE-tax income needed in today's dollars:	$57,696
12	Annual BEFORE-tax income needed as a percent of total portfolio:	10.10%
13	Annual BEFORE-tax income needed in next year's dollars:	$60,004
14	*(Input)* Class of Fixed Income security to consider:	Corporate
15	ESTIMATED amount needed for income in 2004 and beyond	$571,042
16	As Percent of Initial Amount:	100.00%

Future Growth - from Today to End of Planning Horizon:

17	Estimated balance remaining for future growth investment:	$1
18	As Percent of Initial Amount:	0.00%
19	*(Input)* Projected Total Rate of Return on Growth portfolio:	11%
20	Percent of the time the S&P 500 achieved this return over similar spans since 1947:	62%
21	Estimated value of growth portfolio at end in future dollars:	$3
22	Estimated value of growth portfolio at end in today's dollars:	$2
23	Overall Portfolio - Annualized Internal Rate of Return, 2/15/2004 to end:	3.50%

On the other hand, asset dedication could be used to construct two 5-year plans to generate the 10-year income stream. If both sides agreed during a settlement conference, the compromise figure of $530,401 could initially be invested in U.S. Treasuries that would mature sequentially over the next 5 years at a cost of $294,657 (see Table 9.10). The balance of $235,744 would be allocated to the growth portion of the portfolio and invested in an S&P 500 index fund.

Table 9.9

10-Year Portfolio of Corporate Bonds for Structured Legal Settlement

Year	Rating	CUSIP	Name	Matures	Coupon	YTM	Price	Total Income[*]	Target
2004	Aa1/AA−	79549BBE6	Salomon Inc	2/1/2004	7.200	0.845	$101.26	$59,827	$60,004
2005	Aaa/AAA	459056GA9	International Bk For Recon & Dev	2/15/2005	0	1.825	$97.78	$62,163	$62,404
2006	Aaa/AAA	36966RBS4 MTN	General Elec Cap Corp	2/15/2006	2.500	2.904	$99.12	$65,163	$64,900
2007	Aaa/AAA	459056GE1	International Bk For Recon & Dev	2/15/2007	0	3.211	$90.20	$67,038	$67,496
2008	Aaa/AAA	36966RCC8 MTN	General Elec Cap Corp	2/15/2008	3.450	3.693	$99.05	$70,038	$70,196
2009	Aaa/AAA	3133M7UL8	Federal Home Ln Bks	3/2/2009	5.705	3.706	$109.52	$73,279	$73,004
2010	Aaa/AAA	637432CN3	National Rural Utils Coop Fin Corp	1/15/2010	5.700	4.377	$107.06	$76,084	$75,924
2011	Aaa/AAA	459056JJ7	International Bk For Recon & Dev	2/15/2011	0	4.683	$71.52	$78,550	$78,961
2012	Aaa/AAA	36962GXS8 MTN	General Elec Cap Corp	2/15/2012	5.875	4.631	$108.43	$82,550	$82,119
2013	Aaa/AAA	448814FK4	Yankee Canadian Hydro-Quebec	2/1/2013	8.000	4.494	$126.17	$85,320	$85,404
							Total	$720,013	$720,413

[*]Total income includes principal and interest.

Table 9.10

Asset Dedication Applied to Structured Legal Settlement—
Two Successive 5-Year Plans

Scenarios for Dec 3, 2003	2	1
1 *(Input)* Client Name(s):	Bob	Bob
2 *(Input)* Total available for investment:	$400,549	$530,401
Cash and Income Needed for 2003:		
3 *(Input)* 2003 cash plus income BEFORE taxes from today to 2/15/2004:	$0	$0
4 *(Input)* Interest earned on 2003 cash:	0%	0%
5 Initial amount needed in cash BEFORE taxes:	$0	$0
6 As Percent of Initial Amount:	0.00%	0.00%
7 Balance remaining for future growth and income:	$400,549	$530,401
Future Income Needs - 2004 and Beyond:		
8 *(Input)* Planning horizon - 2003 plus an additional:	5 yrs	5 yrs
9 *(Input)* Select inflation rate to apply to future income:	4%	4%
10 *(Input)* Monthly BEFORE-tax income needed in today's dollars:	$5,849	$4,808
11 Annual BEFORE-tax income needed in today's dollars:	$70,191	$57,692
12 Annual BEFORE-tax income needed as a percent of total portfolio:	**17.50%**	10.90%
13 Annual BEFORE-tax income needed in next year's dollars:	$72,999	$60,000
14 *(Input)* Class of Fixed Income security to consider:	US Gov't	US Gov't
15 ESTIMATED amount needed for income in 2004 and beyond	$358,691	$294,657
16 As Percent of Initial Amount:	**89.50%**	55.60%
Future Growth - from Today to End of Planning Horizon:		
17 Estimated balance remaining for future growth investment:	$41,858	$235,744
18 As Percent of Initial Amount:	**10.50%**	44.40%
19 *(Input)* Projected Total Rate of Return on Growth portfolio:	11%	11%
20 Percent of the time the S&P 500 achieved this return over similar spans since 1947:	66%	66%
21 Estimated value of growth portfolio at end in future dollars:	$71,120	$400,549
22 Estimated value of growth portfolio at end in today's dollars:	$58,273	$328,198
23 Overall Portfolio - Annualized Internal Rate of Return to 2/15/2004:	**3.60%**	6.40%

Assuming a total return on the S&P of 11 percent per year (which has a 66 percent probability of being realized), the growth portfolio will be worth $400,459 5 years hence. If interest rates decline no lower than current levels on similar bonds in 5 years, the cost of supplying the second 5-year income stream, after adjusting for inflation, would be $358,691. This would leave a balance of $41,858, which could be split between the two parties, thereby mitigating what each one gave up in compromise.

There is the possibility that the S&P 500 index fund will fail to achieve 11 percent growth. It would need to grow at 8.8 percent to reach the $358,691 needed to purchase the next 5-year stream. The probability of this happening is 80 percent. The two sides could agree that, just as they would split any excess, they would also split any deficiency at that time. Such agreements are the essence of what are called *structured settlements*, and asset dedication could represent a compromise approach for both sides.

SUPPORTING GRANTS FROM THE J FOUNDATION

Making a Charitable Foundation's Portfolio Efficient

The J Foundation was attached to a large university, and every year it provided grants of up to $50,000 for projects by faculty and staff that fit the criteria for the causes it supported. The fund had a portfolio of $20 million at its disposal, and the total amount it could fund each year depended on how well the fund's portfolio had done.

When the foundation was originally set up in the early 1970s, its administrators had used the $20 million to purchase 10-year U.S. Treasury bonds. The interest that the bonds paid had varied, depending on interest rates at the time the next bonds had to be purchased. At the prior repurchase point, the bonds had happened to be paying 5 percent coupon interest. The $1,000,000 interest meant the foundation could fund up to 18 projects after paying $100,000 for administrative expenses (mostly dinners, travel, and so on for the foundation's benefactors and administrators plus office and proposal review expenses).

One of the issues that the administrators faced was the fact that under the original guidelines, they had failed to consider the slow erosion caused by inflation. The magnitude and quality of the project proposals they funded had slowly declined over the years. One of the members of the group that oversaw the fund pointed out that the basic funding guidelines had not been changed in 30 years. Over that time, inflation had averaged 4.7 percent per year, meaning that the original $50,000 limit in real dollar terms represented only $11,797 at current prices. Had they kept up with inflation, they should have a current funding limit of $198,322 (see Table 9.11).

Another problem was the fact that the interest rate paid by bonds was currently quite low. Lower interest meant that they would not be able to earn enough to fund even 18 projects in the coming years.

One of the administrators had learned of asset dedication and suggested that the foundation should consider restructuring its investment and funding policies. By moving to asset dedication, the fund could harness the power of the stock market through index funds but meet its inflation-adjusted funding needs each year without having to use any of the foundation's money to pay for financial advisory fees.

After a spirited discussion at the foundation's annual meeting, and despite the protests of the financial adviser who had managed the fund for years, the J Foundation went ahead with the asset dedication plan with a 5-year horizon. Interest rates were low, so the 5-year horizon seemed appropriate, and it would allow the administrators to evaluate how well the new policies were working. They decided to increase the funding limit to $100,000. They also decided to not put in an automatic inflation adjustment, but rather to wait and see how the funds did. They would track inflation and consider potential adjustments as a regular part of the agenda at their annual policy meeting.

The investment in bonds for a 5-year plan with U.S. Treasuries was $4,555,927 (Table 9.12). The balance would be invested in an S&P 500 index fund. Assuming that the fund grew at 11 percent, it would reach $26,233,339 by the end of 5 years. If it did, in fact, achieve this level, the administrators would then consider revising the award amounts and perhaps extend the planning horizon to 10 years. All of the members understood the idea of asset dedication and felt that they were doing a better job of directing the foundation toward making the contribution to society that it was intended to fulfill.

The J Foundation could also make use of asset dedication to fund a charitable giving program for its donors. A number of charities now offer the equivalent of annuities. The main attraction is that the donor gets an immediate tax deduction plus the knowledge

Table 9.11

J Foundation with Stated Funding
Limit, Real Funding Limit with 4.7
Percent Inflation, and How Funding
Limits Should Increase with Inflation
at 4.7 Percent

Year	Inflation Adjustment		
	0%	−4.7%	4.7%
0	$50,000	$50,000	$50,000
1	$50,000	$47,650	$52,350
2	$50,000	$45,410	$54,810
3	$50,000	$43,276	$57,387
4	$50,000	$41,242	$60,084
5	$50,000	$39,304	$62,908
6	$50,000	$37,457	$65,864
7	$50,000	$35,696	$68,960
8	$50,000	$34,018	$72,201
9	$50,000	$32,419	$75,594
10	$50,000	$30,896	$79,147
11	$50,000	$29,444	$82,867
12	$50,000	$28,060	$86,762
13	$50,000	$26,741	$90,840
14	$50,000	$25,484	$95,109
15	$50,000	$24,286	$99,580
16	$50,000	$23,145	$104,260
17	$50,000	$22,057	$109,160
18	$50,000	$21,020	$114,291
19	$50,000	$20,032	$119,662
20	$50,000	$19,091	$125,286
21	$50,000	$18,194	$131,175
22	$50,000	$17,339	$137,340
23	$50,000	$16,524	$143,795
24	$50,000	$15,747	$150,553
25	$50,000	$15,007	$157,629
26	$50,000	$14,302	$165,038
27	$50,000	$13,629	$172,795
28	$50,000	$12,989	$180,916
29	$50,000	$12,378	$189,419
30	$50,000	$11,797	$198,322

Table 9.12

$20 Million J Foundation Asset Dedication Plan

Scenario for Dec 4, 2003	
1 (Input) Client Name(s):	J Foundation
2 (Input) Total available for investment:	$20,000,000
Cash and Income Needed for 2003:	
3 (Input) 2003 cash plus income BEFORE taxes from today to 2/15/2004:	$0
4 (Input) Interest earned on 2003 cash:	0%
5 Initial amount needed in cash BEFORE taxes:	$0
6 As Percent of Initial Amount:	0.00%
7 Balance remaining for future growth and income:	$20,000,000
Future Income Needs – 2004 and Beyond:	
8 (Input) Planning horizon - 2003 plus an additional:	5 yrs
9 (Input) Select inflation rate to apply to future income:	0%
10 (Input) Monthly BEFORE-tax income needed in today's dollars:	$83,333
11 Annual BEFORE-tax income needed in today's dollars:	$1,000,000
12 Annual BEFORE-tax income needed as a percent of total portfolio:	5.00%
13 Annual BEFORE-tax income needed in next year's dollars:	$1,000,000
14 (Input) Class of Fixed Income security to consider:	US Gov't
15 ESTIMATED amount needed for income in 2004 and beyond	$4,555,927
16 As Percent of Initial Amount:	22.80%
Future Growth - from Today to End of Planning Horizon:	
17 Estimated balance remaining for future growth investment:	$15,444,073
18 As Percent of Initial Amount:	77.20%
19 (Input) Projected Total Rate of Return on Growth portfolio:	11%
20 Percent of the time the S&P 500 achieved this return over similar spans since 1947:	66%
21 Estimated value of growth portfolio at end in future dollars:	$26,233,339
22 Estimated value of growth portfolio at end in today's dollars:	$26,233,339
23 Overall Portfolio-Annualized Internal Rate of Return, 2/15/2004	8.20%

that if she dies shortly after setting up the annuity, the charity will benefit rather than an insurance company. Using asset dedication, the administrators could lock up a payment stream for the donor's chosen planning horizon with the income portion, then invest the balance in the S&P 500.

ASSET DEDICATION WITH A ROLLING HORIZON

Frank and Flora Green are like Bob and Helen Brown. They are also 10 years from retirement, but they are fortunate enough to have already accumulated a nest egg of $600,000 in their retirement portfolio. They are extremely conservative, and over their lifetimes they have realized that they simply do not sleep well at night when they have their entire portfolio invested in stocks. They are fully aware of the higher average growth rates that stocks achieve over the long run, but they still do not like to go to bed worrying about it. They want to buffer themselves against the volatility they hear talked about on the news every day.

The Greens decide to use a rolling-horizon asset dedication strategy with a twist. They will initially purchase a 10-year income stream, but at the end of each year, when each bond matures, they will use that money plus whatever interest has accumulated from coupon payments to purchase a new 10-year bond. This will keep their horizon 10 years out. That is, they will maintain a perpetual 10-year income stream in front of them. If the new 10-year bond costs less than the available cash, which it is likely to do, then any excess will be deposited in stocks. By the time they retire, they will have an income stream for the next 10 years already in place.

Assume the same parameters for the Greens as for Ms. Smith from Chapter 3: a $600,000 portfolio and a $30,000 income stream plus 4 percent inflation. Assume further that it is 1990, and the 10-year horizon covers 1990 to 2000, the same period used in the Dorfman study discussed in Chapter 2 and for the first test period in Chapter 4.

At bond prices prevailing in 1990, purchasing the initial set of bonds required an investment of $230,869 (38.9 percent of the total portfolio), with the balance being invested in an S&P 500 index fund. Ten years later, in 2000, this portfolio would have been worth $2,520,994, having earned an annualized total return of 15.4 percent, better than any of the brokers presented in Chapter 2 (see Figure 9.2). Note that 15.4 percent is slightly less than the fixed-horizon return demonstrated in Chapter 4. That is due to the fact that the fixed-horizon model kept more on average in stocks, which produced extremely high returns over the period from 1990 to 2000. The available cash from the maturing bonds and interest each year averaged about $12,000 over and above the cost of the new 10-year bonds over the entire horizon. This excess was added to the stock portion of the portfolio.

Note that the absolute amount in bonds does not grow significantly. This stems from the fact that the cost of the bonds did not

Figure 9.2

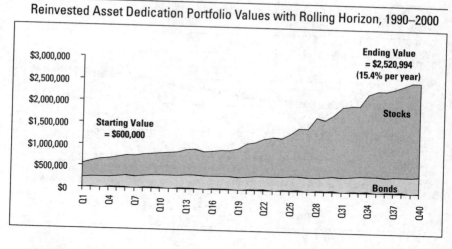

Reinvested Asset Dedication Portfolio Values with Rolling Horizon, 1990–2000

Table 9.13

Initial and Ending Values of the Portfolio in Dollars and Percentages

Portion	Initial		Ending	
Dedicated	$230,826	38%	$364,700	14%
Stocks	$369,174	62%	$2,141,555	85%
Cash	$0	0%	$14,739	1%
Total	$600,000	100%	$2,520,994	100%

change nearly as much as the value of the stocks did over this period. Because the dollar value of the bonds did not grow as quickly as the value of the stocks, it declined as a percentage of the portfolio (remember that there is no rebalancing to arbitrary formulas in asset dedication). Cash plays a very minor role during the planning horizon; the amount is so small that it cannot be seen at the bottom of the chart.

Table 9.13 shows the initial and ending values and allocations of the portfolio.

Figure 9.3 also demonstrates the declining proportion of bonds as a percentage of the overall portfolio. This is a natural consequence of the growth of stocks, which dominated bonds over this period.

Figure 9.3

Stocks, Bonds, and Cash as a Percentage of Total Portfolio Value

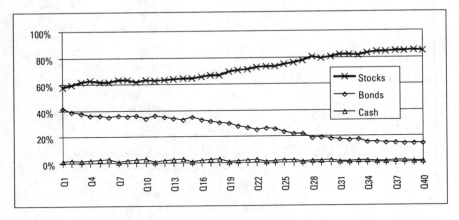

PROFESSIONAL ATHLETES, PENSION FUNDS, CORPORATE CONTROLLERS, PUBLIC AGENCIES

Anyone Facing a Projected Future Income Stream Can Use Asset Dedication

Professional athletes tend to have high but brief earnings during their careers. It is easy for them to squander their incomes on "big-boy" toys or to fall prey to financial predators. They seldom have the appropriate training or insight to understand exactly what it is they are investing in. They may try to take care of their friends or family by setting up trusts, but if they fail to invest the money wisely, these trusts will be worthless.

Because of their schedules, they have little time to monitor their own financial affairs, let alone the affairs of those whom they are trying to help. They often end up paying dearly for advisers. If they are fortunate enough to hook up with a competent and scrupulous adviser, they may be OK, but they are constantly bombarded with offers from advisers of other types. Asset dedication represents a very low-cost approach that offers them the opportunity to support whomever they wish in an independent way that is better than either simply putting them on the dole or giving them a lump sum of cash.

Pension funds also are clear candidates for asset dedication. It would allow the fund to manage its cash flows with a minimum of administrative expense. Because passive management is used, there will be no need for the fund to hire expensive money managers. Those who operate 401(k) plans would benefit from lower operating costs. As mentioned very early in the book, dedicated portfolios have been utilized for many years by pension fund managers and others who manage large funds with predictable cash flows.

Public agencies such as local governments whose treasurers are sufficiently sophisticated to be able to forecast their cash flows can also apply asset dedication. They might face a shorter time horizon and plan in terms of weeks or months, but because they often deal with very large sums of money, even minor improvements on the amount of interest they can capture can generate significant sums. One percent of $100 million is $1 million, or a little over $2700 per day. Unfortunately, many county treasurers are not very entrepreneurial, because they have little incentive to innovate. It takes intellectual courage for civil servants to think outside the box and professional courage to act outside it. Most do not do so. They tend to focus entirely on making sure that no checks bounce, and they end up being so conservative that they waste taxpayers' money by not exploring the available options. But so long as they continue to get reelected, no one will ever know how much could have been saved.

Corporations, on the other hand, have a clear incentive to manage their cash flows so as to minimize costs. Again, the key is being able to successfully forecast future cash flows. Asset dedication promises to make it worthwhile to investigate ways to make accurate cash flow predictions.

CONCLUSION

This chapter presented some additional examples of how asset dedication can be applied in a variety of settings. Others could be included. The approach is actually quite rich in terms of research possibilities: testing the effects of longer planning horizons, adding confidence intervals to the critical path, finding sweet spots in the trade-offs among planning horizon lengths, different bond types, withdrawal rates, and so on. Academic researchers have a way of ferreting out the implications of new investment approaches quickly.

The bottom line will be whether financial advisers and leaders in the financial community decide to put the interests of investors ahead of their own. Asset allocation proponents will not give up peacefully because asset allocation offers such great advantages to those who benefit from investors' ignorance. Asset dedication may be viewed as a competitive threat to their preferred way of doing business.

In the final part of this book, we will explore the theoretical underpinnings of asset dedication and also explore the murky world of forecasting. Researchers face formidable obstacles in attempting to find the Holy Grail of accurate stock market predictions. Some predictions can be made with perfect accuracy, but others defy the ability of serious researchers to unravel the factors that drive the market.

NOTES

1. In actual court cases, worklife expectancy rather than retirement age is often used. Worklife expectancy factors in expected times of unemployment and the probability of leaving the workforce early. In this case, we assume that a worklife expectancy to age 63 applies.
2. The argument in favor of plaintiff's attorneys getting a share of the award is that it gives anyone access to legal representation, even someone who cannot pay an attorney up front. The attorney who takes the case will do so only if he thinks it is winnable and worth his while. The system thus provides a screening effect. Cases that do not have merit or significant economic consequences will not reach the courts. On the other hand, our clogged court system suggests that we may have so many attorneys that at any point in time, there may be one who will be willing to take on even the most questionable claim. The hope is to get a victory in court, or at least to negotiate a settlement that will cost the defense side less than going to court.
3. The economists may also dispute the appropriate rate of inflation to use, but we have assumed in this case that both sides have agreed to use 4 percent per year.

PART 3

Theoretical Underpinnings of Asset Dedication: A Few Fundamentals

Scott Peck's book *The Road Less Traveled* has a great opening line: "Life is difficult." So is financial planning, especially if you are unfamiliar with the basic concepts and vocabulary. If you are relatively new to investing, you may have been forced to accept some of the discussions in the earlier chapters as a matter of faith. Those chapters outlined the approach that asset dedication takes in order to achieve its goals.

The purpose of this part of the book is not to introduce anything particularly new, but rather to explain what is going on behind the scenes in financial investing decisions. It explains why markets work the way they do, the tools that are used to make investing decisions, and a number of the common mistakes that people make when they are dealing with interest rates and growth projections.

Chapter 10 will present some of the background elements that form the environment in which financial decisions must be made. Much of the chapter presents basic economic theory concerning why companies and individuals as "economic decision makers" behave in certain ways in making choices over time. An old joke among economists is that economics is the mother of all business phenomena; we just do not know who the father is.

Chapter 11 delves into the world of investing itself. It traces a company from its initial start-up phase to the final stage of becoming a publicly traded corporation. As we follow this story, many of the various elements of the financial industry will come up in a natural way so that we can see how they fit into the overall picture.

Chapter 12 begins the more technically difficult chapters. It explains the mathematical foundation for the types of analyses that researchers use as they attempt to understand markets. Approaching investing from a scientific point of view automatically entails the use of measurements, and with measurements come numbers, and with numbers, mathematics. Hopefully, reading these chapters will prove to be worth the trouble.

Chapter 13 continues the mathematics, explaining the quantitative tools of optimization and Monte Carlo analysis that more sophisticated financial analysts utilize to try to improve portfolio performance. It highlights the eternal battle between return and risk, and how portfolio managers have attempted to deal with it.

Chapter 14 finishes the book with a look at forecasting, the bane of all financial planning. It points out the situations when investment returns can be forecast with near perfect accuracy and when they cannot. It demonstrates the best and worst consequences of trying to time the market. It closes with a look at the ugly side of the financial industry, the scam artists and some of their favorite tricks for exploiting investors' unquenchable thirst for precognition.

CHAPTER 10

Life, Death, Economics, and Time

Fortune favors the prepared mind.

—Louis Pasteur

Recall from Chapter 5 that most financial advisers separate the stages of life into three financial phases:

1. The accumulation phase—when money is added (the working years)
2. The distribution phase—when money is withdrawn (retirement)
3. The transfer phase—when money is passed on to heirs

Note that when we describe life in these terms, the time element is automatically introduced. Time is a dimension in which we all exist. It is something of a mystery, if you think much about it. Physicists and cosmologists probably think about it the most, but it infuses everything we do. It even plays a central, if unseen, role in financial markets because of its dynamic irreversibility. The phrase that economists use is the *time value of money*. It is one of the fundamental reasons for the existence of interest rates.

THE TIME VALUE OF MONEY

Why Interest Rates Exist

Earlier chapters describing asset dedication emphasized that bonds have lower but predictable rates of return through interest payments at specified points in time and the ultimate return of the principal listed on the face value of the bond. Stocks carry higher but more volatile returns that are based on the profits that the companies earn, but even their returns represent a form of interest in which the rate is uncertain.[1]

Clearly, interest rates affect everyone's lives, whether through mortgages, credit card charges, auto loans, or whatever. They can have a tremendous impact on bond prices directly and on all financial markets indirectly. They permeate our existence.

This brings up a simple question: Why does money earn interest in the first place? Positive interest rates cause $0.95 to be worth about $1 a year later (at 5 percent) and vice versa. But why are interest rates always positive? When I ask this question of my students in class, they say that it is because banks or other institutions will pay you interest. But that begs the question: Why do the banks pay interest? The simple answer is because they lend the money to other borrowers at a higher rate and make a profit. But then why do the other borrowers pay it? It becomes circular reasoning.

The real question is: Why do we have positive interest rates in the first place? Here are some root causes:

1. *Compensation for deferred gratification.* Most of us have a positive time preference: When we want something, we want it now—not later, now. In fact, we expect compensation if we have to postpone our gratification to a later time because our natural preference is to have what we want when we want it. We will wait if there is some inducement or reward for doing so, but the default preference is for immediate gratification. Little children usually want dessert before a meal, not after—why wait for the good stuff? It is an interesting exercise to offer a small child a small-size ice cream cone now or a giant-size if he waits an hour (assuming that you can put up with the continuing "How much longer?"). Positive time preference is considered to be an innate characteristic of human nature and is one of the two "deep" reasons why

interest rates exist and always have in all societies since recorded time.

2. *Compensation for risk.* Positive time preferences are not just the result of childish impatience. They are also quite rational as a result of the dynamic irreversibility of time and the risk it creates. Within the financial community, several types of risk are often mentioned, including market risk, inflation risk, reinvestment risk, and default risk. But where does the risk come from?

It has to do with the nature of time. Time is a mysterious element of our existence that perhaps only cosmologists understand. One of its properties is referred to as *dynamic irreversibility*: Time moves in only one direction. This is what causes risk. Once a dollar leaves my direct control, there is always some probability that I will never be able to use it to gratify my desires. The person I gave it to may not give it back (the bank may go out of business, the stock may drop, and so on). If I invested that dollar for a year, but I need it back in 6 months because of an emergency, it may be worth less because of a decline in the market at that point. Or the person I gave it to may be ready to give it back at the end of the year, but I may no longer be here to receive it (I may be dead, incapacitated, or whatever). I cannot go back in time to recapture the deferred gratification because time moves only forward. My gratification was not simply deferred, it was lost forever. This type of risk is considered to be the second deep reason for the existence of interest rates.[2]

3. *Inflation.* Inflation is a perennial part of our economy, and most people expect that it always will be. Price increases may be faster or slower, but deflation (an actual decline in overall prices) appears unlikely over any extended period of time. As a result, one of the functions of interest is to keep up with inflation so that purchasing power parity is maintained. If prices rise by 3 percent, you need to earn at least 3 percent on your money to make the principal worth the same amount (neglecting taxes). The U.S. Treasury now sells inflation-proof bonds ("I bonds") that pay a return equal to the stated interest rate plus inflation.[3]

4. *Expectation of a higher standard of living.* The United States has generally enjoyed a rising standard of living

since its inception in 1776. There have been notable lapses, such as the Great Depression, but money income on average has risen about 4 percent a year. Prices have also risen, but at only about half that rate. The difference, about 2 percent per year, represents the rise in the standard of living. Each generation has generally enjoyed greater real income than the preceding generation. This has created an expectation that this rise will continue indefinitely. I always thought I would be better off than my parents and that my kids would be better off than I am.[4]

If each of these causes accounted for 1 percent at some point in time, the prevailing interest rate would be 4 percent. The ebb and flow of expectations, risk, and so on constantly fluctuate, of course, and interest rates follow. In addition, there are institutional factors that influence the level of interest rates at any given point in time. The Federal Reserve Bank can raise or lower the rate it charges member banks for money that they borrow to support the fractional banking system. Banks can raise or lower the interest that they charge customers based on the demand for loans. The relative assessments of the trade-offs between stocks and bonds as investments play a role. But all of these factors are layered on top of the root causes listed here and would have little effect if the root causes themselves disappeared—which they will never do because they are an intrinsic part of life, time, and human nature.

TRADE-OFFS
More of This Usually Means Less of That

Trade-offs are a fact of life and extend to every part of it. To get more of this, you must get less of that. To have more leisure, you must spend less time working. To have a more attractive waistline, you must eat less food. To have more money later, you must spend less now. Each of us must make our choices and accept the consequences.

I still remember the day my daughter realized this. She was about four years old, and she had been invited to two friends' separate birthday parties on the same day at the same time. She wanted to go to both. When her mother explained that it was impossible for her to do both, she paused and thought about it for a moment, then suddenly burst into tears as she grasped the truth. At that instant, she took a step closer to maturity.

The trade-off between stocks and bonds is a classic example. To get more investment growth, you must get less investment security. Stocks provide higher returns but lower security. Bonds provide higher security but lower returns. Exploiting the virtues of each type of investment is the essence of asset dedication. One of the advantages of asset dedication is that it clarifies the trade-offs that must be made. To provide a protected stream of income for a longer span of time, more bonds must be purchased. We know exactly what less exposure to risk is going to cost us because it is measured in the length of the planning horizon.

THE TRINITY STUDY OF SUSTAINABLE WITHDRAWAL RATES

Three Goals: Don't Go Broke, Preserve the Corpus, or Preserve Buying Power

One of the clearest trade-offs in retirement is how much can be safely withdrawn from a portfolio. The answer depends on how long you want the portfolio to last and how much you want to leave to your heirs. Many advisers use the 4 percent rule. Ms. Smith in Chapter 3 withdrew at the rate of 5 percent.

A number of researchers have investigated the impact of various withdrawal rates to see what general recommendations can be made to help retirees determine an appropriate withdrawal rate. One of the best of these studies is called the Trinity study. Its name is derived from Trinity University in Texas, where its three coauthors were professors. In 1998 they published an article entitled "Retirement Savings: Choosing a Withdrawal Rate That Is Sustainable."[5]

The idea behind the study was fairly simple. It asked, "What is your goal for the ending value of this portfolio?" and it gave three possible goals: staying above zero (don't go broke), retaining principal, or retaining buying power (i.e., maintaining the inflation-adjusted principal). These are probably the three most common goals specified by investors.

A web site owned by the Zunna Corporation (www.zunna.com) offers a free demonstration version of the software that was built to perform the Trinity study. You tell it how long you want the portfolio to last (2 to 40 years); how certain you want to be that it will achieve its goal based on the historical performance of stocks, bonds, and cash; and how much you want to withdraw initially. It automatically incorporates historical inflation rates for all similar periods and adjusts each year's withdrawals for the prior year's inflation rate to maintain buying power. The software then simulates what would have happened in all spans of similar length based on the actual historical performance of stocks, bonds, and cash (T bills) since 1926.

It turns out that the critical rate for the initial withdrawal is about 4 percent. That means that it is possible to find an asset allocation plan that, in 100 percent of all 31-year periods since 1926, could support up to a 4 percent initial withdrawal rate without reducing the portfolio to a zero balance. The software assumes a fixed-formula approach to asset allocation and reports the allocation plan that achieves the goal, namely, 65 percent large-cap stocks and 35 percent bonds.[6] It does not incorporate the asset dedication concept, nor does it consider sequence risk. It simply says that, given the actual historical returns and inflation rates for each year, this is what would have happened. Nevertheless, the software takes the fixed-formula allocation approach to a much higher level of sophistication because it provides a mathematically defensible rationale for the allocation it suggests.

What differentiates this approach from the usual Monte Carlo simulation is that it uses the actual historical record. The advantage of this is that it does not incorporate the usual assumption in Monte Carlo simulations that each time period is independent of the next. That is, it does not ignore the autocorrelation that results in many economic time series between successive time periods. If this year has a high return, it may influence the return in the following year, increasing or decreasing the likelihood that that year's return will be lower than usual. Autocorrelation may extend over periods longer than 1 year, and it is difficult, if not impossible, to explore all the potential lead and lag effects that one variable can have on another. Most Monte Carlo analyses simply ignore this effect. The historical record, on the other hand, captures these effects automatically because they are embedded in the data set itself.

The disadvantage of using the historical record is that it is based only on the empirical experience from this particular time span in the database. This means that the impact of world events on the market is also included, such as World War II, the deregulation of the financial industry, the end of the Cold War, and so on. It therefore assumes that history will repeat itself—i.e., that equivalent earth-shaking events and random shocks will occur in the same sequence and will have the same effect on market performance. If history does not repeat itself, then the historical record will not be a good predictor of future market performance. This casts doubt on whether the relationships will continue in the same fashion.

But this is an inherent problem with any projecting procedure. All methods rely in one way or another on the past behavior of the data, whether directly, with mathematical equations, or indirectly, with experience and judgment. Those who claim not to use the past to make projections into the future often seem to forget that their perceptions and interpretations are based on the past. They simply have not figured out how to convert their beliefs into formal mathematical relationships.

TAKING ADVANTAGE OF FAVORABLE TAX LAWS: PENSION AND RETIREMENT PLANS

How the Government Encourages People to Provide for Themselves

The plethora of rules and regulations surrounding retirement, the fact that it requires facing unpleasant realities or making unpleasant choices, and the mathematical tediousness of the calculations all contribute to the fact that most people are woefully unprepared for retirement. Studies of the general public's understanding or awareness of retirement issues are worrisome to most policymakers. Here are some of the more glaring examples: (1) Only 16 percent of those in a random survey could correctly give the age at which they will be eligible for Social Security; (2) only 40 percent have bothered to perform any retirement calculations whatsoever (or had them done by a financial adviser); (3) only about 48 percent have invested any of their retirement savings in stocks. These are only the highlights of the 2003 Retirement Confidence Survey.[7]

The best news from this survey is that about 80 percent of the survey respondents are not "very confident" about their ability to live comfortably in retirement. This suggests an underlying level of anxiety that may give them the motivation to overcome their ignorance about retirement issues. As is often the case, those who will face the worst problems are the least likely to do anything about it. Presumably, they intend to rely on others to take care of them and will probably vote for whatever political hack promises to do so.

Myriad rules surround the various pension and retirement plans, and the rules change periodically whenever Congress or state legislatures alter the tax code. A full discussion is entirely beyond the scope of this book. If you are looking for detailed information on the different types of plans that people can use to save money for retirement, it is best to seek professional help, read a book devoted entirely to that topic, or visit a web site focusing on the subject.[8]

One retirement detail that bears mentioning, however, is the changing age of eligibility for retirement. Most of us think of age 65 as the traditional retirement age, and Social Security used to pay full benefits beginning at 65. But the earliest age when people can receive full benefits is receding as a result of changes made by the government in order to keep the system solvent.[9] It now depends on when you were born. Anyone born in 1943 or after must wait until the age of 66, and anyone born in 1960 or after must wait until age 67. There are intermediate ages for those born between these years, as shown in Table 10.1.

Anyone who is covered by the system can elect to retire as early as 62 or as late as 70.5. If you wait, you will receive higher monthly benefits. The sobering trade-off is that you may not reach

Table 10.1

Changing Retirement Ages to Receive Full
Social Security Benefits

Year of Birth[*]	Full Retirement Age	Percent of Full Benefit If Retire at 62
1937 or earlier	65	80.0%
1938	65 and 2 months	79.2%
1939	65 and 4 months	78.3%
1940	65 and 6 months	77.5%
1941	65 and 8 months	76.7%
1942	65 and 10 months	75.8%
1943–1954	66	75.0%
1955	66 and 2 months	74.2%
1956	66 and 4 months	73.3%
1957	66 and 6 months	72.5%
1958	66 and 8 months	71.7%
1959	66 and 10 months	70.8%
1960 and later	67	70.0%

*If you were born on January 1, you should refer to the previous year. If you were born on the first of the month, the benefit is computed as if your birthday was in the previous month.

Source: Social Security Administration (www.socialsecurity.gov).

that age, in which case the higher benefits won't matter. The social security web site (www.socialsecurity.gov) has a calculator that allows you to see how long it will take before the higher payments balance out what you gave up by waiting the extra few years before you started collecting.

FINDING A FINANCIAL ADVISER

Getting the Help You Need but Not More than You Need

Putting your financial affairs in order can be a daunting task. That is the primary reason that financial advisers are in business. They can be especially helpful in determining the proper types of accounts to set up for retirement and other financial goals.

But finding a competent financial adviser to help you with your retirement planning can be a challenge. Unfortunately, many financial advisers are little more than salespeople. Some of my MBA students get excited when they secure an internship at a mainstream broker. They think they are going to be able to use the financial tools they have learned in their studies. Imagine how disheartened they feel when they are placed at a desk with a phone and told to begin dialing for dollars like a telemarketer to find prospective customers. Their bitterness is quite understandable.

Stockbrokers often like to pass themselves off as financial advisers. But thinking that stockbrokers are experts in financial planning is equivalent to thinking that shoestore sales clerks are podiatrists. They both deal with feet, but only one can give informed advice.

Partly because of the abuses within the brokerage industry, many qualified people have left the larger mainstream companies and gone into the financial planning business on their own. They set much higher standards of professional and ethical conduct with stiff eligibility requirements in order to bring integrity into the system. Certified Financial Planners must pass the most comprehensive tests available on personal financial matters and are considered to have the highest level of educational qualifications. They are trained to see the big picture when it comes to personal finances and related "life planning" issues—estate planning, trusts and wills, taxes, long-term health insurance, and so on. You can recognize them by the letters CFP after their name.[10] This credential can be verified by checking the Internet at www.cfp.net/search.

You are more likely to get solid, accurate advice from a CFP than from a stockbroker or anyone else who does not have this designation. It is not so much that brokers will lie to you (although some will). More often, they simply do not have the knowledge or training to provide a holistic approach to your situation. Companies will sometimes invite financial advisers to come to the company so that employees can learn about retirement and other financial matters. It pays to sign up for these workshops and seminars.[11]

One of the issues that always comes up is how much it costs to have a professional financial adviser. Nothing is free, of course. That includes financial services.

Until about 10 or 20 years ago, most financial advice was dispensed by stockbrokers. They received commissions on every stock (or bond or other product) that was either bought or sold. It did not matter whether the transaction was good or bad for the client. The point was to generate transactions for the brokerage house because the clients were charged a percentage of the value of the stocks involved, and part of this transaction fee (usually 30 percent or more) was given to the broker as a commission.

While many abuses continue to persist, one step in the right direction has been the rise of the "fee-only" adviser.[12] Fees are based entirely on assets under management, not on transaction commissions. Because they have separated compensation from trading, these advisers have no incentive to churn accounts.

Most fee-only advisers charge 1 percent of assets under management. A client with a $500,000 portfolio will have to pay $5,000 per year for the adviser's help. Thus, if they need an 8 percent return per year to reach some goal, they will have to earn 9 percent in order to pay for the adviser. Only they can decide if the value added by the adviser is worth it.

One of the strangest consumer behaviors in our society is that many people would rather pay several thousand dollars a year by having it deducted from their account than write a check for $200 or $300 whenever they need advice. These people would not be fooled by such an arrangement if they were shopping for a refrigerator or automobile. It is difficult to explain this irrational behavior when it comes to financial services, but it is nearly universal, and mainstream brokers know how to capitalize on it.

Even the fee-based compensation arrangement has its flaws. It creates an incentive for advisers to spend most of their time trying to find new clients so that they can gather more assets to manage and increase their incomes. They also get their 1 percent regardless of whether the client makes any money from their advice. One perennial suggestion is to base compensation on how much the portfolio earns each year. The problem is that no one can control or predict what the market will do. If the market declines because of a turn in the economy or some other random shock, it does not mean that the adviser has not done her job (unless clairvoyance was part of the sales pitch). No one can predict the market perfectly. When the market does decline, the adviser will get stuck with no compensation. Such an arrangement may make the adviser gamble more with her client's money and lose far more than he would otherwise.

Other compensation plans are also used. Some fee-only advisers charge an annual fee or a combination of an annual fee plus a smaller percentage of assets under management, such as ½ or ¼ of 1 percent. CFPs who are members of the National Association of Personal Financial Advisors (www.napfa.org) also refuse any type of kickback or compensation from any financial products they sell, such as insurance. They believe this to be a more equitable and fair way to charge their clients for the service they provide. In these cases, the advice you get will be objective and uncontaminated. With a CFP, the advice is much more likely to be accurate. Unfortunately, such fee arrangements are the exception rather than the rule.[13]

Once you have lined up several possible prospects, it is obviously a good idea to make a personal visit. Most financial advisers will give an initial consultation for free if you ask. The main idea is make sure the personal chemistry between you and the adviser works, since you may be spending quite a bit of time with this person and discussing very private matters. It is important for you to feel comfortable with your adviser.

Another way to check out the background of a prospective adviser is to ask if he or she is a Registered Investment Advisor (RIA). If so, you must be given a copy of both parts of the official "ADV" form, which provides information in great detail about the person and the company. The first part of the ADV form will contain information about any legal or disciplinary history the adviser may have and the fees he charges for his services. You should read both parts carefully to make sure nothing raises any red flags. You are also entitled to ask the adviser if he receives commissions on anything he sells to you or advises you to invest in. If the adviser appears to be evasive or uncomfortable with these kinds of questions, you may be better off with someone else. There are many others to choose from.

CONCLUSION

This chapter covered some of the basic issues that underlie the financial markets that provide the opportunity to invest in the free-market economy. It is all intertwined in a remarkably complex manner. To someone who is just starting, it may seem quite intimidating. Unfortunately, that is what many unscrupulous brokers rely on to gather in more customers and their assets. Nearly every day, the *Wall Street Journal* and other newspapers carry reports of scandals and unethical practices perpetrated by the dark side of the financial community. Because asset dedication portfolios can be constructed so simply and can be set up in a one-time transaction, they offer the significant advantage of keeping their owners out of the clutches of the financial predators. More on the predators in Chapter 14.

NOTES

1. Inflation is an insidious factor, a sort of negative interest rate that keeps eating away at whatever has been saved in terms of financial instruments.
2. Here is an example that my hormone-filled college students readily understand. Let's say a boy asks his girl for a kiss after a nice date one evening. She refuses, but she promises to give him two kisses tomorrow night. He protests: "If you give me a kiss tonight, we can still do two kisses tomorrow night. But if tomorrow should never come, the dynamic irreversibility of time will prevent us from ever coming back to tonight to get this kiss now. It is gone forever." What girl could argue with that logic?
3. More information on I-bonds can be found at the U.S. Treasury web site: http://www.publicdebt.treas.gov/sav/sav.htm.
4. This expectation began to break down, however, sometime in the 1980s. At that time, I noticed that many of the students in my college classes no longer felt that they would be better off than their parents. The cost of education has soared, credit cards abound, and many young graduates now leave school with a much higher debt load than I did or than most of my contemporaries did. The extent to which this forces them to postpone buying a house or starting their families is not known with certainty, but young people seem to be marrying and having kids later in life than those of a generation ago.
5. Philip Cooley, Daniel Walz, and Carlin Hubbard, "Retirement Savings: Choosing a Withdrawal Rate That Is Sustainable," *The AAII Journal*, February 1998. A synopsis of the article can be found on the Zunna Corporation web site (www.zunna.com). Researchers at Zunna developed software to refine and improve the Trinity study

methodology. [The software, called WATS, is reasonably priced (in 2003) at $49 for the Personal Edition and $199 for the Advisor Edition, and is quite clever, although you need to understand the finer points of Monte Carlo analysis to fully appreciate its advantages.]

6. The precise initial withdrawal rate reported is 3.94 percent, based on the record since 1946. These numbers change slightly as each year passes and another data point is added. Also, this asset allocation is only one of perhaps many that would have achieved the same result.

7. A fuller version of the study can be found at www.ebri.org/rcs/index.htm. The description from the web site follows: "The RCS is the country's most established and comprehensive study of the attitudes and behavior of American workers and retirees towards all aspects of saving, retirement planning, and long-term financial security. Sponsored by the Employee Benefit Research Institute (EBRI), the American Savings Education Council (ASEC), and Mathew Greenwald & Associates (Greenwald), the 13th annual RCS is a random, nationally representative survey of 1,000 individuals age 25 and over."

8. Some web sites that provide solid information and educational content on retirement accounts and basic investing are as follows:

    Nonprofit: The American Savings Education Council (www.asec.org), the Employee Benefit Research Institute (www.ebri.org), Boston College Center for Retirement Research (http://www.bc.edu/centers/crr/), AARP (formerly called the American Association of Retired Persons; www.aarp.org/financial), Choose to Save Education Program (www.choosetosave.org)

    For profit: Fidelity mutual funds (www.fidelity.com), Yahoo! (biz.yahoo.com/edu/ed_retire.html), the Motley Fool (www.fool.com), Financial Engines (www.financialengines.com), Quicken (www.quicken.com/retirement/planner), George H. Coughlin II, CFP (www.IRAplanning.com).

9. Actually, social security distributes more money to most retired workers than they ever put into it. Social security remains solvent through current contributions by existing workers.

10. The designation CFP is now trademarked.

11. My wife, Patricia O'Healy Huxley, CFP, works for one such company: Financial Knowledge Network (http://www.financialknowledge.com/).

12. One of the best but most depressing accounts of problems in the financial services industry can be found in *Take on the Street* by Arthur Levitt, former chairman of the Securities and Exchange Commission (New York: Pantheon Books, 2002).

13. I agree with Arthur Levitt's assessment: Anyone who has less than about $50,000 does not need a financial planner—just put it in an index fund (a small-cap index fund if the money can remain untouched for 10 years or more, large-cap otherwise).

CHAPTER 11

A Few Investment Fundamentals

Everybody is ignorant, only on different subjects.
—WILL ROGERS

The asset dedication approach separated the Browns' portfolio into three distinct portions, each with a specific purpose. The cash portion was designed to meet their immediate needs; the bond portion, to meet their income needs; and the stock portion, their growth needs. The cash portion is easy to understand, but the income and growth portions can be a bit confusing. This chapter covers some stock market basics, highlights the differences between stocks and bonds, and shows how these investments fit into an asset dedication portfolio.

When teaching classes to entering MBA students, I find that their questions often indicate that they do not quite understand exactly how the stock market works and how it is related to the listed companies. The next section tells the story of Zapper, a little company that goes from start-up to a publicly traded company whose stock is eventually purchased by a mutual fund. Many of the terms used by the financial community are boldfaced in the story for easy recognition. Following the Zapper story, a few of these terms and how they relate to asset dedication will be covered in greater detail.

STOCKS AS FINANCIAL INSTRUMENTS: FROM START-UP TO WALL STREET

In the Beginning—Venture Capital and High Risk for the Zapper Company

Joe Zapper has a great idea for a business venture. He is going to start a company that will supply replacement batteries for all kinds of laptop computers (his ads will call them "lapper zappers"). He needs $1 million to start the company. To get the money, he develops a business plan with all the details and presents the plan to a group of **venture capitalists** (professionally savvy investors who are looking for investments in start-ups) and to some **"angels"** (rich relatives, friends, or potential customers). After some negotiation, the investors put in $1 million and get 20 percent of Joe's company.

Investing in Joe's business is risky. According to the U.S. Census Bureau's Business Information Tracking Series, less than 40 percent of all start-ups make it past 6 years, and even then they are not necessarily profitable.[1] A 1999 PricewaterhouseCoopers report indicated that only 10 to 30 percent of venture capital funds produce profitable companies.[2]

Fast-forward 6 years. Joe has made it, and all his enthusiasm proved correct. He is now in business as the Zapper Corporation. In addition to cash, accounts receivable, inventory, and furniture and fixtures, the company owns a piece of land with a warehouse on it. Zapper Corporation has total assets of $15 million and total liabilities of $5 million. The difference of $10 million between total assets and liabilities represents the **book value** of the company as reported on the balance sheets prepared by the certified public accountants (**CPA**s) hired to audit the books.

Going Public: An IPO

Joe wants to go public to raise some capital for new growth initiatives and to allow his original investors to sell their shares in the **secondary market**. Next year the company is expected to earn $2 million in net profit, or $2.00 per share based on 1 million shares outstanding. Zapper's board of directors could decide to give all of this $2 million profit to the shareholders in the form of a $2 **dividend**, or they could decide to keep all or some of it as **retained earnings** to fund internal growth so that they would not have to borrow from a bank whenever they need money. The **underwriter,** an investment banking firm that is helping Joe and his board of directors orchestrate the **initial public offering** (**IPO**), has suggested a share price of $20. That would make the **price/earnings** (**P/E**) **ratio** $20/$2 = 10. (The long-term average for established public companies is between 15 and 20, so a P/E ratio of 10 is reasonable for a brand new public company like Zapper.)

Although the odds were against him, Joe's success has generated a good return for his initial investors. At $20 per share, the **market capitalization** of the company is $20 * 1 million shares = $20 million. This is considerably less than the $1 billion cutoff to be considered to be a **small-cap** company and even below the $150 million cutoff for a **micro-cap** company. The original venture capitalists still own 20 percent of the company, meaning that their initial $1 million investment 5 years ago is now worth $4 million. This corresponds to an annualized return of about 32 percent per year, slightly better than the common target of 30 percent for most venture capitalists. If the board of directors pays out the $2 per share dividend, the **dividend yield** on the stock will be $2/$20 = 10 percent.[3]

The ratio of the market capitalization value ($20 million) to the company's book value ($10 million) is 2.0. If this ratio puts Zapper in the bottom 30 percent of the **price-to-book** ratio for similar-sized companies, then Zapper would be considered a **value** company; if it puts Zapper in the top 30 percent, it would be considered a **growth** company.

The Zapper Corporation was assigned ZAPR as its **symbol** or **ticker** to identify it on the exchange where thousands of other firms are also listed. Investors who want to find its latest stock price in the newspaper will have to learn its reference (which may be different than its symbol) and which exchange it is traded on.

After the IPO, the company's shares can be freely traded, and the price of the stock will fluctuate along with the prices of thousands of other companies' stocks traded on the **National Association of Securities Dealers Automatic Quotation System** (**NASDAQ**), the **New York Stock Exchange** (**NYSE,** sometimes called the **"Big Board"**), the **American Stock Exchange** (**AMEX**), or one of the regional stock exchanges. Zapper will not be one of the 30 **"blue chip"** stocks tracked by the **Dow Jones Industrial Average** (**the Dow**) nor one of the 500 stocks of large companies tracked by **Standard & Poor's**, a firm that publishes information about stocks. The **S&P 500** index is one of several broad summary measures used to monitor the overall stock market (others are the **Wilshire 5000 total market index** and the **Russell 2000 small cap index**).

WHAT IS A STOCK WORTH?

Zapper's Stock Price and Why It Fluctuates

The story just given traced Zapper's progress from a start-up to a full-fledged publicly traded company whose shares may be purchased by anyone. If you buy one share of stock in the Zapper Corporation, you are buying one share of the company's profits. Zapper issued 1,000,000 shares, so you are entitled to one one-millionth of its profits for each share you own. If Zapper earns $2 million in profit next year and pays all the profit out in dividends, then you will receive $2 for each share you own. Hypothetically, if Zapper earns exactly the same profit every year in the future, then your share entitles you to an income stream of $2 per year forever or as long as you own it. If you sell it to someone else, that person will get $2 per year for as long as she owns it.

How much is your one share worth? Recall that the underwriter set the share price at $20 initially. Once Zapper has gone public, however, the shares are worth whatever investors think they are worth. Nobody sets the price. It is like an auction, where the highest bidder determines the prices of items. The prices reported in the newspaper are the opening, highest, lowest, and closing prices that were paid for the stock that day. Most statistical databases report only the closing prices on the day that marks the end of the period covered, or the final trade. That means that for annual data, you see the closing price as of December 31 or the last trading day in December. The closing price on that date or any other date reflects the price that some investor somewhere in the world with a stock account was willing to pay for the shares he wanted and that someone else who had bought them previously was willing to sell them.

Nobody knows for sure what will happen to the price of Zapper stock in the future, of course. That is why share prices fluctuate from one moment to the next. Everyone's guesses converge in the marketplace, which nets out the ultimate result. If something happens—a new discovery, a political event, a better opportunity to invest some other way, what people think other people will think, and so on—then everyone's projections, whether formal or informal, will change.

There are a million reasons why people buy and sell stocks at the prices and times they do. It is the interaction of all these forces—the uncertainty of future earnings, dividends, and prices and of how other investors will act—that introduces volatility into the price of a stock. The beginning of modern portfolio theory was the explicit recognition of the fact that the earnings stream was uncertain. At a time of general optimism, people tend to bid the prices of stocks up to higher levels than the earnings of the underlying company suggest they should be at and vice versa.

Figure 11.1 shows just how volatile the price/earnings ratio is over the long run. It tracks the P/E ratio for the S&P 500 from 1926 to 2003. Although its long-term average is around 16, its meandering pattern is a nightmare for analysts, researchers, and anyone else who is attempting to produce reliable and accurate forecasts. Guessing other people's guesses is an art, not a science. In Chapter 14 we will discuss the forecasting problems created by the unpredictability of the P/E ratio.

So, back to the original question: How much is one share worth? It depends entirely on how much other investors will pay at that moment for the anticipated income stream (or what they think others

Figure 11.1

Price/Earnings Ratios, 1926–2003

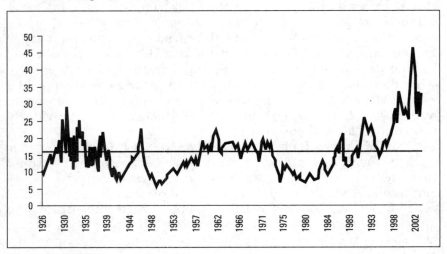

Source: Data from Global Financial Data (www.globalfindata.com).

will pay later). If another investor pays you $40, that investor will be earning an annual rate of return of 5 percent (P/E ratio of 20). If the investor pays you $20, he will be earning 10 percent (P/E ratio of 10). If he pays you $80, he will be earning 2.5 percent (P/E ratio of 40).

The conventional wisdom is that investors will pay no more than whatever they think they can earn elsewhere with their investment dollars. If the rate of return on similar types of companies at the time you want to sell is 10 percent and everyone believes the $2 earnings per share is accurate for future profits, then one share will be worth $20. If the rate of return for similar companies is 20 percent, one share will be worth $10. As people's expectations fluctuate minute by minute, so does the value of your share. That is why stocks are considered more volatile than bonds. The extreme price sensitivity of one or just a few stocks makes concentrated portfolios far riskier to hold in the growth portion of a dedicated portfolio. Buying stocks in different companies, called *diversification*, helps reduce the sensitivity of the overall growth portion to the change in price of any one stock.

MUTUAL FUNDS

How Diversification Reduces Risk

Assume that Zapper stock has been purchased by the managers of some of the 8000 or so **mutual funds** that pool money from many investors to buy stocks in a variety of companies. Most investors buy mutual funds because a mutual fund diversifies their stock holdings across many companies and thereby reduces their risk compared to buying just one company's shares. While there can often be a significant drop in the fortunes of one company, it is much rarer for such a drop to happen to many companies all at the same time. The overall market may go up or down, but by definition, half of the companies will suffer a worse-than-average decline and half will not. If you buy shares in only one company, and it happens to be one of those in the bottom half, your losses will be greater (if you have to sell) than they would be if you had shares in many companies, because it is much more likely that you will not pick all losers. By investing in many companies, mutual funds automatically provide diversification.

There is no guarantee that diversity will protect you, of course. There is no guarantee that the manager of the mutual fund will be smart enough to avoid all the worst stocks. If she is especially inept (or unlucky), then anyone who bought shares (sometimes called *units*) will suffer. When you buy a share in a mutual fund, you are essentially buying fractions of shares in the companies that the mutual fund manager has already bought. This means that you trust his judgment that the stocks in the fund will perform better than what you could do on your own.

Thus, the true benefit that mutual funds provide to investors comes from diversification. Holding a single stock, like Zapper, puts your portfolio at greater risk than holding several stocks. Granted, if you had held Microsoft or Cisco from the beginning, you would have received stellar returns. But what if you had held only Enron? You would have seen spectacular highs, followed by a devastating collapse. The more stocks you hold, the more closely the performance of your portfolio will track the general stock market.[4] If you hold only one company in your portfolio and something bad happens to that company, your portfolio could be wiped out. If you have 499 other companies in your portfolio, the impact is greatly reduced. In addition, diversifying across industries helps buffer the impact of negative conditions within a specific industrial sector. Thus, holding a diversified portfolio in the growth portion of your portfolio will help reduce catastrophic risk and stabilize returns.

INDEXED VERSUS ACTIVE INVESTING
Getting Your Money's Worth

Index funds are a special type of mutual fund. Rather than trying to guess which stocks will go up and which stocks will go down, the managers of index funds simply buy an equivalent amount of stock in all companies or a very large sample of them—hundreds or even thousands of companies are included. The idea here is that you will not beat the market, but neither will it beat you because you are simply duplicating whatever it does.

The classic index fund is the **Vanguard 500 Index Fund**. Pioneered by John Bogle in 1976, this fund buys the same stocks that are in the S&P 500 in equivalent quantities (General Motors, IBM, and Microsoft, are typical examples of the 500 companies whose stocks are included in the S&P 500). This fund therefore mirrors the performance of the S&P 500, which, in turn, mirrors closely what would happen to a portfolio that consisted of every stock listed on all exchanges. Barclay's **Exchange Traded Funds**

(**ETF**) and other index funds track all or a large sample of the stocks within one of the categories that are used to classify stocks (the classification scheme will be described later).

Index funds are an example of *passive* management because the managers do not try to actively select specific stocks or time the market. They simply own whatever stocks are included in the S&P 500 (or some other category of stocks). They are not trying to beat the market, but only to make it a tie game. Because they do not try to select stocks or time the market, they do not have to hire people with stock-picking talent or make a large number of trades. This saves on salaries and trading costs. Because people who buy their funds seldom withdraw the money, they do not have to keep much around in cash reserves to pay off those who want their money.

The reverse is true for actively managed funds. Their managers are constantly trying to beat the market, even though Brinson's study clearly demonstrated the flaw in this approach. They pay big salaries to people who claim to be talented stock pickers. They pull money in and out of the market as they trade stocks, paying for each transaction just like any other investor. And they must keep some of their funds in cash at all times for those who want to redeem their shares. Load funds must also pay the sales commissions to the brokers and financial advisers who sell their shares to clients. All of these costs add up (the next section discusses how much fees can matter; also see Table 11.1). Active managers are typically no better and no worse stock pickers and market timers than anyone else, but they have the extra expenses that they must cover just to equal the market return. They cannot just tie the market; they must beat it by more than their extra expenses. And most of them cannot do this on a consistent basis except by luck.

Index funds tend to do better than most actively managed mutual funds in the same category. This fact, borne out by nearly all academic and practitioner research, is a source of continual embarrassment to mutual fund managers. It is even more remarkable that many investors are unaware of it or ignore it. Their irrational behavior represents what economic theorists politely refer to as *bounded rationality*. It allows mutual fund managers to often live a lavish lifestyle in spite of being rather poor at what they are paid to do.

One situation in which selecting an actively managed fund makes sense is socially responsible investing. Ethical investors who dislike the idea of their dollars being used to support companies that engage in activities that they feel are socially or morally irresponsible can buy mutual funds whose managers refuse to invest in companies that earn any profits from tobacco, pornography, or gambling, for example, or that have a poor record in such areas as pollution, workers' human rights, or other such factors. Such investors care not only about the magnitude of returns but also about how those returns are earned. They believe in the old adage about "putting your money where your mouth is," and they act accordingly. Fortunately, research has demonstrated that the performance of socially responsible funds is not significantly different from the performance of benchmark index funds in the same investment categories (small cap, large cap, value, growth, and so on).[5]

THE HIDDEN COSTS OF OWNING MUTUAL FUNDS

How the Fees Add Up

The fees that a mutual fund charges investors for sales and management have a large impact on the return that investors actually see in their accounts. Most companies are not very forthcoming about the fees that they charge, but they are required to disclose these fees in the fund's prospectus. Any investor who seriously considers investing in any mutual fund should make sure that she knows exactly what fees she is being charged. Again, Arthur Levitt suggests that although firms must comply with the law about disclosing their fees, some do whatever they can to hide this information by burying it deep in the fine print. It can make a big difference over the long run. Using the SEC's cost calculator, Table 11.1 shows the difference between the average sales and management fees charged by large-cap mutual funds and those charged by an average S&P 500 index fund. Over 10 years, fees cost the mutual fund investor nearly $80,000 ($810,181 − $730,930 = $79,251).

Some mutual funds (which are monitored by Morningstar, a company that compiles statistics on mutual funds) charge a sales fee, often called a *load*. Recently, mutual funds have changed to a new system and sell several classes of shares. With class A shares, when investors first buy in, 2 to 8 percent of the value of the initial purchase is paid as a commission to the stockbroker who sold the mutual fund to the investor. With class B shares, a back-end load or exit fee

Table 11.1

The Impact of High Fees over 10 Years

	Initial Growth Portion	Initial Sales Fee	Ongoing Operating Expenses	Fees and Lost Earnings	Ending Value
Average mutual fund	$300,000	1.1%	1.41%	$120,896	$730,930
Index fund	$300,000	0%	0.50%	$41,646	**$810,181**

Source: Securities and Exchange Commission (www.sec.org).

is charged. Class C shares have no front-end or back-end fees, but they charge higher ongoing fees as long as the investor stays in the fund. Proponents of the new system say that it gives investors more options as to how they can pay the fees. Cynics have suggested that the new system is really designed to create greater confusion in the mind of the investor and further mask the actual fees so that only the savviest investors can accurately determine them.

No-load or low-load funds pay much lower commissions or no commissions at all to the brokers who sell them. This puts them way ahead of most funds, but even they must charge fees of some sort (e.g., management fees, 12b-1 fees, or administrative cost fees). These fees determine each fund's expense ratio. The most efficient mutual funds keep their expense ratios below 1 percent, and some of the index funds even keep their expenses below ¼ or ½ of 1 percent.[6]

The transaction cost component of a fund's cost of operation, as mentioned earlier, can sometimes be quite significant. Unlike the majority of index funds, actively managed mutual funds can have very high turnover in the stocks held in the portfolio. It is not uncommon to see managers turn over the entire portfolio five times in a year, incurring trading costs with each transaction. That means that the entire portfolio was changed more than five times and that a commission was paid every time a share was bought or sold. This generates huge payments to the brokerage houses by the mutual fund. This is money that is lost to the investor. In addition, each time that a stock is sold at a profit, a capital gains tax is triggered. This creates an additional tax burden for the investor. These fees and taxes drain a portfolio's value, and ignoring them can be hazardous to the investor's wealth, to say the least.

LARGE-CAP, MID-CAP, SMALL-CAP, VALUE, AND GROWTH STOCKS

Characteristics Used to Classify Stocks and Mutual Funds

In the 1980s and early 1990s, research on the factors that cause some stocks to rise more quickly than others culminated in a 1992 paper by Eugene Fama and Kenneth French.[7] They concluded that the primary factors contributing to higher or lower returns on stocks over the long term are (1) company size, (2) the ratio of the company's book value to its market capitalization, and (3) general movements in the overall stock market. These factors are important to consider when choosing equity investments in the growth portion.

This led to a classification system based on two of the Fama-French factors. Stocks are separated by size ("small-cap," "mid-cap," or "large-cap") and by the ratio of book value to size ("value" or "growth"). *Cap* stands for capitalization and is the number of a company's shares outstanding (shares owned by the public) multiplied by the price per share. A company with 1 million shares whose current market price is $50 would have a market capitalization of $50 million. This is a loose definition, but it captures the concept. There is no agreement as to exactly where to draw the lines between these categories, but "small-cap" generally means companies with a capitalization of under $1 billion; "mid-cap," companies with a capitalization between $1 billion and $5 to $10 billion; and "large-cap," companies with a capitalization of over $5 to $10 billion.

Often both book value and market capitalization are divided by the number of shares. The result is called the *price-to-book ratio*. Sometimes, its inverse is calculated and called the book-to-price ratio. Unfortunately, the book value used to compute the ratios can be dubious because it is difficult to get a precise estimate of everything a company owns. For example, brand image is valuable, but how valuable is it? What is the extra value of owning the product name "Coca Cola" as opposed to owning "Sam's Soda Pop?" Or consider the value of a half-empty building where the company does some manufacturing. What would that property fetch on the real estate market? Should appraisers be hired every year to estimate it? How reliable is the appraiser? Book value is the difference between what all these assets add up to minus what is owed. Estimates are based only on the figures that appear on company balance sheets, which may be based only on historical, out-of-date costs or subjective valuations.

The theory is that investors who think that a company's future earnings will grow to be much higher than current earnings will bid up the price of the stock relative to the prices of other stocks and make the price-to-book ratio larger, hence the name *growth*. The opposite is true for companies that investors think will not earn much more than they do now. In this case, the stock prices of value companies will be relatively less than those of growth companies with identical assets.

People in the financial community love to toss around terms like "mid-cap value" or "small-cap growth" when referring to mutual funds. This means that the fund invests mostly in the stocks of mid-cap value or small-cap growth companies.

BONDS: HOW THEY DIFFER FUNDAMENTALLY FROM STOCKS

Safety and Predictability

Bonds are fundamentally different from stocks. A bond is actually the equivalent of a loan. The predictable nature of bonds *that are held to maturity* plays the central role in asset dedication because it provides a stable foundation for immunizing the income stream against the vagaries of the stock market.

Unlike stocks, bonds are not directly related to profits at all. When a company or a government agency sells a bond for $1000, it promises to pay that $1000 back on the date the bond matures. It will pay interest each year until that date. The $1000 is called the *face value* of the bond. If you buy the bond for its face value, then you have paid *par* for the bond. The interest the bond pays is called the *coupon* interest. A 5 percent coupon interest rate means that the company promises to pay $50 per year per $1000 bond. Figure 11.2 presents the process schematically for a $1000 bond with a maturity date of 5 years and coupon interest of 5 percent.

How much is this bond worth? Again, it depends on what people are willing to pay for it. If they can get no more than 5 percent on any other equivalent investment, then they will pay exactly the amount printed on the face of the bond (the par value), namely $1000. If prevailing interest rates are higher, they will pay less (for example, if the prevailing interest rate is 10 percent, they will pay only $778 for a 5-year 5 percent coupon bond). When bonds are issued, the coupon payment amount is set, and it does not change over the life of the bond. Therefore, in order to receive coupon payments equivalent to those from a bond with a 10 percent coupon

Figure11.2

Cash Flows for a 5-Year 5 Percent $1000 Coupon Bond Sold at Par

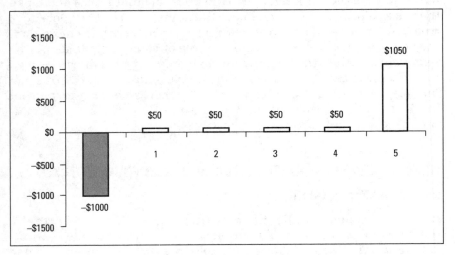

over the life of the bond, you must adjust the price of the bond down. Similarly, if prevailing rates are 2.5 percent, an investor who is seeking that return will pay up to $1140 for a $1000 bond. Bonds therefore can fluctuate in price just as stocks do, but only during the intermediate time period *before* they mature. The closer they get to their maturity date, the less they differ from their face value at maturity. On the date they mature, they are worth exactly what their face value says. Bond pricing is described in greater detail later in this chapter.

    Because changes in interest rates can change the intermediate values of bonds, professional financial money managers have created bond mutual funds. Managers of bond funds buy many different bonds with varying maturities and coupon rates. Whenever interest rates go down, the value of the bonds they own goes up. From the mid-1990s into the early years of the new millennium, interest rates generally went down, and bond funds therefore went up in value. Once interest rates began to rise, however, the value of the bonds began to fall. Many investors then learned the market risks associated with bond funds the hard way. Owning individual bonds and holding them to maturity is the only way to avoid the market risk caused by rising interest rates.

The basic bonds just described are called *noncallable* bonds. However, some bonds are issued as *callable*. These terms refer to the maturity date. Noncallable bonds have a single, definite maturity date. If the bond says February 15, 2010, you will receive the principal on February 15, 2010. But with bonds that are designated as callable, the issuer can "call" the bonds back at any time from a specified call date until the maturity date specified on the bond. Thus, the predictable nature of coupon bonds does not apply to callable bonds.

For instance, a callable bond may indicate that it can be called any time between February 15, 2010, and February 15, 2015. Whoever issued the bond can pay the money back at any time during that 5-year interval. If interest rates happen to be low when February 15, 2010, arrives, the issuer can sell new bonds at the lower rate and use the proceeds to pay off the older bonds that were paying a higher rate. Issuers will do this because they will save money for themselves, just as consumers shop around to get the lowest mortgage interest rates and credit card interest rates.[8]

The issuers will usually warn the owners of the bond a few months ahead of time. The fact that a bond is callable must always be disclosed at the time it is purchased, so there is never an issue of not knowing whether a bond is callable or not. Callable bonds should always be purchased with that understanding. Because their maturity date cannot be predicted with certainty, callable bonds do not work for the asset dedication approach.

WHO ISSUES BONDS?

The U.S. Treasury and Federal Agencies, Corporations, State and Local Governments

The financial community generally sorts domestic bonds into three classifications, depending on who issues them: government, corporate, and municipal. The following outline highlights the different characteristics of each type of bond.

1. *Federal government bonds.* The federal government issues several types of bonds, all of which are considered to be the safest financial investment instruments on earth. Foremost among these are U.S. Treasury bonds. They are backed by the full faith and credit of the U.S. government. The chance that they will not pay the interest or the prin-

cipal when due is nil (that is, the default risk is zero, since the Treasury can always print more money). At one time, the government issued a bond that matured in 30 years, but 20 years is now the longest for new issues. Treasury notes have maturities of less than 10 years, and Treasury bills have maturities of less than a year.

Some Treasuries, called "strips" or "zeros," pay only the principal and make no intervening interest payments before the principal is paid.[9] Zeros are issued at a discount from par and increase in value each year until they reach $1000 at maturity. That means that the price you pay for them is much lower than the price you pay for coupon bonds because it takes into consideration the fact that you will receive nothing until the bond matures, when you will receive the entire amount—interest plus principal.

In addition to the U.S. Treasury, federal government agencies also issue bonds. These bonds cannot be said to be backed by the full faith and credit of the U.S. government, but they are considered moral obligations that the government would never allow to default. Agencies that issue bonds include the following:

> Federal National Mortgage Association (Fannie Mae)
> Federal Home Loan Mortgage Corporation
>   (Freddie Mac)
> Farm Credit System Financial Assistance Corporation
> Federal Agricultural Mortgage Corporation
>   (Farmer Mac)
> Federal Home Loan Banks
> Student Loan Marketing Association (Sallie Mae)
> College Construction Loan Insurance Association
>   (Connie Lee)
> Small Business Administration (SBA)
> Tennessee Valley Authority (TVA)

2. *Corporate bonds.* "Corporates" are issued by companies such as IBM and General Electric. They sometimes have maturities of 40 years or more. The likelihood that these companies will default on either the interest or the principal payment becomes a factor to consider because there is always some chance that a private company will go bankrupt (think Enron). Chapter 14 and Appendix 2 present statistics on default rates.

3. *Municipal bonds.* "Munis" are issued by state or local governments, agencies, districts, and so on. They also can have maturities of 40 years or longer and receive ratings like corporate bonds. But munis have one great feature: The interest on them is not taxable by the federal government. Many states do not levy taxes on their own bonds, meaning that those bonds are "double tax-free" for residents of those states. But the catch is that munis usually pay lower interest rates. Theoretically, their tax-free feature offsets their lower interest.[10] But anomalies in the market sometimes create inversions in which munis pay more that taxable bonds of equivalent maturity and quality. This does not happen very often, and when it does, it seldom lasts for very long.

HOW SAFE ARE BONDS?

Rating Bonds: Higher Ratings Equal Higher Safety

Several companies rate bonds according to their creditworthiness: Moody's and Standard & Poor's are the best known. The ratings (see Appendix 1 for definitions) correspond roughly to grades on a school student's report card or transcript. The highest rating is called *triple A* and is symbolized as either Aaa or AAA.[11] This means that there is little chance of these bonds' ever defaulting. They are considered nearly as safe as federal government issues, but they usually pay a slightly higher interest rate. Double-A-rated bonds (Aa or AA) are nearly but not quite as safe as triple A, so they usually pay a very slightly higher rate of interest. And so it goes down into the B and C range. Bonds at the high end of the quality scale are called "investment grade," while those at the low end, which have much higher default rates, are called "speculative" or "junk" bonds. (Table 14.1 shows the historical record on the safety of investment-grade corporate bonds—they pay off over 99 percent of the time, and even when they are considered officially "in default," this usually means they simply were late on an interest payment, not that the bondholders lost all their principal.) Speculative bonds pay high interest rates but carry a much higher risk of default and are unsuitable for asset dedication. Investment-grade bonds should always be used when building an asset dedication portfolio.

INTEREST RATES AND BOND PRICES:
THE TEETER-TOTTER EFFECT

Market Risk—Selling Bonds Early

There is an inverse relationship between bond prices and interest rates. The math can be tricky, but the concept is simple. Figure 11.3 shows the relationships as interest rates rise, bond prices fall, and vice versa. Changing interest rates or expectations of a change create fluctuations in the market value of a bond until the day it finally matures and pays back its principal. For example, suppose you pay $1000 for a bond that promises to pay back $1000 at the end of 5 years plus a $50 interest payment at the end of each year until then (starting with the end of the first year—see Figure 11.2). In the language of bond investing, you would have bought the bond at par and be earning a coupon interest rate of 5 percent.

What if for some reason you have to sell the bond before the 5 years are up? If prevailing interest rates have not changed since you bought the bond and are still at 5 percent, then you will be able to sell it for $1000. But if interest rates have gone up, then you will have to sell it for less.

For instance, assume that at the end of the first year, you need to sell the bond. If interest rates on the same type and quality of bonds maturing in 4 years are now at 10 percent, you will be able to sell the bond only for $807. Because the buyer could now get $100 a year over the next 4 years from other bonds selling for $1000 (because 10 percent of $1000 equals $100), the 5 percent coupon

Figure 11.3

The Inverse Relationship between Interest Rates and Bond Prices

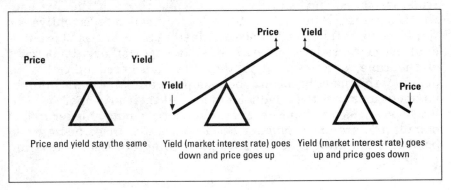

Price and yield stay the same   Yield (market interest rate) goes   Yield (market interest rate) goes
                                 down and price goes up   up and price goes down

bond, paying only $50, is worth less than $1000. The difference between your original investment of $1000 one year earlier and the current value of $807 is a capital loss for you. It might seem that your bond should be worth only $500, since $50 is 10 percent of $500. This would be true if the bond were a *perpetuity* and had no ultimate maturity date. But remember that your bond will pay $1000 back in 4 years when it matures. Also, $807 is more than the figure used earlier in the chapter, since the bond was then a 5-year bond and is now a 4-year bond. This is a good example of the tricky mathematics involved in these sorts of calculations, but the good news is that there are many calculators, programs, and web sites that will do it for anyone who is interested.[12]

But the intervening values of a bond before it matures are relevant if and only if—and this is the critical if—you need to sell it before it matures. If you do not need to sell it, then it does not matter that at the end of the first year it is worth only $807. If you hold it to maturity, you will still get your original $1000 principal back. This simple fact makes all the difference in the world.

The odd thing is that the market value of your bond—even a Treasury bond—will show up as $807 in any statement you receive. But in reality, this is only a temporary change in the value of the bond. It is called a *paper loss* because it appears on the paper temporarily. It is guaranteed to disappear if you hold the bond until it matures because the U.S. Treasury will not default on its bonds. There is no real loss, and there never will be if the bond is held to maturity.

The reverse is true if interest rates fall. In this case, the market value of the bond will rise, and you will enjoy a capital gain on paper. For example, if interest had dropped to 2.5 percent, then your bond would have risen in value to $1117 because the $50 per year is equivalent to a 2.5 percent return on a bond of $1117, adjusted for the fact that you will receive $1000 in 4 years. Your paper gain will be $117. If you actually sell the bond, you will actually achieve the gain. If you don't sell it, it will eventually drop back in value to $1000 when it matures. This teeter-totter effect between bond prices and interest rates is an inherent part of bond investing. It is always there. And it is always irrelevant if you hold the bond to maturity.

At this point, people often wonder why not sell it when it is worth more? The answer is that you would then have to reinvest the $1117. Buying an equivalent bond to replace the one that you just sold paying $50 per year will cost you exactly $1117. Theoretically you are no better off from a cash flow perspective if you originally bought the bond to get the $50 per year. But you would have incurred a transaction cost from selling the bond. The proceeds would have to be invested somewhere else immediately to continue earning a return.

CONCLUSION

This chapter and the other chapters in Part 3 of the book cover a few of the fundamentals associated with economics, math, and investing. But these should be sufficient to allow you to understand what goes on in the financial world and how stocks and bonds are used in asset dedication. The predictable nature of bonds that are held to maturity is the foundation of the income portion of an asset dedication portfolio. When you purchase the income portion, you know the exact cash flow stream that it will generate over the time horizon that you choose. By specifying your time horizon, you can use the income portion to control the risk in your portfolio by using time to buffer the volatility of stocks in the growth portion.

NOTES

1. Brian Headd, "Redefining Business Success: Distinguishing between Closure and Failure," *Small Business Economics* 21, 2003.
2. Figures on the latest trends in venture capital are available from the PricewaterhouseCoopers/Thomson Venture Economics/National Venture Capital Association Money Tree Survey web site (www.pwcmoneytree.com). The figures reported here were compiled in 1999.
3. If the board of directors had decided to keep 75 percent of the profits as retained earnings, it would have kept $1.50 and paid only $0.50, meaning that the dividend yield would be only 2.5 percent ($0.50/$20.00 = 2.5 percent).
4. Vladimir DeVassal, "Risk Diversification Benefits of Multiple Stock Portfolios," *Journal of Portfolio Management*, Winter 2001.
5. One of the most recent articles on this topic is by Mary Naber, "Catholic Investing: The Effects of Screens on Financial Returns," *The Journal of Investing*, Winter 2001. Interested readers can visit several web sites related to socially responsible investing. Two such web sites are www.socialinvest.org, www.socialfunds.com, and www.crosswalk.com/family/finances/.
6. In the vernacular of the financial community, fees are sometimes quoted in *basis points*. One percent per year is the same as 100 basis points. Firms do this because the decimal points can get confusing when talking about percentages, and using the term *basis point* avoids this confusion. (Unfortunately, the real estate community also uses the term *points*, but in that industry, one point means one percentage point or 100 basis points.)
7. Eugene P. Fama and Kenneth R. French, "Cross-Section of Variation in Expected Stock Returns," *Journal of Finance*, June 1992.
8. The economic reason for callable bonds has to do with the level of interest rates. For example, in the early 1980s, interest rates were extremely high, reaching over

10 percent for U.S. Treasuries. Anticipating that interest rates would be lower in the future, the government issued bonds that were callable sooner than their ultimate maturity date so that when interest rates dropped, it could save the taxpayers some money by paying off the bonds early. Instead of paying really high interest rates for 20 years, it would have to pay those rates for only 15 years.

9. The term *strips* comes from the fact that the interest payments have been stripped off from the payment of the principal. The term *zero* comes from the idea that zero coupon interest is paid on the bond. *Zeros* is a more generic term and can apply to corporate or muni bonds as well as to U.S. Treasuries.

10. Actually, it is the other way around: Munis pay less interest because they are tax-free and everyone knows it. Most bond vendors indicate the "tax equivalent yield" based on an assumed investor tax bracket of 35 percent. If a muni yields 4 percent, its tax equivalent yield would be 0.04/0.65 = 6.15 percent.

11. The rating systems vary slightly, but Moody's and Standard & Poor's seldom disagree. Their web sites (www.moodys.com and www.standardandpoor.com) allow you to verify any company's rating.

12. Recognizing the inverse relationship between prices and interest rates is the important thing, not knowing the math behind the calculations.

CHAPTER 12

Understanding the Numbers

Figures don't lie, but liars figure.

—MARK TWAIN

Because dollars represent numerical values, mathematics becomes involved in any serious discussion of investment analysis. And because a lot of numbers are used, statistics becomes involved. Some brokers use mathematical and statistical terms as a shield to deflect questions. By quoting some mumbo jumbo about standard deviations or correlation analysis, they hope to intimidate their more inquisitive clients and stop them from asking questions that might reveal the true extent of the broker's ignorance. Most brokers have a quite limited technical knowledge of mathematics and statistics, but they cover themselves well.

In defense of the financial community, it needs to be said that even those with Ph.D.s in mathematics find the complexities of the market bordering on the infinite.[1] Such people may be a hundred times more sophisticated than the typical broker or adviser in terms of mathematics, but this is still a drop in the bucket—a bigger drop, but still a drop—compared to the magnitude of the problem. An Olympic swimmer on a cruise ship that sinks in the middle of the ocean may get a lot farther than most of us, but he or she will still never make it to shore.

On the other hand, knowing a modicum of the fundamentals will help you to avoid some of the most common errors in dealing with investments. To get deeply into the academic research literature requires a higher level of mathematical and statistical sophistication, but the fundamentals are not difficult. In fact, if you understand the fundamentals here, you may well know more than your broker.

TOTAL RETURN

Appreciation plus Yield

An investment increases in value for two reasons: appreciation and yield. When the price of Company ABC stock goes up, it has appreciated. If ABC also pays a dividend, it has provided yield. The same is true for bonds, but the yield comes in the form of interest rather than dividends. Bonds can appreciate or depreciate like stocks, but only until they reach maturity. At maturity, their face value is locked in. Before maturity, their intervening values can fluctuate.

When you hear or read the word *return*, it unfortunately can mean several things. In the simplest calculation, it refers only to appreciation. If you buy a stock at $100 and 1 year later you could sell it for $110, then you have earned a return of 10 percent on the appreciated price of the stock, assuming that it paid no dividend. If it earns 10 percent again the next year, then it would be worth $121 at the end of that year, because 10 percent of $110 is $11. Starting at $100 and ending at $121 after 2 years means that you have earned an average return of 10 percent per year as a result of the appreciation of the stock.

"Total return" is the sum of appreciation plus yield. Continuing with the same example, assume that you had also received a 5 percent dividend, or $5, in the first year. Your total return on the initial investment would be 10 percent from appreciation and 5 percent from yield, for a total of $15, or a 15 percent total return for the first year.[2]

Over 2 years, the total return calculation gets a little more complicated. Total return assumes that the yield portion is automatically reinvested instantly in the stock or bond, allowing you to "earn interest on the interest," so to speak. It means that you are compounding the returns on your investment. If you choose to spend the interest or dividends instead of automatically reinvesting them, then you will not achieve total return.

For example, assume that at the end of the first year, you immediately reinvest the $5 dividend you earned in the stock and stay in the market. Assume that the second year is identical to the first in that appreciation continues at 10 percent and you receive another 5 percent dividend. You will now have $100 (initial capital) + $10 (first-year appreciation) + $5 (first-year dividend) + $11.50 (second-year appreciation) + $5.75 (second-year dividend) = $132.25. Total return would be exactly 15 percent over 2 years. Total return can be achieved only by reinvesting the dividends to allow them to appreciate as well. If you spend the dividends, you will have a lower return because they did not get the opportunity to compound. By spending the dividends, you have created a cash flow out of the investment/reinvestment loop, and, unfortunately, a different calculation is needed to compute the return accurately. It is called the *internal rate of return*, and there is an amusing story about it that became known as the "Beardstown Blunder" (discussed later in the chapter).

It needs to be noted that total return is not what you hear on radio or TV stock market reports or read in newspapers. Even many financial web sites do not report total return because calculating it requires information on dividends (when they were paid and how much they paid) that is troublesome to obtain. Instead, these sources report only the appreciation component of total return: They report the change in prices of stocks as listed in the indexes (such as the Dow, the S&P 500, or NASDAQ). Ignoring the dividends and interest paid on financial instruments understates the actual returns that investors earn if they reinvest everything automatically.

How much difference does it make? That is, how much difference is there between total return and return excluding dividends? The answer is about 4 percent per year, but it depends on what time frame you are talking about and whether or not you want to include the great bull market of 1995 to 1999.

Table 12.1 shows the average annual total return and its components in the S&P 500 index fund for various time periods during the postwar era ending December 1994 (*before* the great bull market) and December 2002 (*after* the 2000–2002 decline). Yields were fairly consistent at about 4.4 percent through 1994, varying from a low of 4.2 percent to a high of 4.7 percent. But over the longer spans, they averaged only 3.4 percent, varying from 2.4 percent to 4.0 percent. The wider variation in yield is a reflection of the rapid appreciation of stock prices from 1995 to 1999. Figures 12.1 and 12.2 provide graphical representations of the same data.

Table 12.1

Average Annual Total Returns Components

Before the Great Bull Market of 1995–1999

	Total Return	Appreciation	Yield
1950–1994	12.3%	7.8%	4.5%
1960–1994	10.4%	6.2%	4.2%
1970–1994	11.5%	6.9%	4.5%
1980–1994	15.6%	10.9%	4.7%
1990–1994	11.0%	6.8%	4.2%
Average	12.2%	7.7%	4.4%

After the 2000–2002 Decline

	Total Return	Appreciation	Yield
1950–2002	11.8%	7.8%	4.0%
1960–2002	10.1%	6.5%	3.6%
1970–2002	10.8%	7.1%	3.7%
1980–2002	13.0%	9.6%	3.5%
1990–2002	9.7%	7.3%	2.4%
Average	11.1%	7.6%	3.4%

Figure 12.1

Yield and Appreciation *before the Great Bull Market of 1995 through 1999*

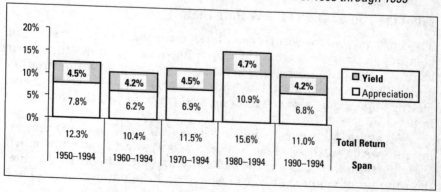

Figure 12.2

Yield and Appreciation *after* the 2000–2002 Decline

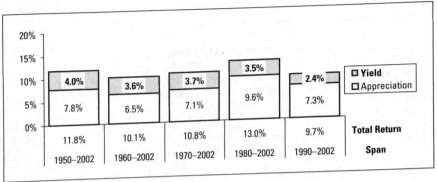

Total return is the appropriate return rate to use for an asset dedication strategy, because all dividends in the growth portion are automatically reinvested and thus capture total return. Investment strategies that try to generate income from the stock portfolio miss out on total return. The asset dedication approach avoids using dividends as part of the income stream. Bonds are far better suited to providing predictable cash flows, since companies can change their dividend policy, but bonds cannot change their coupons. Dividends are far more useful in contributing to growth as part of total return.

INTERNAL RATE OF RETURN (IRR) AND THE BEARDSTOWN BLUNDER

What the Ladies Didn't Know Hurt Them

The internal rate of return calculates a constant growth rate that best fits an irregular stream of cash inflows and outflows that occur at different points in time. This is a very messy situation mathematically. The calculation has to consider not only the starting and ending values, but also the amount and timing of all the cash flows in between.

Most portfolio calculations assume that there are no intervening inflows or outflows of cash. When people want to see how much their portfolio has grown, they usually look at the starting value, the number of years that have passed, and the ending value. They assume that it has grown (or declined) solely by itself. No money from any outside source has been added, and no money has been withdrawn. That makes the calculation simple.

But if external cash flows occur, which is what happens when retirees withdraw funds from their portfolio for living expenses, it is a whole new ball game. This is also true before retirement, when people are adding savings to their account. The external cash flows into or out of the portfolio make the calculation much more complicated. In fact, this happened in what became known as the "Beardstown Blunder." An investment club in Beardstown, Illinois, consisting of 16 ladies ranging in age from 41 to 82, wrote a book in 1994 about their wonderful investment success. In the prior 10 years, the press reported from their book, they had earned an astounding 23.4 percent annual rate of return. They had no special financial expertise; they made decisions based on simple common sense. They became famous, appeared on national TV talk shows, wrote five more books on investing and investment clubs, and so on. It had all the appeal of the classic Cinderella story.

The only problem was that their figures were wrong. They did not do the math correctly. They apparently included the starting and ending values over 10 years and calculated the average annual growth rate needed. But they failed to do the internal rate of return calculation, meaning that they failed to factor in all the monthly deposits that they had made into the account. It would be sort of like starting the year with $1000 and adding $100 per month. At the end of the year, the portfolio would be $2200. If you just look at the beginning and ending values, it appears that the return is 120 percent. This is what they did.[3]

When the mistake was discovered and admitted (in 1998), an accurate IRR analysis revealed they had actually earned only 9.1 percent per year, less than the S&P 500 over the same time period. The Beardstown balloon popped.

The IRR is the correct measure to use when external cash flow streams (additions and withdrawals) are involved because it takes the timing and size of the flows into consideration. In the case of the Beardstown Blunder, there was no intention to mislead anyone. The error was an honest mistake, and the ladies were quite embarrassed and remorseful.[4] But the publisher got sued anyway. The true loss came from the subsequent cynicism that caused women who had been encouraged to take charge of their finances to give up. They felt that the Beardstown Ladies had damaged the whole idea of combining femininity and finance, making women the butt of many jokes in the financial community (sort of like the "woman driver" jokes of the 1950s, or the blonde jokes of today, which also have no merit).

RISK VERSUS VOLATILITY

A Necessary Distinction

An average annual total return of 15 percent does not mean that the investment will grow exactly 15 percent each and every year. Stock prices move up and down in fits and starts, never in a steady progression. The term used to describe this oscillating behavior is *volatility*.

Over the long run, the jumps in the market outweigh the drops. But over any short run, it can be the other way around. Volatility by itself is harmless, but the bumpy ride makes most investors nervous. They fear that a drop will occur at just the wrong time. If they have to sell when their stocks are down, they will lose the money that they had earned before the market dropped. It is like being in a car that hits a big bump or stops suddenly. If you are strapped into your seat, no problem. But if you happen to be unbuckled when it happens, you are vulnerable to injury from being thrown against the dashboard. The chance of real injury, not the bumpy ride itself, is the true risk.

How can risk be avoided? Never driving the car very fast will let you avoid being hurt very badly, even if you are vulnerable when the car stops suddenly. But driving slowly means that it will take you much longer to reach your destination. The same is true for investing. If your investments are not very volatile—that is, if they do not go up or down by very much—you will have less risk. But it will take you much longer to reach your financial goal because higher stability means lower return. This is why allocating too much money to bonds worsens the overall performance of a portfolio. The fixed-formula asset allocation approach often allocates too much to bonds because it ignores the primary advantage that bonds offer, namely, a predictable cash flow when held to maturity.

Asset dedication reduces risk in a different and more efficient way than asset allocation commonly does. Recall that asset dedication uses time, rather than an arbitrary XYZ formula, to allocate assets. Those who want to protect themselves from volatility for longer periods of time can simply lengthen their planning horizon and buy whatever bonds are needed to supply the income they need over that time span. They will have a greater allocation to bonds than someone with a shorter horizon, but they will understand why they have this allocation. They are not following some blind formula that does not consider their individual situation or even specify what bonds are to be purchased.

Recall that the asset dedication web site allows for horizons of 3 to 10 years automatically. Longer fixed horizons can be custombuilt, or rolling horizons can be used to make the buffer perpetual. It is the length of the planning horizon that determines the best allocation of assets. Once the proper percentage of assets has been allocated to the income portion, the rest is allocated to stocks, where it can grow the fastest, and volatility does not matter. In fact, because higher returns are associated with greater volatility, investments in the growth portion should welcome volatility if it does in fact produce higher returns over the long run, as index funds of small-cap value stocks appear to do.

There are a couple of conceptual problems that need to be mentioned before we leave this discussion of risk. First, the idea that volatility is a bad thing stems entirely from investors' fear that they may have to sell at just the wrong time, when the market is temporarily down (or at least lower than what it was). But someone who is stashing money away in a retirement account will not be selling for a very long time. Therefore, as mentioned before, fluctuations during the interim period are meaningless. If reducing fluctuations means giving up return, why do it?[5] The vast majority of people never touch their 401(k) and related accounts until they retire. At that point, what will matter is the ending value.

If investors buy bonds or any other sort of sluggish investment to avoid the intermediate fluctuations and end up with $100,000 less to retire on, they will have made a foolish choice. Whatever will have happened over the preceding 30 years looking back from then will be immaterial and irrelevant. It is a little like worrying about the weather 10 years ago in terms of today. Does it matter? The true focus ought to be on achieving the greatest return so as to reach the highest ending value. Once a person begins to sell funds out of the portfolio, then volatility needs to be factored into the judgments made about the portfolio, but until then, there really is no need to do so.

A second conceptual problem has to do with exactly what the term "selling when the market is down" means. Down from where? If the benchmark is some prior high-water market, then the fear of a down market seems misplaced because the market always goes up and down. For example, assume that an investor has averaged a return of, say, 15 percent per year over the past 10 years, and last year her portfolio went up 30 percent. But for the first 6 months of this year, it is down 10 percent. It is difficult to have much sympathy for whining from this investor. She may lament that she missed the high-water mark, but if she had sold halfway through last year, she would lament that she had sold too soon and could have made more. The only time such investors will be happy is if they have the foresight to know exactly when their portfolio has reached its peak and will decline thereafter. It is equivalent to whining about not knowing which numbers to pick for the lottery.

RATE OF RETURN RISK VERSUS MAGNITUDE OF DOLLARS RISK

Researchers Think in Terms of Rates, but Investors Think in Terms of Dollars

There are a few other things about financial risk that need to be explained before we move on to other topics. Risk measures are usually based on return rates, not on the actual dollar amounts involved. That is, all calculations look at fluctuations in the percentage rate of return rather than the dollars at risk. So the risk measure for two portfolios, one of $10,000 and another of $10 million, would be exactly the same if both portfolios owned the same stocks and bonds in the same proportions. The presumption is that by removing the magnitude component from the calculation, whatever theory or results evolve are assumed to be generally valid for all portfolios regardless of size. This is very convenient from an academic and theoretical perspective. But from the individual investor's perspective, it does not really capture the essence of risk. By ignoring the magnitude of the absolute dollar amount involved, it ignores the element that is of greatest importance to the individual investor.

For example, assume that on the day you retire, you have a $500,000 portfolio, all of it invested in an index fund with a growth rate of 10 percent but a standard deviation of 20 percent. If you were to pull out $200,000 to pay off a mortgage or for some other reason but left the remaining $300,000 invested in the same fund, the rate of return and its standard deviation would be exactly the same. But most individuals would believe that 40 percent less money is now "at risk" because $200,000 has been taken off the table, so to speak.

Calculations based solely on rates of return fail to capture the fact that the portfolio is now only 60 percent of its original size. This is a weakness of any risk measure based only on the rate of return. Academic purists would point out that the rate of return on the house that the mortgage covered should now be factored into the overall portfolio. But such calculations become very complicated and difficult to interpret.

There are no easy, nonarbitrary answers to these questions, and most researchers simply ignore the problem and focus entirely on rates of return. But clearly the number of dollars involved ought to be factored in somehow. Otherwise, poor decisions may be made.

As a case in point, I once had a friend who talked to me about how much time he was spending trying to get the highest return on some money that he had in a savings account. This was prior to the Internet, and he had spent hours on the phone calling various banks to see what rates they were paying. He finally found one that was paying 25 basis points above the others (¼ of 1 percent). I asked him how much money was involved. It was only about $10,000. If you do the math, you will realize that this is a difference of $25 per year, about the cost of one dinner out. Was it really worth his time and effort to gain $25? He might well have spent this much on long distance phone calls or on gasoline driving to the bank to fill out the paperwork.

One of the few measures that incorporates absolute dollar amounts in calculating risk is "value at risk." This measure calculates how much would be lost in actual dollars if the stock market were to drop from whatever its current level is to a dramatically lower level at the end of the planning horizon. An arbitrary definition of "dramatically lower" is that it drops by 95 percent of its historically worst drop over the same time horizon. For example, based on its record since 1947, the S&P 500 index has lost more than 11 percent in a single year only 5 percent of the time. Thus, a $1000 investment in an S&P 500 index fund over a 1-year period would have a value at risk of $110 because there is a 5 percent chance that it would drop below $890 in a single year. The value-at-risk measure attempts to factor in absolute dollar magnitudes, but it can do so only in an arbitrary way. Finding the best way to factor in absolute dollar amounts remains a theoretical problem for researchers.

There is yet another problem with the way in which risk is commonly measured, whether through the standard deviation or the value-at-risk calculation. It has to do with the investor's intent.

Consider the asset dedication strategy that Ms. Smith used in Chapter 3. All the bonds she purchased were designated for a clear purpose: income for a specified year. She was not trying to guess future interest rates or future stock prices or to engage in any other form of speculation. Each bond would be held to maturity, so there was no question as to its future value at the time when it would be needed. Its value before maturity might go up or go down, depending on market conditions, but these fluctuations were irrelevant to her investment strategy. In a sense, she took the money off the table when she allocated it to the bonds that were needed to provide her income. Is it really correct to incorporate these fluctuations in judging the riskiness of her portfolio? I don't think so.

The growth portion of her portfolio is another matter. If this is entirely stocks, then we do not know what its ending value will be, as we do for bonds. So using the standard deviation for this portion of her portfolio may make sense. Even for this portion, however, her intention is to buy and hold until the end of the 10-year planning horizon, so a year-to-year volatility measure does not make as much sense as a 10-year volatility measure. But for bonds that are intended to be held to maturity, it does not make much sense to calculate the intervening fluctuations, as they are meaningless.

HOW TO LOOK AT AVERAGES AND VARIATIONS

How Average Is an Average?

People sometimes get nervous when they have to interpret a statistical report or a set of data. If you happen to be one of these people, there is an easy way to avoid confusion. Just remember what information you wanted when you were a student getting a test back in school. What exactly did you want the teacher to tell you?

Intuitively, you wanted to know not only your own score, but also how the class did overall. That is, you wanted to hear the average class score plus the highest and lowest scores. If your score was 75 percent, and the teacher said that the average was 75, then you knew that you were somewhere in the middle between the best and the worst in the class. But you still did not know exactly what the best and the worst were. If the teacher said that the highest was 99 percent and the lowest was 50 percent, then your 75 percent means that you beat someone else by a wide margin, but someone else beat you by a wide margin. The variation of test scores around the average was pretty wide.

But what if the teacher said that the highest score was 76 percent and the lowest was 74 percent? In this case, the variation around the average is much less, and the difference between the best and the worst is almost negligible. Everyone is about the same, and your average score is quite close to what the best student got.

The same is true of any set of numbers, whether the numbers relate to test scores, rates of return, or any other data set. At the most fundamental level, the purpose of the arithmetic average, or "mean," is to summarize the individual values of all the test scores (statisticians call it a measure of *central tendency*) to give you a sense of the typical value of the results.[6] The highest and lowest scores give you a sense of how typical the mean is. An average score of 75 percent for a class with a high of 76 percent and a low of 74 percent is obviously a different situation from that of a class where the mean was 75 percent with a high of 99 percent and a low of 50 percent. The mean is entirely independent of the variation. This is why both pieces of information are needed—central tendency and dispersion.

As a student, you had a pretty good idea of how the class did and where you stood if you knew only three numbers: the mean, the high, and the low. Any statistical report should contain these three elements at a minimum.

If your teacher was conscientious, he also listed the frequency distribution of all the scores—how many people got 90 percent or more, how many got 80 to 90 percent, and so on. A frequency distribution makes a statistical report better because it gives you more information than simply the best and worst values. A frequency distribution indicates how the individual values are scattered around their average.

If you apply these simple ideas to any set of numerical measures, you are beginning to look at the world the way a statistician does. These principles are universal and apply to any set of data, regardless of their origin or context. They form the essential foundation of any statistical analysis.

As you might imagine, a number of other measures have been developed to portray the central tendency and dispersion of data, but the differences among these other measures are often minor. Each one captures some little aspect that others miss and deletes something that they include, but conceptually they are all equivalent in purpose. The problem that researchers face is that putting down all these measures confuses the casual reader who is uninterested in or unknowledgeable about the little nuances that differentiate the proper interpretation of the various measures.

In financial analyses, the *standard deviation* is the measure most frequently used to describe dispersion in the returns on stocks and bonds as they go up and down over time. The standard deviation measures how much returns differ from their long-term average rate over a number of quarters or years.[7] It is not as good as seeing a frequency distribution, but it is a better measure of dispersion than just the two extremes of highest and lowest values because it includes all the data points in the entire data set. In essence, it tries to crystallize the information in the frequency distribution of the fluctuations in returns around their average over many quarters or years into a single number. A higher standard deviation means greater volatility (the fluctuations were more pronounced).

The standard deviation has a number of theoretical properties that make it useful for mathematical analysis. Nearly all statistical tabulations of stock returns include the standard deviation as part of their coverage.

Because it measures volatility, the standard deviation plays a central role in measuring portfolio performance. Recall the fundamental trade-off between return and stability—higher return means less stability.[8] Therefore, if you want your portfolio to grow faster (higher average returns), you must be prepared to accept more volatility (higher standard deviations). If you are getting the higher volatility without the higher returns, then your portfolio is considered to be *inefficient*. As we shall see, one of the most popular ways to measure portfolio efficiency is the ratio of the portfolio's return to its standard deviation: the higher, the better.[9]

However, the standard deviation has some disadvantages. Figure 4.9 demonstrated that volatility and risk are not exactly the same thing. If a portfolio fluctuates widely, but even at its worst downtick stays above the highest uptick of a less volatile portfolio, then clearly the first portfolio is better. But the standard deviation for the first portfolio would be higher, and thus it would be considered more volatile and riskier than the second. This is a common fallacy that investors (and even their brokers) sometimes make. Simple logic gets lost in the confusion and ignorance of the fundamentals.

Sometimes the "semi-deviation" is used instead of the standard deviation.[10] The semi-deviation counts only the downticks of the market because they are what can hurt you. The upticks are ignored because they help you and so can hardly be called risk. But all volatility measures are based on the same principle: the degree to which your experience in any single year deviates in either direction from the average of all years or from some predetermined target, such as the target portfolio value along the critical path.

Another measure of volatility is called *beta*. It is based on the idea of how closely a portfolio parallels the movements of the overall market. If a 5 percent movement in the market (as measured by the S&P 500) corresponds to a 7.5 percent movement in a portfolio (on average), the beta of that portfolio would be 1.5 (7.5/5.0 = 1.5).[11] Because it is a relative measure, beta is one step removed from the actual magnitude of volatility. That is, knowing that your portfolio's beta is 1.5 is somewhat different from knowing that your portfolio may go up or down by 30 percent of its value each year.

Other ways of measuring volatility have been and will continue to be developed, but the standard deviation of the annual (sometimes quarterly) rate of return seems to be the measure of choice. It can be calculated automatically by computers, it is reported by most stock tracking services, and anyone with at least one college or high school course in statistics has been exposed to the concept. If you would like to shock your broker, ask him to explain it to you by showing you an example of how it is calculated.

ANNUALIZED VERSUS AVERAGE ANNUAL TOTAL RETURN
Growth Rates Are Not Entirely Intuitive

Total return is a growth rate. It determines how fast a portfolio grows over time. Growth rates are not as intuitive as most people think. Errors are common. The errors would be harmless academic distinctions except that they sometimes cause people to make wrong decisions that will affect their chances of success or failure in their long-term financial plans. Failing to do the math correctly led to the famous Beardstown Blunder discussed earlier.

Two types of compound growth rates need to be distinguished: (1) the annualized and (2) the average annual. The annualized growth rate will always be a little smaller than the average annual growth rate. But these small differences in growth rate can lead to large differences in outcomes over 10 or 20 years because of the effect of compounding.

To explain the difference between the two growth rates, consider the two portfolios in Table 12.2. Both Portfolio A and Portfolio B start with $100, and both have the identical average return, 15 percent. Which portfolio will be worth more at the end of 20 years, assuming no additions or withdrawals?

Table 12.2

Two Portfolios, Same Average Return

	Annual Return	
Period	Portfolio A	Portfolio B
First 10 years	5%	15%
Second 10 years	25%	15%

Most people believe that the two portfolios would have the same ending value because they both have the same average annual growth rate, 15 percent.

But they do not have the same ending value. Portfolio B is better. Table 12.3 shows the year-by-year growth. The ending value of Portfolio A is $1517 and that of Portfolio B is $1637, or about 8 percent more after 20 years.

The reason that this happens is actually a minor mathematical phenomenon. It is true that when you average the two growth rates for each portfolio, the result for both portfolios equals 15 percent. However, multiplying the growth rates together yields a different result: The portfolio with the constant 15 percent growth rate grows slightly faster than the portfolio with the 15 percent average growth:

A: $1.05 * 1.25 = 1.3125$
B: $1.15 * 1.15 = 1.3225$.

In this case, it turns out that Portfolio B would have to grow at a constant rate of only 14.56 percent to reach the same ending point of $1517. In other words, $1.1456 * 1.1456 = 1.3125$.

Why is it that constant growth rates that are equal to an average of variable growth rates produce faster growth? The mathematical derivation is shown as a footnote for the interested reader, but a simple riddle with a piece of wood may be the easiest way to explain it:[12]

Assume that a rich lumberjack gives you a piece of wood that was 30 feet long. You can cut it into only two pieces. After you cut it, you must lay down the two pieces perpendicular to each other so that they form two sides of a rectangle or square. He will give you $1000 for each square foot that the rectangle or square covers. How should you cut the board to maximize your payout?

Table 12.3

Average Annual versus Annualized Compound
Rate of Return

	Portfolio A		Portfolio B	
Year	Principal	Rate of Return	Principal	Rate of Return
0	$100	5%	$100	15%
1	$105	5%	$115	15%
2	$110	5%	$132	15%
3	$116	5%	$152	15%
4	$122	5%	$175	15%
5	$128	5%	$201	15%
6	$134	5%	$231	15%
7	$141	5%	$266	15%
8	$148	5%	$306	15%
9	$155	5%	$352	15%
10	$163	25%	$405	15%
11	$204	25%	$465	15%
12	$255	25%	$535	15%
13	$318	25%	$615	15%
14	$398	25%	$708	15%
15	$497	25%	$814	15%
16	$621	25%	$936	15%
17	$777	25%	$1,076	15%
18	$971	25%	$1,238	15%
19	$1,214	25%	$1,423	15%
20	$1,517		$1,637	
Average annual rate of return	15.00%		15.00%	
Annualized compound rate of return	14.56%		15.00%	

Answer: If you cut it into a 5-foot and a 25-foot piece and lay them down, the resulting rectangle will cover only 125 square feet. But if you cut them into two equal 15-foot lengths, the rectangle will cover 225 square feet, netting you $225,000. There is no combination of lengths that are unequal in size that can beat $225,000.[13]

The same is true for growth rates. It also needs to be pointed out that the 14.56 percent growth rate is unique. It is the only rate that will connect the starting value and the ending value of a portfolio with a single number. Therefore, it is the lowest possible rate that will convert $100 into $1517 after 20 years. Any other rate will lead to a different result. Mathematicians call it the geometric mean.[14] The financial community calls it the annualized rate of return. It will always be lower than the average for any other combination of rates.[15] This will be true for any asset class for any time frame. It explains why researchers have to be very precise in their reports, because otherwise, it is difficult to know which rate is being referred to. These reports may sound pedantic, but there is a good reason for it.

CONCLUSION

This chapter provided some background on a few of the quantitative fundamentals associated with investing. Learning these fundamentals will equip any investor to make more informed decisions about her investments. It will also make her a harder target for brokers who are not used to dealing with knowledgeable clients.

The next chapters will present some of the most common errors committed by investors (and often by brokers) when they fail to appreciate the true nature of what it is they are dealing with when they enter the world of investments. It is easy to get misled when you do not know the fundamentals. It sometimes appears that brokers who advise clients about these matters represent the proverbial case of the blind leading the blind.

NOTES

1. For a mathematician's take on the stock market in a highly readable style, see John Allen Paulos, *A Mathematician Plays the Stock Market* (New York: Basic Books, 2003).
2. This explains the intuitive idea of total return. For this to be technically correct, the date and dollar amount of the dividend paid within the year must also be factored in (called *reinvestment return*), but the mathematics become complicated.
3. The actual mathematics needed to perform the IRR calculation are beyond the scope of this book. It involves what mathematicians call polynomial equations, where variables are raised to higher powers (such as $aX + bX^2 + cX^3 + dX^4 + \cdots$). Fortunately, Excel and similar software programs have a built-in worksheet function that will perform the calculation using approximation techniques as long as the data are correctly lined up in a column as described in the program's Help menu (=IRR(...)).
4. The following note now appears on the Amazon.com web site where the book is still listed:

ERRATUM:

Dear Reader,

We recently discovered that there were mistakes in the way we calculated our club's returns. More specifically, the 23.4 percent return rate referred to in various places in this book actually related to a two-year period ending December 31, 1992, and the return for 1991 was 54.4 percent. The annual rate of return for our investment club during the 10 years from its inception through 1993 was 9.1 percent, and through the end of 1997 it was 15.3 percent.

We are distressed that there were any inaccuracies in our financial figures. Our priorities are still, as they always have been, education, enjoyment, and enrichment, in that order.

We've included recipes in the past, and now we would like to share with you our recipe for humble pie: a full measure of regret mixed with our sincere apologies. We thank everyone for their support.

Sincerely,

The Beardstown Ladies

5. In fact, one mutual fund, Dimensional Fund Advisors (www.dfaus.com), welcomes fluctuations by harnessing the greater volatility to achieve higher returns for its clients, all of whom are supposed to be long-term investors.
6. The three most common "averages" are the mean, or the common arithmetic average; the median, or the midpoint of the data when they are sorted from highest to lowest; and the mode, or the most frequently occuring value. All three have different statistical properties, but for symmetrical distributions, all three are the same. Most theoretical work in statistics focuses on the mean, which is what most people think of when they refer to the "average" and is the value calculated by Excel's "=average($\cdots$)" function.
7. The basis of the standard deviation calculation is to square the difference between each individual data point and the mean, then add these up and take the square root of the total. (see Endnote 10 in Chapter 4).
8. The raw figures bear this out if you compare the historical record of large-company stocks with that of small-company stocks. Tables 3.3 and 3.4, plotted in Figures 3.5 and 3.6, demonstrated that small-company stocks have higher returns but a wider range between the highest and lowest returns over any given period of investment.
9. The numerator in the Sharpe ratio is actually the portfolio's return over and above the return on "risk-free" Treasury bills. The denominator is the portfolio's standard deviation.
10. The term *semi-variance* is sometimes used synonymously with *semi-deviation*. The core idea of both is that only downward movements below the mean or some other target are tabulated.
11. Theoretically, an S&P index fund by definition has a beta of 1.0, assuming that the market is measured as usual by movements in the S&P 500. However, an actual fund's beta may not be a perfect 1.0 because of tracking errors, meaning that the price movements of the index fund are slightly off from the true index movements because of the costs associated with running the computer programs to manage the fund, operational costs, and so on. But a beta of 0.999 is considered equivalent to 1.0.

12. The 14.56 percent was derived from the fundamental equation for compound interest. The raw data for the calculation are the starting or present value (PV) and the
ending value of the investment in the future (FV) after some time span of n years.
We then compute the annualized rate of return, r, using the fundamental compound growth equation:

$$FV = PV - (1 + r)^n$$

To solve for r, we must use basic algebra to get

$$r = [-(FV/PV)^{1/n}] - 1$$

From the example in Table 12.2 for Portfolio A, $r = [(\$1517/\$100)^{1/20}] - 1 = 0.1456$.

13. The same result can be verified with calculus. Let X = fraction of board to cut. Let
Y = square footage formed. Therefore, $Y = X(1 - X) = X - X^2$. Setting the first
derivative = 0 yields $X = 1/2$.
14. If you have 10 values as data points, the arithmetic mean is computed by adding up
the 10 values and dividing by 10. The geometric mean is computed by multiplying
the 10 values together and taking the tenth root.
15. A calculator that will compute the annualized rate of return for any starting value,
ending value, and intervening additions or withdrawals can be found at
http://cgi.money.cnn.com/tools/returnrate/returnrate.jsp.

CHAPTER 13

Portfolio Management Tools

I not only use all the brains I have, but all I can borrow.
—WOODROW WILSON

Managing a portfolio means deciding how to invest the money—which mutual funds, stocks, bonds, or other investments to buy and how much of each. Once these decisions have been made, the next step is to wait and see how the investments do.

MEASURING PORTFOLIO PERFORMANCE

The Risk-Return Dance

Most measures of portfolio performance attempt to incorporate both return and risk. These two elements are at the heart of most performance measures in some way or other. The simplest measure that captures both is the ratio of return divided by risk. A 10 percent return with a 20 percent standard deviation would have a ratio of 0.5. A better portfolio would be one that had a return of 15 percent with a 20 percent standard deviation, a ratio of 0.75. The idea is that you get more return per unit of risk in the second case. It is a productivity measure of output per unit of input.

This ratio is actually the inverse of what statisticians call the *coefficient of variation*, which is the standard deviation divided by the mean. It can be found in most basic statistics books. William Sharpe, the Nobel Prize winner mentioned in Chapter 3, popularized the idea of dividing the return by its standard deviation, and this is now called the *Sharpe ratio*. The actual calculation is a bit more complicated in that most financial researchers first subtract the return on U.S. Treasury bills because Treasury bills earn what is considered to be the risk-free rate of return. Risk is measured as the standard deviation of the returns (usually based on annual values).

One of the problems with ratios is that they are one step removed from the actual values themselves. Portfolios can have identical Sharpe ratios of 0.75 but differ greatly in terms of how they behave. Portfolio A may have an average return of 15 percent with a standard deviation of 20 percent; Portfolio B, an average return of 9 percent with a standard deviation of 12 percent; and Portfolio C, an average return of 3 percent with a standard deviation of 4 percent. Few people would consider these three portfolios to be equivalent. Combining two measures that are designed to measure separate, distinct aspects of portfolio behavior means that information is lost. For that reason, it is necessary to always know both of the values that are included in the calculation.

The obvious goal of most investors is to get the "best" portfolio performance they can. Researchers have a number of mathematical tools that strive to do this. None of them work perfectly because they all require various questionable assumptions, but knowing the ideas behind them will allow you to better understand what they are attempting to do.

OPTIMIZATION—SEEKING THE BEST SOLUTION

Maximizing Return or Minimizing Risk

When researchers apply mathematics to solve real-world problems, they usually use two different approaches: optimization and simulation. In the simplest of terms, these might be called the "what's best?" approach and the "what if?" approach.

Optimization seeks to find the best possible answer: a maximum or a minimum. In general, the assumption is that any decision maker has a goal or objective in mind, such as maximizing return or minimizing risk. Figure 13.1 illustrates this idea.

Figure 13.1

Optimization: Maximizing Return or Minimizing Risk

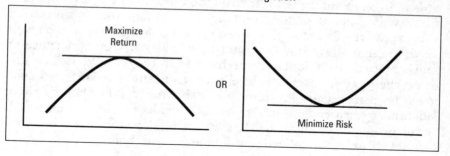

Analysts try to find mathematical equations that show how all the factors involved are related to one another and to the objective. The factors are usually sorted into two categories: controllable factors (decision variables) and uncontrollable factors (parameters). Once the researchers have quantified the relationships, they use mathematical techniques to determine the best (optimal) values for the controllable factors to achieve the objective.[1]

The mathematical techniques for determining the optimal values, whether the goal is to maximize or to minimize, are complex and require training to understand and utilize. The classic technique of calculus, discovered in the 1700s, was used in some of its earliest applications to determine maximums and minimums. In more recent times, mathematical programming has become the workhorse of applied mathematics. It is incorporated into Microsoft's Excel spreadsheet as the add-in "Solver."

Optimization was an essential element in the development of modern portfolio theory, and it remains a centerpiece of many studies in academic financial research. Its use in the investment world will be explained more fully in later sections of this chapter. Optimization is always the best tool to use whenever possible because it does provide the optimal answer. In an ideal world, it should be applied in all decision situations. But unfortunately, it is not applied nearly as often as it could be.

The complexity of the techniques themselves is partly responsible for the reluctance of those in the financial community (and other industries as well) to embrace optimization. Getting the training that is needed to understand and feel comfortable with the mathematical aspects of optimization requires significant time and effort.

Our society has a habit of disdaining things, like mathematics, that are complex and hard to understand. Perhaps this is a defense mechanism to excuse our reluctance to do the work necessary to reach proficiency. Perhaps it is due to managers who fear that optimization will expose the fact that they have not been doing their jobs as well as they might have done, or that it will reveal their ignorance of mathematical techniques, something that they would rather not draw their boss's attention to. As a consultant, I have found that lower-level managers are often defensive about how they do their jobs and regard consultants more as intruders than as helpers. A softer explanation might be that they really are unaware that this technology exists or believe that it cannot help them.

MODERN PORTFOLIO THEORY

Getting the Highest Return for a Given Level of Risk

Modern portfolio theory (MPT) is a portfolio optimization tool that was originally developed by Harry Markowitz in 1952 while he was a graduate student at the University of Chicago. William Sharpe (developer of the Sharpe ratio described earlier) worked under the tutelage of Markowitz and refined the concept. The elegance of the mathematics that serve as the foundation of MPT generated accolades from academics and quantitative investment managers around the world. The two won the Nobel Prize in Economics in 1990 for their contribution to investment management.[2]

The essence of MPT is to create efficient portfolios that maximize expected investment returns for any given level of risk. If the standard deviation of two portfolios is 20 percent, but Portfolio A has a return of 15 percent and Portfolio B has a return of only 12 percent, then clearly A is better than B. If we compared the returns for many portfolios that all had standard deviations of 20 percent, the one that provided the highest return (and therefore would have the highest Sharpe ratio) would be considered the best of all for that level of volatility.

Now do the same sort of evaluation for all portfolios that have a standard deviation of 21 percent. Whichever one has the highest return would be considered the best for that class of risk.

If you do this for many different portfolios and plot the highest return for each level of risk (i.e., higher standard deviation), you will ultimately trace out a curve along the upper edge of all possible combinations similar to that shown in Figure 13.2. The line

Figure 13.2

Simple Efficient Frontier

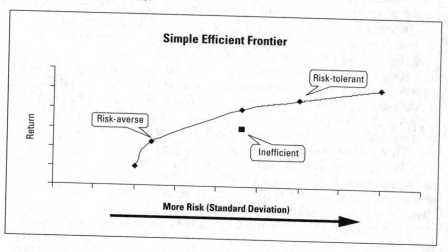

itself, which represents the highest return for each level of risk, is referred to in MPT as the *efficient frontier*. Any portfolio that offers a lower return for the same level of risk, such as the one shown in Figure 13.2, is considered "inefficient" because it does not compensate the investor for assuming that level of risk. Portfolios on the left end of the curve, with lower risk (and correspondingly lower returns), are considered better for "risk-averse" investors. These investors tend to allocate more of their assets to bonds and cash than to stocks. Portfolios further to the right are considered better for "risk-tolerant" investors and allocate more to stocks than to bonds or cash. Any portfolios on the line are considered to be efficient for their given levels of risk. This sort of analysis is sometimes called the *mean-variance* model.

Problems with MPT

MPT offered a significant potential for improving investment management. It provided portfolio managers with a mathematical rationale for making investment decisions that recognized what were considered to be the two fundamental elements of portfolio performance: returns and risk. But MPT is not without its problems.

MPT hinges on several key factors that have proved to be elusive, including accurate forecasts of expected returns, the quantification of an investor's true risk tolerance, and measuring risk.

Forecasting market returns is a monumentally difficult task, as evidenced by the dismal performance of the brokers in Dorfman's *Wall Street Journal* study. The obstacles that serious forecasters face have yet to be overcome successfully. Investments are allocated based on forecasted returns, but when the market deviates from the predictions, the impact on portfolio performance is dramatic. If a portfolio is heavily weighted in a security or asset class that is expected to have a high return, but that in fact has a low return, the effect of the miscalculation is magnified.

Identifying the investor's risk tolerance presents another problem: how to define the level of risk tolerance. MPT requires a quantifiable value, but that information is generally nothing more than a guess. Typically, an investor is presented with a risk-tolerance questionnaire that includes quantitative questions about market returns that they do not understand or qualitative questions about their attitudes toward risk that do not lead to a directly quantifiable value. Either way, defining risk tolerance becomes an art rather than a science and therefore leads to imprecision in portfolio selection.

Finally, the fact that the standard deviation is a good measure for volatility but a questionable one for risk casts doubt on its use as a fundamental element MPT. Its problems as a risk measure were explained earlier.

Although MPT is conceptually simple, the real-world challenges to it have robbed it of much of its usefulness in practice. The model has too many variables that are difficult to forecast or estimate. It simply cannot optimize an unknown future.

MONTE CARLO ANALYSIS

Simulating Investment Returns

Another reason that optimization has not come into widespread use has to do with the very nature of real-world problems. Often, the relationships are not easily quantified. Nuances and subtleties are difficult to capture in mathematical equations. Another practical problem is the presence of random variables. Because their values cannot be determined with certainty, the random elements in a situation are even more difficult—in fact, almost intractable—for optimization techniques to handle very well, given the current state of the art. Unfortunately, future rates of return (or anything involving forecasting the future) inherently include randomness, often as the dominant element. This section describes a different tool that was developed to handle situations involving random variables.

The most common tool whenever optimization cannot be used is *simulation*. It is based on the simple idea of trial and error: testing different scenarios to see what the consequences would be. What if we did this? What if we did that? We try different values for the controllable factors until we find one that produces a satisfactory solution most of the time.

Simulation has actually been around much longer than the classic optimization tools. Archeological evidence suggests that maps and models were used in ancient Greek and Roman times to train military officers on how to develop strategic battle plans and test different options for troop movements in upcoming battles.

Applied mathematicians split simulation into two types: deterministic simulation and stochastic simulation. Deterministic simulation is what many people do when they try to see how changes in one variable affect other variables in their spreadsheets. Randomness does not play a part in these situations, and the people doing the testing may not even realize that they are engaged in deterministic simulation.

The word *stochastic* takes its name from a Greek word meaning "to guess at." It now is used to refer to any situation involving a random variable. Stochastic simulation goes by the much sexier name *Monte Carlo analysis* because of the association of randomness with gambling. It probably helps that Monte Carlo evokes images of worldly aplomb and James Bond, making it sound appealing, especially to stodgy mathematicians.

Monte Carlo simulation was developed in the early 1950s shortly after the invention of large-scale computers. This was not a coincidence. Monte Carlo analysis reaches its conclusions based on systematic trial and error. Thousands or millions of trials may be needed to duplicate the behavior of random variables. Only a computer can do this quickly. Although the finer points of Monte Carlo analysis can become very complex, the basic idea is simple.

For investment purposes, Monte Carlo analysis can estimate the probability of achieving a given rate of return based on the historical record. For example, assume that in 80 percent of the years since 1946, the market had 20 percent gains, but in the other years, it lost 10 percent. To simulate this behavior with dice, you would have to purchase a 10-sided die.[3] You would then toss it for each year to simulate that year's gain or loss. If it lands on a 1 or a 2, it would represent a year in which the market lost 10 percent. If it landed on 3 through 10, it would represent a year in which there was a gain of 20 percent. Do this several thousand times, and you have simulated, at least crudely, the behavior of the market. A more refined Monte Carlo would ask what percentage of the time the market gained 0 to 10 percent, 10 to 20 percent, and so on and base the simulations on finer gradations of return rates.

Although Monte Carlo simulation has its advantages, it also has weaknesses. One is the underlying assumption that history provides a good guide to the future. Will the probabilities from yesterday hold true for tomorrow? It is a good guess that they will, but it is still just a guess.

Relying on the past seems like an obvious thing to do, but surprisingly, something of a debate about this has developed in financial circles. Some people claim that the past cannot or should not be used to make forecasts because the world is constantly changing. All advertising by mutual funds must carry a warning that a fund's past performance is no guarantee of its future performance.

But the claim that the past is entirely irrelevant to the future is questionable itself. The proposition that the past should be ignored seems self-contradictory because the question then becomes, what happened in the past to make anyone think that? Anyone who thinks that the future patterns of returns will be based on something other than the past must be basing his opinion on some perception of how the many factors involved have interacted in the past. Therefore, any projections are, in a sense, products of the historical record, either directly or indirectly.

Another hidden complication in Monte Carlo analysis is autocorrelation. If we treat each year as a separate experience, we fail to capture any relationship that exists between this year's return and last year's return. If there was a big gain last year, does that influence the probability of getting another big gain this year? How about a big loss? Are successive years truly independent, or are they correlated? How about links between this year and 2 years ago? What about factoring in the impact of inflation or other elements in our economy?

For these reasons, it is considered better to simulate returns over any 10-year span by using the distribution of average annualized returns over all past 10-year spans rather than by using the distribution of returns for a single year 10 times in a row. Presumably, when we use the return distribution of past 10-year spans, we will automatically capture wherever conditional linkages existed within each of these spans. The same is true for 5-year spans or spans of any other length.

All too often, advisers who have little training in mathematics will simply use a single rate of return (usually the annualized rate) when making projections. The problem with this is that there is a 50 percent chance that the rate will be higher and a 50 percent chance that it will be lower. How much higher or lower it will be varies with the time spans involved, and it is not possible to know what rate will occur. But knowing that an 11 percent rate of return has a 62 percent chance of occurring, whereas an 8 percent return has a 77 percent chance of occurring will lead to more informed decision making (see Table 5.4).

THE EXPERT COIN FLIPPER—10 HEADS IN A ROW
50-50 Chance That One out of a Thousand Will Get It by Luck

Once the idea that the return on an investment in any given year is a random variable is accepted, Monte Carlo analysis is a natural way to analyze the probabilities of any given return. But probability theory itself, the foundation of Monte Carlo analysis, offers other tidbits of insight into the world of portfolio performance.

One example is the advertising by mutual fund managers that appears regularly, pointing out successful calls on the market that have led to big returns over 3, 5, or even 10 years. Are these managers prescient, have they developed a system, or is it luck? How likely is it that they will get a series of successes as a result of luck?

Assume that you have a large room with 1000 people in it. Everyone is asked to flip a coin. If a person gets tails he or she sits down; if the person gets heads, he or she remains standing and flips again. How long will it be before there is only one person standing?

Table 13.1 shows the expected progression of the number standing after each flip. On average, probability theory predicts that after 10 flips, one person will have gotten 10 heads in a row and will remain standing. This is our champion coin flipper. She may be interviewed by the press to explain how she was able to perform such an amazing feat. She may appear on talk shows to explain her techniques. She may write a book about coin flipping.

Does this sound far-fetched? Substitute the words *mutual fund manager* or *investment expert* for *coin flipper*, and the scenario

Table 13.1

1000 Coin Flippers: How Many Get
10 Heads in a Row?

	Coin Flippers Getting Heads
After flip 1	500
After flip 2	250
After flip 3	125
After flip 4	63
After flip 5	31
After flip 6	16
After flip 7	8
After flip 8	4
After flip 9	2
After flip 10	1

is not rare at all. Some fund managers have made a short career out of a lucky streak and are smart enough to get out while they are ahead. A 10-year record of success at beating the market will often be reported in glowing terms by the press. Left out are the critical details that would allow an informed reader to understand what really happened. Furthermore, the fact that one person would be left after 10 flips is only the average. There is a 50 percent probability that more than one person will get 10 heads in a row. Enough success stories appear in the media and advertising to make the general public believe that coin flippers are clairvoyant, not lucky. The lack of a 10-year winner (like buildings that don't burn) would not make the news.

Here is another coin-flipping question for your intuition: Which has a greater probability, getting 6 heads (or more) out of 10 flips or getting 60 (or more) out of 100 flips?

Most people think that this is a trick question. They think the answer is that both have equal probability. In fact, getting or beating 6 heads out of 10 is much more likely than getting or beating 60 out of 100. The probability of getting 6 or more heads in 10 flips is about 38 percent. But the probability of getting 60 or more heads in 100 flips is only about 3 percent. The explanation is that getting 60 heads out of 100 flips would be like getting 6 heads out of 10 flips 10 times in a row. Lucky money managers hope that you will make the mistake of extrapolating their short-term streak into long-term success. The chances that this will actually happen are very small.

CONCLUSION

As earlier chapters sought to explain, one of the advantages of asset dedication is that it is based on some very simple principles. It employs optimization to build the computer routines that find the right bonds in the right quantities to provide and protect the income at the lowest possible cost, and the web site www.assetdedication.com uses Monte Carlo analysis to determine the probability of your meeting your financial goals. It thus manages both risk and return using techniques that require some level of mathematical sophistication. But the basic ideas are not difficult to understand. There are no formulas masked in mathematical mystery. The investor using asset dedication knows exactly why he or she has each investment. Every dollar has a reason for being where it is. Compare this to the ambiguous explanations of the XYZ formulas in asset allocation. The difference in clarity should be quite distinct.

NOTES

1. For the classic formulation of the mathematical approach to portfolio optimization, see www-fp.mcs.anl.gov/otc/Guide/CaseStudies/port/index.html.
2. The development of MPT is well chronicled in the book *Capital Ideas: The Improbable Origins of Modern Wall Street* by Peter L. Bernstein (New York: The Free Press [A Division of Simon & Schuster], 1992).
3. In explaining Monte Carlo simulation to a class once, I stated that I did not know where to find a 10-sided die. In the next class meeting, a student brought me a 10-sided die that he had from a game and a 100-sided die (which looked like a golf ball) from another game. I have used those dice for classroom demonstrations of Monte Carlo concepts.

14

Forecasting: The Good, the Bad, and the Ugly

Experience is a good teacher, but she sends in terrific bills.
—MINNA ANTRIM

Clairvoyance. Divination. Precognition. Prescience. Prophecy. These are the siren songs of investing. Everybody wonders if there is magic out there somewhere that will allow us to predict the future. Surely, some brilliant "mathemagician" with a powerful computer has somehow figured out how to predict the stock market—and wants to share it with us.

Unfortunately, nothing could be further from the truth. But that does not seem to stop people from believing that someone, somewhere, somehow knows how to predict the market with accuracy. Forecasting has an allure that fascinates most people. A joke among statisticians is that forecasting is a little like sex: Everybody has a favorite way of doing it but wonders how others do it and if there is a better way.

The purpose of this final chapter is to encourage skepticism by pointing out the problems associated with forecasting. It is important to have some basic knowledge of forecasting in order to understand why the degrees of accuracy about the future behavior of financial markets vary from 100 percent down to practically nothing.[1] Too many investment advisers play to the typical client's desire for quick and easy returns by implying that they or their research department can correctly anticipate the market and will help the client take advantage of the next big move.

Asset dedication makes no such claim. Its "plain vanilla" approach of holding bonds to maturity and using index funds for growth may not be sexy compared to promises of quick riches, but in the long run, it keeps its promises.

We will first examine some of the good news regarding the prediction of financial phenomena: the areas where accuracy is 100 percent. Then comes the far more prevalent bad news, as demonstrated by a famous University of Michigan study on market timing that calculated the impact of stock market extremes. Missing just a few of the "biggest days" in the market leads to radically different results over the long run. As we will see later in the chapter, a perfect timer would have converted $1 in 1926 into $690 million by 1993, but an inept timer would have converted $100 million in 1926 into $1000 by 1993. Predicting the size and timing of these randomly spaced biggest-day jolts remains as elusive today as it was 50 years ago. Finally, we will look at scams, the ugly side of forecasting and some of the ways in which predators prey on people's hope, greed, and ignorance.

The web site that supports this book lists in its research link a short paper on 12 of the most common obstacles that serious researchers face when they attempt to forecast financial markets. But it needs to be said that there is no way to prove that systematic, accurate predictions are not possible. Nor is there any way to prove that no one has ever done it over an extended period of time. But it is doubtful that anyone has.

THE GOOD: FORECASTING RETURNS ON BONDS HELD TO MATURITY

Perfect Forecasts: Future Value Is Guaranteed If Bonds Are Held to Maturity

The good news about forecasting financial markets starts with the one case in which returns can be predicted with 100 percent accuracy: the returns on bonds that are held to maturity. If bonds are held to maturity, we can project their exact cash flows to the dollar and the day. This is what makes bonds unique as financial instruments. Nothing else in portfolio management compares to them.

If you buy a $1000 U.S. Treasury bond with a coupon rate of 5 percent that expires in 2015, you can predict with certainty that you will receive $50 every year between now and then, and you will get $1000 the day the bond matures. There is no chance that this will not happen.[2] Asset dedication is founded on this certainty.

Academic researchers refer to the return on Treasury bills as the *risk-free rate*.[3] They use this term to indicate that there is no uncertainty about getting the money back. The return on Treasury bills is the benchmark against which all other returns are measured. Any return higher than the risk-free rate is considered to be the reward for tolerating the fact that the investment may return less than the risk-free rate. They call the difference the *risk premium*.

But all bonds and notes of the U.S. Treasury are also risk-free *if* they are held to maturity. We can forecast their cash flows, both interest and principal, with 100 percent assurance. The only reason that researchers do not consider Treasury bonds and notes to be as risk-free as T bills is that researchers measure risk by assessing the value of the asset held at the end of each year. Since T bills pay off within 1 year, they always provide the expected return. But other U.S. government bonds last longer than 1 year, and researchers totally ignore the intent of the investor. They do not care whether the bonds held in a portfolio are designed to be held to maturity or not. They value everything at whatever it would be worth if it were sold at the end of every period.

Is this a valid measure? It is sort of like appraising the value of your home or your car. The appraisal may be of interest, but it does not really have any significance for you until you are actually ready to sell. Another analogy might be the case where a $100,000 diamond necklace goes on sale for $80,000 at Tiffany's. Does this really matter to you if you are not in the market for diamond necklaces of that caliber? The logic is easy to understand in this context, but investors sometimes fail to apply it when dealing with financial assets.

Theoretically, the 100 percent guarantee of forecast accuracy applies only to bills, bonds, and notes issued by the U.S. Treasury. But in practice, something very close to this guarantee also applies to bonds issued or backed by any federal agency. A partial list of the best known such agencies was given in Chapter 11 (such as the Federal National Mortgage Association, Federal Home Loan Mortgage Corporation, and so on).

Is there any danger that these agencies might ever fail to make their interest or principal payments? If that happened, it would send shock waves through the economy that would destroy the political and professional careers of everyone associated with it. Not likely!

To be technically correct on these matters, the fact that we can accurately forecast the cash flows from U.S. government securities does not mean that there is no risk whatsoever. It depends on what you include in "risk." Recall from Chapter 5 that there is always some possibility that you will face an emergency that will force you to sell a bond before it matures in order to get the cash immediately. Second, there is the chance that inflation may be higher than you allowed for, and therefore the purchasing power of the cash flows may be less than you anticipated. Third, if you have to reinvest the coupon interest, you may receive a lower interest rate. Fourth, there is always the risk that you may die before the bond matures, meaning that you never get to enjoy the gratification that the money could have brought you. However, your heirs will get it. These basic risks apply to any investment, of course.

Once we move out of the federal government domain, bonds issued by corporations, states, and local government agencies are less secure, but only very slightly so—they are in the 99+ percent range instead of 100 percent if they are held to maturity. They still offer much greater security than stocks because of their fundamental nature. The only financial risk when they are held to maturity is default.

Default usually means that the bond issuer is late with an interest or principal payment. Only rarely do investors lose any of the principal they invested. Like most normal people, there are times when businesses are late paying their bills. It is very, very rare for bondholders to end up losing all or even most of their principal. Because this is so rare, when it does happen, the news media tend to report it as a major story if the defaulting company is well known. This exacerbates the general public's distorted perspective of the risk of bonds. Even in cases where a company declares bankruptcy, bondholders usually get whatever proceeds are available from salvage values, and many warning signals show up in the bond ratings before then. An Enron-type scandal is always possible, of course, but so is getting killed by lightning.

The good news is that default rates for the highest-rated bonds (Aaa or Aa for Moody's, AAA or AA for Standard & Poor's) are extremely low. Thus, the likelihood of getting the return you expect is extremely high. How high? Table 14.1 shows the probability of bonds with different initial ratings meeting their return expectation 1 to 10 years after the bonds were issued. The probabilities never dip below 99.2 percent. (See Appendix 2 for default rates on lower-rated bonds and other historical data on bonds.)

Table 14.1

Probability of Meeting Projected Rates of Return for Bonds
Rated Aa or Higher, 1970–2000

	U.S. Treasury or Agency	Muni Aaa	Muni Aa	Corporate Aaa	Corporate Aa
Year 1	100.000%	100.000%	100.000%	100.000%	99.977%
Year 2	100.000%	100.000%	99.998%	100.000%	99.965%
Year 3	100.000%	100.000%	99.995%	100.000%	99.925%
Year 4	100.000%	100.000%	99.992%	99.961%	99.820%
Year 5	100.000%	100.000%	99.989%	99.876%	99.718%
Year 6	100.000%	100.000%	99.985%	99.784%	99.603%
Year 7	100.000%	100.000%	99.981%	99.684%	99.495%
Year 8	100.000%	100.000%	99.977%	99.575%	99.373%
Year 9	100.000%	100.000%	99.972%	99.456%	99.290%
Year 10	100.000%	100.000%	99.967%	99.325%	99.197%

Source: Moody's U.S. Municipal Bond Rating Scale, Special Comment, November 2002, Report Number 76553.

The worst overall default rate in U.S. history occurred in 1932, at the depth of the Great Depression, when the overall bond default rate reached 9.2 percent, meaning that the companies issuing 90.8 percent of all bonds continued to meet all their obligations. Compare this to stocks during that time, and you can see why bonds are far and away a more secure investment

THE BAD: FORECASTING STOCK RETURNS

The Funneling Effect: Returns over Longer Spans Are Easier to Predict

The stock market is the real challenge in forecasting. Because stocks have no legal obligation to pay anything, they have no fixed value in the future. They have none of the legally mandated cash flow obligations or defined maturity dates that bonds have. Stocks represent a share of the value of the company, which ebbs and flows based on how well the company performs in the business world. It depends entirely on the fortunes of the company. Another joke among statisticians is that the most common method of forecasting the stock market is the "WAG Method," short for Wild Ass Guess (Wild Approximate Guess in polite company).

The problem is that with stocks, there is nothing definite upon which to base the forecast, as there is with bonds. Stock prices live in a very messy environment from a mathematical point of view, which explains why researchers usually treat the returns on stocks as random variables. Accuracy now becomes a matter of luck as well as number crunching

One of the interesting aspects of forecasting stock returns is that long-term forecasts are likely to be better than short-term forecasts. This is the reverse of the normal situation, and it helps if you remember this so that you will know when to roll up your pant legs the next time a broker or any other purveyor of forecasting systems begins to spread his "wisdom" on predicting short-term moves.

To show why long-term averages are easier to predict than short-term returns, Figures 14.1, 14.2, and 14.3 present the average rates of return over 1-, 5-, and 10-year spans for large-company stocks as measured by the S&P 500 index since 1926. Notice how the charts settle down as the time spans lengthen. The 1-year returns are very choppy and abrupt, but the 5-year averages are smoother and the 10-year averages smoother yet. This is a natural consequence of including more years in the average. If we ultimately included all 77 years in a single span, there would be no variation, only a flat line representing the overall average, 10.1 percent.

This smoothing process results from the canceling effect of averaging. Deviations from the mean in either direction—gains or

Figure 14.1

Year-to-Year Returns in Stocks (S&P 500), 1926–2002

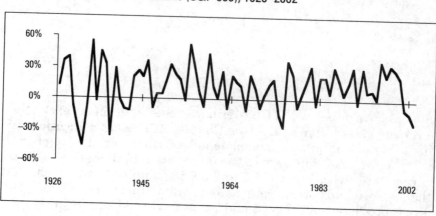

Figure 14.2

5-Year Average Returns in Stocks (S&P 500), 1926–2002

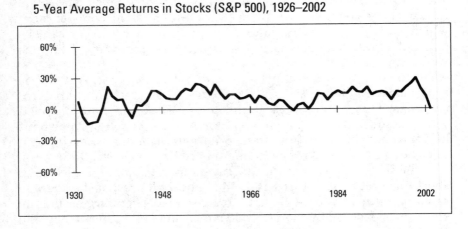

Figure 14.3

10-Year Average Returns in Stocks (S&P 500), 1926–2002

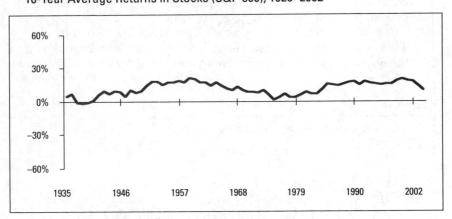

losses above or below the long-term average—will cancel each other out over longer time spans (see Chapter 12). Asset dedication utilizes this serendipitous phenomenon by focusing on the long term.

Figure 14.4 summarizes the information in these three charts. It correlates with Figures 3.5 and 3.6 in Chapter 3, which charted the highest and lowest returns over all 1- to 11-year spans. The difference between the best and worst narrowed significantly over

Figure 14.4

Highest, Lowest, and Average Returns on Large-Company Stocks
(S&P 500) for 1-, 5-, and 10-Year Horizons, 1926–2002

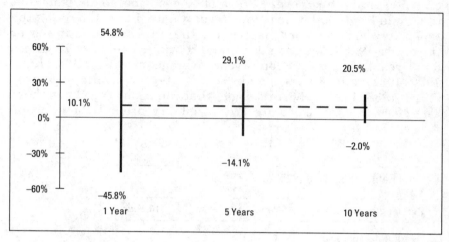

longer spans into the funnel shaped chart. This "funneling" phenomenon should be familiar by now. It occurs for any time series
because of the averaging process. Its effect is to improve the accuracy of forecasting the average rate of return as more periods are
averaged together.

But the shorter the time horizon, the less opportunity there is
for this canceling effect to take place. The problem continues to get
worse as the span drops to quarterly, monthly, or daily returns.
Short-term forecasters are really trying to predict deviations away
from the averages. Deviations are much more difficult to predict
than the averages themselves.

Another, more mundane reason for greater accuracy in predicting average returns over the long term is higher-quality information. People who are not professional statisticians probably do
not realize that one of the biggest obstacles that statisticians have
to overcome in the real world is finding numbers that they can
trust. Much of the time needed to conduct a statistical study is
devoted to simply cleaning up the data—making sure that they are
accurate, valid, and reliable. They should be traceable to an authoritative source and should contain no clerical errors, biases, or missing items.[4] But fresh data that have just arrived may not be

verifiable before decisions must be made. Later on, the figures that were first reported may be revised up or down.

Table 14.2 provides some other basic descriptive statistics for S&P 500 total returns over 1-, 5-, and 10-year time spans. Note that the annualized total return appears only once, in the top row of the table. As explained in Chapter 12, the annualized return over the entire 1926–2002 span is unique. However, there are 77 values for 1-year returns, 73 for 5-year average returns (1926–1930, 1927–1931, and so on), and 68 for 10-year average returns (1926–1935, 1927–1936, and so on) that can be averaged together.[5] Therefore, we can calculate the variability around their means

Table 14.2

Total Return, S&P 500, 1926–2002 (77 Years)

Planning Horizon:	1-Year	5-Year	10-Year
Average Annualized	10.1%	—	—
Mean	12.1%	10.9%	11.2%
Upper Limit (95% Conf.)	16.7%	12.9%	12.5%
Lower Limit (95% Conf.)	7.5%	8.8%	9.8%
Median	14.5%	13.1%	12.3%
High	54.8%	29.1%	20.5%
Low	−45.8%	−14.1%	−2.0%
Std. Deviation	20.5%	8.8%	5.7%
Standard Error	2.3%	1.0%	0.7%
Frequencies: How Often Annualized Total Return Is Between:			
+50-60%	2		
+40-50%	2		
+30-40%	13		
+20-30%	14	9	1
+10-20%	12	34	36
0-10%	11	21	28
−10-0%	14	6	3
−20-10%	4	3	
−30-20%	3		
−40-30%	1		
−50-40%	1		
Total Observations	77	73	68

Note: Upper limit inclusive, e.g., 50–60% is over 50% through 60%.

using the high, the low, and the standard deviation as shown in Table 14.2.

But the big take-away from this section is that short-term forecasting is very challenging for serious researchers. Forecasting short-term movements is essentially forecasting deviations away from the average, and deviations are inherently more difficult to anticipate. The next section provides the results of a very interesting study that points out one of the biggest obstacles to forecasting the market: the impact of the "biggest day."

THE PERILS OF MARKET TIMING—THE IMPACT OF THE BIGGEST DAY

Only 1 Percent of the Trading Days Produce 95 Percent of the Total Gain

Predicting returns over short, specific time periods is precisely what market timers try to do. The particular period that they are trying to foretell is tomorrow, next week, or the next 30 days (a "short-term play"). The mainstream brokerage houses' recommended asset allocations for the next quarter represent the same attempt at divination.

Whether the time frame is months, weeks, days, or hours, Figure 14.5 illustrates the forecasting problem that market timers face. It shows the month-to-month changes in the S&P 500 over the same 924 months used earlier (1926 to 2002, or 77 years). This is what statisticians call a *spark line*. It surges and plunges, producing sharp, abrupt gains or losses in what appears to be a totally random pattern around its monthly mean of 0.97 percent, which works out to an average of 12.1 percent per year (10.1 percent annualized). It is these jumps that the market timer must get right. To succeed perfectly, she must forecast every little jig and jag in the chart.

Market timers risk missing the impact of the biggest days. Dramatic, almost violent shifts in stock market levels in a single day may account for most of a year's loss or gain. There is no way to predict the timing or the size of these biggest days. Market timers are essentially gamblers. Missing the big day in either direction leads to radically different results in the long run. To win the timing game, you need to be very lucky.

The consequences of good and bad timing have been the object of a number of studies. One of the most graphic of these was a University of Michigan study, "Stock Market Extremes and Portfolio

Figure 14.5

Month-to-Month Changes in the S&P 500, 1926–2002

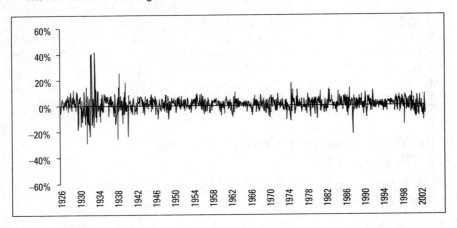

Performance," sponsored by Towneley Capital Management, Inc.[6] The study traced what would have happened to a market timer who made or missed the market's biggest daily changes during the period from 1963 to 1993. The analysis was repeated for the biggest monthly changes from 1926 to 1993.

Figure 14.6 presents the results of the daily study of the 1963–1993 period as published on the Towneley web site (www.towneley.com; the full text of the study is available, brief, and easy to understand). The span covers 31 years, or 7802 trading days. Table 14.3 presents the results in tabular form.

According to the study, any investor who initially invested $10,000 and simply bought and held the index fund of stocks over the entire 31-year period, without trying to time the market, would have had an ending value of approximately $243,000, including their initial $10,000. This corresponds to an average annual return of 11.83 percent (about 10.84 percent annualized).[7] But an investor who tried to time the market and missed the 90 best days during that 30-year period, when the market jumped (about 3 times a year), would have ended up with only about $21,000, an average annual return of only 3.28 over the 7712 days (or 2.45 percent annualized). The gain in the first case is $233,000; that in the second is $11,000. By missing the best 1.2 percent of the trading days, this investor would have missed about 95 percent of the gain ($11,000/$233,000 = 0.047, or about 5 percent)!

Figure 14.6

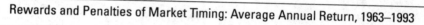

Rewards and Penalties of Market Timing: Average Annual Return, 1963–1993

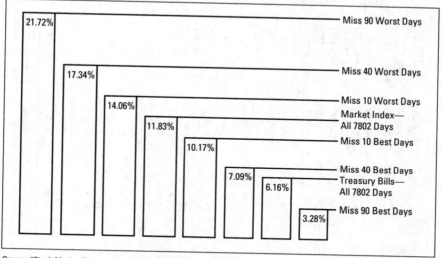

Source: "Stock Market Extremes and Portfolio Performance," a study commissioned by Towneley Capital Management, Inc., and conducted by Professor H. Nejat Seyhun, University of Michigan. For the complete text of the study, see www.towneley.com.

Missing the 90 worst days and thus avoiding those losses also generates radically different results. Without those days, the final portfolio would have been worth $3,264,000. The swing from $21,000 to $3,264,000 is quite a gap and should strike fear into the heart of anyone who thinks that she can time the market!

Figure 14.7 and Table 14.4 present equivalent results for the 68-year period from 1926 to 1993. Daily figures for this period were not available at the time of the study, so monthly figures were used. In this case, missing the "biggest month" produces the same types of radical changes that missing the biggest days did in the 1963–1993 time frame.

The buy-and-hold strategy would have generated an average annual return of 12.02 percent (9.96 percent annualized), with an ending value of $6,383,000. Missing the best 48 months (5.9 percent of the 816 trading months) would have dropped the average annual return to 2.86 percent (1.50 percent annualized) and an ending value of only $26,000. What a difference a few months can make! Other studies have consistently demonstrated the same phe-

Table 14.3

Returns Excluding Extreme Daily Observations for Period January 1, 1963 to December 31, 1993 (31 years)

Condition	Number of Days	Average Annual Return on Index	Standard Deviation of Returns	Average Annual Return on T-Bills	Cumulative Return on Index
All days	7,802	11.83%	12.9%	6.16%	23.3
Exclude best 10 days	7,792	10.17	12.6	6.16	14.4
Exclude best 20 "	7,782	8.98	12.5	6.15	10.1
Exclude best 30 "	7,772	7.99	12.4	6.15	7.4
Exclude best 40 "	7,762	7.09	12.3	6.15	5.5
Exclude best 50 "	7,752	6.26	12.2	6.15	4.1
Exclude best 60 "	7,742	5.47	12.1	6.15	3.1
Exclude best 90 "	7,712	3.28	12.0	6.15	1.1
Exclude worst 10 days	7,792	14.06	12.2	6.16	44.8
Exclude worst 20 "	7,782	15.28	12.1	6.15	62.6
Exclude worst 30 "	7,772	16.36	12.0	6.15	83.4
Exclude worst 40	7,762	17.34	11.9	6.15	107.9
Exclude worst 50	7,752	18.28	11.8	6.15	137.5
Exclude worst 60 "	7,742	19.17	11.7	6.15	172.8
Exclude worst 90 "	7,712	21.72	11.6	6.14	325.4
Exclude best & worst 10	7,782	12.37	11.9	6.15	28.1
Exclude best & worst 20	7,762	12.36	11.6	6.15	28.0
Exclude best & worst 30	7,742	12.37	11.4	6.15	28.1
Exclude best & worst 40	7,722	12.37	11.2	6.15	28.0
Exclude best & worst 50	7,702	12.39	11.1	6.15	28.1
Exclude best & worst 60	7,682	12.40	10.9	6.15	28.0
Exclude best & worst 90	7,622	12.42	10.6	6.15	27.8

The value-weighted index of NYSE, AMEX, and NASDAQ stocks is used to measure the market returns. All returns and standard deviations are annualized by compounding the arithmetic average of the daily returns. Ending value measures the holding period returns to $10,000 invested at the beginning of the period. Hence, the cumulative return of 23.3 means that $1 would grow to $24.30 if invested continuously from January 1, 1963, to December 31, 1993.

Source: "Stock Market Extremes and Portfolio Performance," a study commissioned by Towneley Capital Management, Inc., and conducted by Professor H. Nejat Seyhun, University of Michigan. For the complete text of the study, see www.towneley.com.

Figure 14.7

Rewards and Penalties of Market Timing: Average Annual Return, 1926–1993

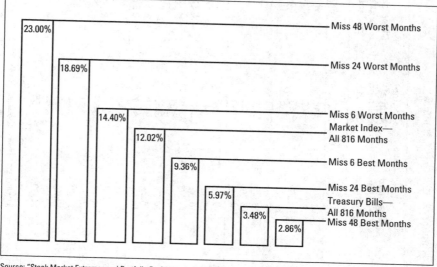

Source: "Stock Market Extremes and Portfolio Performance," a study commissioned by Towneley Capital Management, Inc., and conducted by Professor H. Nejat Seyhun, University of Michigan. For the complete text of the study, see www.towneley.com.

nomenon for other time periods.[8] Investing as a market timer might be described as months of boredom punctuated by days of sheer elation or sheer panic.

The final element in the Michigan study is also insightful. It traced the performance of a "perfect" market timer who made all the right decisions, and an "inept" market timer who made all the wrong decisions. The period covered was the 816 months from January 1, 1926, to December 31, 1993. The perfect timer would have transferred all funds into stocks during each of the 507 months when stocks had positive returns and transferred all funds into risk-free Treasury bills during the 309 months when stocks returns were negative, guessing right every time. The inept timer would have done exactly the opposite, guessing wrong every time.

Table 14.5 shows what would have happened. Starting with $1 in 1926, the perfect timer would have an ending portfolio in 1993 of $690 million. The inept timer would have turned $100 million in 1926 into $1000 in 1993. These two extremes represent the outer limits of what market timing can do. By contrast, a buy-and-hold

Table 14.4

Returns Excluding Extreme Monthly Observations for Period January 1, 1926 to December 31, 1993 (68 Years)

Condition	Number of Months	Average Annual Return on Index	Standard Deviation of Returns	Average Annual Return on T-Bills	Cumulative Return on Index
All months	816	12.02%	19.30%	3.48%	637.3
Exclude best 1 month	815	11.41	18.90	3.48	460.6
Exclude best 2 months	814	10.84	18.37	3.49	337.2
Exclude best 3 "	813	10.31	17.96	3.49	253.1
Exclude best 6 "	810	9.36	17.50	3.49	144.7
Exclude best 12 "	804	8.07	17.09	3.51	65.0
Exclude best 24 "	792	5.97	16.58	3.49	16.9
Exclude best 36 "	780	4.31	16.28	3.50	5.3
Exclude best 48 "	768	2.86	16.08	3.51	1.6
Exclude worst 1 month	815	12.51	19.05	3.48	898.0
Exclude worst 2 months	814	12.92	18.83	3.49	1,176.1
Exclude worst 3 "	813	13.30	18.62	3.49	1,516.1
Exclude worst 6 "	810	14.40	18.08	3.49	3,052.1
Exclude worst 12 "	804	15.99	17.51	3.51	7,850.1
Exclude worst 24 "	792	18.69	16.77	3.50	34,233.9
Exclude worst 36 "	780	20.96	16.27	3.52	106,522.9
Exclude worst 48 "	768	23.00	15.91	3.51	270,592.8
Exclude best & worst 1	814	11.90	18.51	3.49	649.2
Exclude best & worst 2	812	11.72	17.78	3.49	622.7
Exclude best & worst 3	810	11.58	17.13	3.50	603.0
Exclude best & worst 6	804	11.69	16.04	3.51	696.0
Exclude best & worst 12	792	11.92	14.93	3.55	810.3
Exclude best & worst 24	768	12.32	13.39	3.51	958.1
Exclude best & worst 36	744	12.73	12.37	3.54	1,051.6
Exclude best & worst 48	720	13.10	11.60	3.55	1,080.9

The value-weighted index of NYSE, AMEX, and NASDAQ stocks is used to measure the market returns. All returns and standard deviations are annualized by compounding the arithmetic average of monthly returns. Cumulative return measures the holding period dollar returns to $1 invested at the beginning of the period. Hence, the cumulative return of 637.3 means that $1 grows to $638.30 if invested continuously from January 1, 1926 to December 31, 1993.

Source: "Stock Market Extremes and Portfolio Performance," A study commissioned by Townley Capital Management, Inc. and conducted by Professor H. Nejat Seyhun, University of Michigan. For the complete text of the study, see www.towneley.com.

Table 14.5

Performance of Perfect Timer/Inept Timer for period January 1926 to December 1993 (816 Months)

Condition	Number of Stock Returns	Number of Risk-free Returns	Average Annual Return on Index	Standard Deviation of Returns	Cumulative Returns to $1
Perfect timer (see Note 1)	507	309	35.82%	12.4%	$690 million
Inept timer (see Note 2)	309	507	−15.03%	11.5%	(see Note 2)
Treasury bills – all months	—	816	3.38%	—	$9.20
Stock index – all months	816	—	12.02%	19.30%	$637.3

1. Perfect timer invests in the value-weighted index when returns are positive and in one-month Treasury bills when market returns are negative. From January 1926 to December 1993, there were 507 months when the value-weighted index had positive returns and 309 months when the value-weighted index had negative returns.
2. The inept timer does the converse, investing in Treasury bills when market returns are positive and in the market when market returns are negative. The inept timer would have converted $100 million in 1926 into $1000 by 1993.

Source: "Stock Market Extremes and Portfolio Performance," A study commissioned by Towneley Capital Management, Inc. and conducted by Professor H. Nejat Seyhun, University of Michigan. For the complete text of the study, see www.towneley.com.

strategy for Treasury bills would have returned $9.20 for each $1 invested, and a buy-and-hold strategy for stocks, $637.30 for each $1 invested.

These random jolts, which are unpredictable in their timing and their strength, appear to defy any systematic success in forecasting the market. It is difficult to prove that no mathematical equation will ever be discovered that can predict them, but as of now, market timing appears to be mathematically intractable. It is not really investing. It is gambling.

SEQUENCE RISK

Those Who Were Planning to Retire in 2001 or 2002 Know It Well

Yet another problem faced by forecasters is the problem of *sequence risk*. Not only does the average return over the period of time relevant to a client's goals need to be predicted accurately, but the actual sequence of returns if funds are being added to or withdrawn from the portfolio must also be predicted.

Recall the Beardstown Blunder, where the internal rate of return calculation was explained. In that case, the additions that the Beardstown Ladies made to their portfolio introduced a new external factor and created a dynamic situation that required a different way to calculate the return on the portfolio. The situation is no longer a static, closed system, and both the timing and the amount of the new money that was added to the portfolio each month has to be factored in (which they failed to do). The same thing is true if withdrawals are made. The precise pattern of cash flows and returns must be considered.

The source of the Beardstown confusion stems from the non-intuitive nature of the dynamic cash flow situations compared to the relatively intuitive nature of static situations, where no cash flows are involved. Most schoolchildren who have learned the multiplication table know that 2 times 3 is the same as 3 times 2. Both calculations equal 6. Mathematicians call this the commutative law of multiplication, meaning that you get the same result no matter what the order or sequence in which you multiply numbers.

Intuitively, it seems that the same thing should be true for investment calculations. If a portfolio of $100 invested today earns 10 percent this year and 20 percent next year, then it would grow to $132 at the end of the second year. If the sequence of returns were reversed, with a return of 20 percent the first year and 10 percent the second year, the result would be the same, $132. The basic calculation is multiplicative: $100 * 1.10 * 1.20 = $132 and $100 * 1.20 * 1.10 = $132. Intuition is right in this case because no other factors are involved. This is a static situation.

But intuition is wrong if additions to or withdrawals from the portfolio are being made. When external cash flows are involved, they introduce a new factor that breaks the commutative law and destroys the multiplicative equivalency. You will get different results depending on when the money is withdrawn, how much is withdrawn, and the sequence in which the returns occur, even when the average annual returns are identical and the volatility is the same. Average returns per year and their standard deviations are blind to the sequence of values from which they are calculated. This creates the problem of sequence risk. It is insidious because it is a hidden risk that most investors are unaware of until it happens to them.

To demonstrate this phenomenon, compare two identical portfolios with identical starting balances of $100 and identical fixed dollar withdrawals of $10, but a reversed sequence of returns.

Sequence A: The return is 10 percent in Year 1 and 20 percent in Year 2 (average = 15 percent)

Sequence B: The return is 20 percent in Year 1 and 10 percent in Year 2 (average = 15 percent)

Which sequence will have a higher ending value?

Sequence B wins. Sequence A starts with $100 and grows to $110 at the end of Year 1. Then $10 is withdrawn, say, for income, leaving the balance back at $100. This then grows to $120 at the end of Year 2.

Sequence B starts with $100 and grows to $120 at the end of Year 1. Then $10 is withdrawn, say, for income, leaving the balance at $110. This then grows to $121 at the end of Year 2.

Sequence B is better ($121 versus $120) because it produces a higher ending result. The explanation for this is not difficult to understand. You want the portfolio to grow faster before you take the money out rather than after. If it grows faster after you take the money out, this will do you no good. Extending this to retirees, they are in the process of withdrawing money regularly.[9] Therefore, it is in their best interests for the portfolio to grow most quickly while most of their money is still in the portfolio.

The opposite is true for younger people who are in their accumulation phase. They want the market to grow after they have put most of their money in, not before. It does them no good to have it grow before they have invested.

THE T. ROWE PRICE STUDY OF SEQUENCE RISK

Impact of Reversing the Actual 1969–1999 Record for the S&P 500

This simple example with $100 over 2 years yields only a small difference, $120 versus $121. But for large sums over long periods, the effects can be dramatic. T. Rowe Price made this point in a concise but compelling study.

T. Rowe Price, a mainstream investment company, demonstrated the significance of sequence risk in a study printed by the *Wall Street Journal* that used data from actual stock returns for the period 1969–1999 (see Table 14.6).[10] The study tracked the actual performance of a continually rebalanced portfolio (60 percent S&P 500 stocks, 30 percent bonds, 10 percent cash). Over the entire 30-year period, the average annual rate of return was about 11.73 percent (11.22 percent annualized), with a standard deviation of 10.69 percent. The growth rate was slower during the first half of the period than during the second half. The starting amount in the portfolio was $250,000. If no cash were withdrawn from or added at any time, it would have grown to $6,746,219.

Using actual market conditions over 31 years (1969–1999), the same portfolio of $250,000 (60 percent S&P stocks, 30 percent bonds, and 10 percent cash) was followed, but income was withdrawn annually, starting with $20,000 and increasing each year by 3 percent inflation. The $20,000 initial withdrawal corresponded to 8 percent of the starting value of the portfolio, but this percentage would change because the value of the portfolio changed from year to year and also because of the inflation adjustment.

The study projected that if the average rate had been steady each and every year, the portfolio would in theory have had an ending value of about $117,042. That never happened because the returns were not nice and steady. Instead, they varied from a loss of 14.12 percent (1973–1974) to a high of nearly 27.57 percent (1994–1995). Returns during the first half of the period (1969–1983) were weak, averaging only 8.00 percent. But they nearly doubled in the second half to 14.31 percent.

Table 14.6

Actual versus Reversed Sequence of Returns, 1969–1999
$250,000 Starting Value, $20,000 Withdrawals Increasing Annually
by 3 percent Inflation

	Actual Returns of Portfolio			Same Returns in Reversed Sequence	
Year	Return	Ending Balance	Year	Return	Ending Balance
1968		$250,000			$250,000
1969	−4.63%	$219,351	1	12.28%	$258,244
1970	8.36%	$215,367	2	21.09%	$287,763
1971	11.84%	$217,136	3	22.72%	$327,104
1972	13.18%	$221,019	4	14.72%	$350,182
1973	−6.93%	$184,752	5	27.57%	$418,011
1974	−14.12%	$138,754	6	−0.34%	$393,484
1975	24.84%	$143,407	7	9.68%	$405,380
1976	18.75%	$141,086	8	7.18%	$408,123
1977	−3.41%	$111,804	9	23.52%	$472,819
1978	5.98%	$90,834	10	1.93%	$455,345
1979	13.32%	$72,474	11	23.57%	$529,457
1980	21.75%	$54,531	12	12.52%	$564,594
1981	1.25%	$26,341	13	5.89%	$567,653
1982	22.88%	$0	14	16.55%	$627,369
1983	16.50%	$0	15	26.09%	$752,905
1984	9.13%	$0	16	9.13%	$787,641
1985	26.09%	$0	17	16.50%	$880,212
1986	16.55%	$0	18	22.88%	$1,040,984
1987	5.89%	$0	19	1.25%	$1,019,522
1988	12.52%	$0	20	21.75%	$1,198,570
1989	23.57%	$0	21	13.32%	$1,317,286
1990	1.93%	$0	22	5.98%	$1,356,628
1991	23.52%	$0	23	−3.41%	$1,273,352
1992	7.18%	$0	24	18.75%	$1,465,233
1993	9.68%	$0	25	24.84%	$1,778,442
1994	−0.34%	$0	26	−14.12%	$1,491,363
1995	27.57%	$0	27	−6.93%	$1,347,869
1996	14.72%	$0	28	13.18%	$1,475,237
1997	22.72%	$0	29	11.84%	$1,598,729
1998	21.09%	$0	30	8.36%	$1,681,311
1999	12.28%	$0	31	−4.63%	$1,557,169
Avg. Annual	11.73%			11.73%	
Annualized	11.22%			11.22%	
Std. Dev	10.69%			10.69%	
High	27.57%			27.57%	
Low −	14.12%			−14.12%	

Note: Returns shown are the averages for years 1969–1999, *not* just the years when the account had a balance.

Source: T. Rowe Price. (The portfolio was rebalanced to 60 percent S&P 500 stocks, 30 percent bonds, 10 percent cash; $20,000 was withdrawn in the first year, and this was increased by 3 percent inflation each year thereafter.)

Table 14.6 and Figure 14.8 demonstrate the results. The low growth in the early years was devastating. The portfolio would never have recovered from the early losses. As the third column in Table 14.6 shows, it would have run out of money towards the end of 1982, less than 15 years after the initial withdrawal. This is what actually happened during the 1969–1999 period.

However, if the sequence of returns had been reversed, the impact on the portfolio would have been radically different. Instead of being depleted within 15 years, it would have continued to grow over the entire 30-year period and reached an ending value of $1,557,169. The difference is due entirely to sequence because the average rate of return and standard deviation would have remained the same, at 11.73 percent and 10.69 percent, respectively.

This study by T. Rowe Price should make the importance of sequence risk clear. It is not just the up-and-down fluctuations that determine what happens to a portfolio when dollar withdrawals are being made. The sequence in which the up-and-down movements occurs must also be considered.

Figure 14.8

Actual versus Reversed Sequence of Returns, 1969–1999
$250,000 Starting Value, $20,000 Initial Withdrawal, Increasing
Annually by 3 Percent Inflation

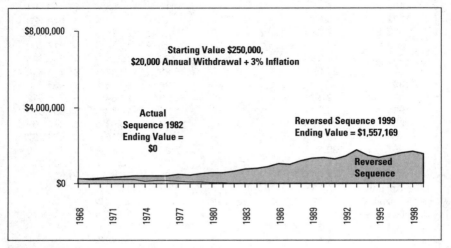

Source: Table 14.6.

Advisers who fail to make their clients aware of this risk may lose those clients. Many people who had planned to retire in 2001 or 2002 could not do so. They had to postpone their retirement because the declines in the market would have had started them off in a very bad situation. Many of them were no doubt disappointed and angry. How many of them switched advisers will never be known, but it is unlikely that none did.

HOW TO AVOID THE SEQUENCING PROBLEM

Two Solutions: Perfect Forecasting or Asset Dedication

There are two ways to avoid the problem of sequencing: accurate short-term forecasting or asset dedication. As was pointed out earlier in this chapter, accurate short-term predictions from the perfect market timer would have turned $1 into $690 million between 1926 and 1993. With perfect forecasts, you would soon be rich enough never to have to worry about financial matters again. Hope springs eternal, of course, but basing the financial foundation of your retirement on the prospect of accurate forecasts is like dancing with the devil—you will ultimately get kicked where it really hurts!

Asset dedication is the other way to avoid the sequencing problem. As described in Chapter 3, it avoids the sequencing problem by splitting the portfolio into two distinct portions, one for income and the other for growth

The income portion avoids the sequencing problem by holding precisely timed bonds to maturity. This immunizes the portfolio from both volatility risk and sequence risk. Both are rendered harmless.

The risk of the growth portion of the asset dedication portfolio is reduced because there are no withdrawals, at least during the fixed horizon. In the case of a fixed 10-year horizon, stocks will be sold only once in a decade. During the intervening years, the fact that there are zero withdrawals again renders volatility and sequence risk nearly impotent. It is a simple solution, but it works.

THE UGLY—STOCK MARKET SCAMS

True Predators

In *Matchstick Men*, a 2003 movie about con artists, the main character (played by Nicolas Cage) defends what he does by saying that he does not force people to give him money. They do it willingly, so he does not feel bad about taking it. In a similar movie, *The Flim-Flam Man* (1967), the main character (played by George C. Scott) makes the same point by quoting the old adage that you cannot cheat an honest man.

Con artists can make a living in the financial community as well. In one of the most common stock market forecasting scams, the predators start by advertising on TV, setting up a booth at a money show, posting junk mail, or sending out e-mails ("spam-scams") to names they buy from mailing list companies, telemarketers, and so on. In their pitch, they extol the virtues of a new system for predicting the future behavior of a stock. For anyone who signs up, they will prove it works by sending you its predictions.

Assume the scam artist gets 10,000 people to agree to receive the predictions. Half of the mail pieces will predict that the market or a stock will be higher in 2 weeks, and half will predict that it will be lower. If the stock goes up, then the 5000 who received the correct "forecast" receive the next mailing. In the third round, 2500 will again predict that the stock or the market will be up, and 2500 will predict that it will be down. The 2500 that receive the correct "prediction"—whatever it is—will again receive the next mailing. The pattern is not hard to understand.

After about five or six correct predictions in a row, the perpetrators give all those who received the sequence of correct "forecasts" a chance to buy the system. Most of them won't buy it, but some will. As long as they can cover their costs plus enough profit to make it worth their while, the organizers of this scam will pull it as often as they can.[11]

ETHICAL VIOLATIONS?

You Be the Judge

Another, less egregious example is the situation in which someone is made slightly better off, but is misled to believe that nothing better could have been done. The justification for this sort of deceit comes from the fact that the client might, in fact, be better off than he or she would have been otherwise. For example, assume that an elderly woman comes into a bank to withdraw money from a passbook savings account that she has had for 30 years and that returns 1 percent per year. Assume that she has $50,000 in her savings account.

The teller guides her to the office or desk of a financial adviser who has been hired by the bank to deal with customers like her. The adviser gains her confidence and puts her money into a bank-managed mutual fund that charges a hefty load and management fee. Assume that the load is 3 percent the first year, management fees also amount to 3 percent every year, and the fund earns 7 percent per year. During the first year, she will net only her usual 1 percent (7 percent less the 3 percent front-end load and the 3 percent management fee). After the first year, she nets 4 percent, which is better than the 1 percent she was getting before.

Is the bank cheating her? This may not be a scam, but she could have earned much more if the bank adviser had steered her toward an index fund or suggested that she see an adviser on her own. It also ignores the fact that if the bank's fund manager is a market timer, she could be in real trouble. No doubt the bank would deny any violation of fiduciary responsibility. Its adviser made the decision convenient for her, gave her information that she otherwise would not have had, increased her annual income after the first year (probably), and so on. But has the bank really done the best for her? Has it acted with the same level of fiduciary responsibility of care and loyalty as is normally required in an agency relationship between an adviser and a client?[12] If traders at the stock exchange failed to get the lowest possible price for a buy order, they would be considered in breach of their ethical standards and lose their jobs. If real estate agents fail to negotiate the best price they can get for their clients, they are considered to be in violation of their ethical standards.

The laws regulating what banks, insurance companies, and brokerage houses can do in terms of handling people's financial matters have been changed in recent years to encourage competition. While removing monopoly power is nearly always a good thing, one of the unresolved areas is the issue of fiduciary responsibility. Acting as an agent on behalf of a person in managing that person's wealth is far different in scope, scale, and accountability from simply handling that person's checking and savings accounts. The banking industry, staid and conservative throughout its history, is used to being held accountable under the traditional contract law that governs relationships between customer and vendor. Responsibilities between the parties in simple circumstances are modest from a legal standpoint. But agency relationships represent a much more inclusive set of responsibilities. The new legislation allows banks, insurance companies, and others in the financial community to begin to serve in agency relationships with their customers, who now attain the status of clients. This has created an extremely fertile environment for conflicts of interest.

A more dramatic way of saying this is that it has created an accident waiting to happen. The scandals of corporate fraud, stock trading, and fund management that have rocked Wall Street in the past few years may begin to appear on Main Street as local banks try to cash in on the new liberalization and realize how ignorant most of their customers really are when it comes to investing. Most people right now are circumspect with regard to corporations and stockbrokers but still trust their bankers. Will the bankers and insurance companies be able to resist the temptation to take advantage of this trust? Which would you bet on to become the dominant force—integrity or greed?

CONCLUSION

Two important things to understand from this chapter are that holding bonds to maturity is the closest thing we have to a sure bet in prediction accuracy and that forecasting stock returns faces many obstacles, especially short-term forecasts. Unfortunately, the technical inability to produce accurate predictions is overwhelmed by the public's emotional desire to believe that this is possible.

What should an investor do in light of the bad news regarding market predictions?

The simplest answer is to take steps to avoid investment strategies that appear to rely on market timing or on picking which stocks will rise more than average. Many investors have gotten this message already, and there has been a steady progression away from investing in individual stocks. First came the mutual funds, which sought to avoid risk by diversifying the stocks held in the portfolio.

Next came the index funds, which did not attempt to time the market or pick stocks, but rather were content to simply tie the market. This was an implicit recognition of the difficulties of attempting to predict the future performance of either individual stocks or the overall market. What is embarrassing for the fund managers is the fact that history has shown that index funds actually end up beating most of the mutual fund managers most of the time just by tying the market.

Now comes asset dedication, the next generation in the progress of portfolio management. It takes advantage of the best that both bonds and index funds have to offer and essentially solves the riddle of how much to put into each without using arbitrary fixed formulas. It renders stock market fluctuations impotent over the entire planning horizon, which is tailored specifically to the need and goals of individual investors by harnessing the power of today's technology. It is easy to understand and simple to implement.

What are you waiting for?

NOTES

1. An excellent web site that covers all the major aspects of forecasting principles is maintained by Professor J. Scott Armstrong of the Wharton School of Business at the University of Pennsylvania, http://www-marketing.wharton.upenn.edu/forecast/welcome.html.

2. In theory, the federal government will never default on its loans because it technically has the authority to simply print the money. Obviously, it is improbable that it would do so because this would generate manifold economic problems that would signal the imminent collapse of the economy, similar to what happened in Germany after World War I.

3. Treasury bills have several different maturities, all within 1 year. Most analysts use the rates on those that mature in 30 days or 90 days for returns on cash.

4. Data points that appear out of place, or "outliers," can create havoc in statistical analyses because of their ability to distort basic trends, characteristics, and interpretations. Each outlier must be patiently and tediously verified before the rest of the analysis can begin. It also helps to have raw data in a suitable computational form.

5. As mentioned in Chapter 12, the three most common averages are the mean, median and mode. Nearly all statistical estimation theory centers on the mean. All three figures have different statistical properties, but for symmetrical distributions, all three are the same.

6. "Stock Market Extremes and Portfolio Performance," a study commissioned by Towneley Capital Management, Inc., and conducted by Professor H. Nejat Seyhun, University of Michigan. For the complete text of the study, see www.towneley.com. The origin of the study, reported on Towneley's web site, is an interesting story in itself.

7. The figures and tables from Towneley are reprinted directly and show the average annual returns as opposed to the annualized returns, although the figures used were annualized based on the number of trading days involved. With the biggest days dropped, the time spans no longer represented a perfectly consecutive succession of days, and the breaks made the calculations tedious and cumbersome. Thus, the returns are reported as average annual returns rather than as single annualized returns, which would be slightly lower than those shown in their tables.

8. The article "You Can't Time the Stock Market Successfully," published by TIAA-CREF in *The Participant* (February 1996), listed a number of similar studies: (1) A study by Nicholas–Applegate Capital Management (www.nacm.com) indicated that missing the 20 best trading days during the 1983–1992 bull market would have cut gains in half. (2) A study by Sanford C. Bernstein & Company on the S&P 500 index from 1926 to 1993 using monthly returns found that in the 60 best months of the

816-month period, returns averaged 11 percent, whereas while in the other 756 months, they averaged only 0.01 percent (one basis point). A summary of a representative 10-year period is given on the Highland Professional Group web site, http://www.4hpg.com/hpg//hfm/Investment_Strategy.asp. (3) Hulbert Financial Services (www.hulbertdigest.com) tracks the performance of the advice of nearly 200 market-timing newsletters. It periodically presents studies demonstrating the futility of timing. One such study found that over the 5-year period ending November 30, 1994, the market timers' advice resulted in a lower return on average (7.1 percent) than simply leaving the money in a Wilshire 5000 index fund (8.9 percent) over the same period.

9. A fixed dollar withdrawal each month, like a paycheck, is the common situation for most retirees. The majority of their monthly expenses are fixed. They have some discretion over how much they spend on food, gifts, and leisure pursuits, but most of the big-ticket items (mortgage, insurance, medicines, and so on) can be changed only by making major life changes. It turns out that if a strict proportional withdrawal is made—say, 4 percent of the total portfolio value each year—then sequence does not matter. But this would mean that the withdrawals would have to match the exact fluctuations of the market. It might be easy to spend more when the market is going up, but if the market drops by 20 percent, most people would find it difficult to cut back this much.

10. Earl C. Gottschalk Jr., "After the Fall," *Wall Street Journal*, March 19, 2001. The T. Rowe Price study is presented as a sidebar to the main article ("When Averages Don't Work").

11. John Allen Paulos described this scheme in his book *Innumeracy* (New York: Vintage Books [a Division of Random House], 1990).

12. Ethical considerations surrounding these issues are covered at a very deep level in Lester A Myers, Ph.D., J.D., CPA, "Accounting for Accountability: A Deontological Foundation for Corporate Financial Disclosure" (unpublished monograph). (Professor Myers can be reached at ethics@mindspring.com). Professor Myers provided valuable insights for this section.

1

Long-Term Bond Ratings

Table A1.1

Moody's	S&P	Fitch	Definitions
Aaa	AAA	AAA	Prime. Maximum safety
Aa1	AA+	AA+	High grade, high quality
Aa2	AA	AA	
Aa3	AA−	AA−	
A1	A+	A+	Upper medium grade
A2	A	A	
A3	A−	A−	
Baa1	BBB+	BBB+	Lower medium grade
Baa2	BBB	BBB	
Baa3	BBB−	BBB−	
Ba1	BB+	BB+	Noninvestment grade
Ba2	BB	BB	Speculative
Ba3	BB−	BB−	
B1	B+	B+	Highly speculative
B2	B	B	
B3	B−	−	
Caa1	CCC+	CCC	Substantial risk
Caa2	CCC	-	In poor standing
Caa3	CCC−	-	
Ca	-	-	Extremely speculative
C	-	-	May be in default
-	-	DDD	Default
-	-	DD	
-	D	D	
-	-	-	

Moody's	Moody's Investor Service (www.moodys.com)	1-212-553-1653
S&P	Standard & Poor's Corp. (www.standardandpoors.com)	1-212-438-7307
Fitch	Fitch Ratings (http://www.fitchratings.com/)	1-212-908-0500

Important Note: Information herein is believed to be reliable but Bondsonline Group, Inc., does not warrant its completeness or accuracy.

Source: Bondsonline Group, Inc. (www.bondsonline.com).

APPENDIX 2

The Safety of Bonds Based on Historical Default Rates

Table 14.1 presented the probability of meeting all projected cash flows for both U.S. Treasury bonds and bonds that were rated in the top two tiers of safety based on the historical record from 1970–2000 by Moody's, one of the premier rating agencies. Additional results are presented here, again based on reports issued by Moody's (see p. 292 for corporate bonds; p. 295 for muni bonds).

CORPORATE BONDS

Table A2.1

Probability of Meeting All Projected Cash Flows for Corporate Bonds, 1970–2000, Based on Cumulative Default Rates over 1 to 10 Years from Date of First Issue

| | Investment Grade | | | | Speculative Grade | | | Combined Invest. Grade | Combined Specul. Grade | All Corporates |
	Aaa	Aa	A	Baa	Ba	B	Caa-C			
Year 1	100.0%	100.0%	100.0%	99.9%	98.7%	93.8%	80.1%	99.9%	95.8%	98.7%
Year 2	100.0%	100.0%	99.9%	99.6%	96.5%	86.5%	66.2%	99.8%	91.0%	97.2%
Year 3	100.0%	99.9%	99.8%	99.2%	93.9%	80.0%	55.6%	99.6%	86.6%	95.9%
Year 4	100.0%	99.8%	99.7%	98.6%	91.2%	74.4%	47.4%	99.4%	82.8%	94.7%
Year 5	99.9%	99.7%	99.5%	98.1%	88.6%	69.4%	42.2%	99.2%	79.4%	93.7%
Year 6	99.8%	99.6%	99.4%	97.6%	86.2%	65.2%	36.9%	98.9%	76.5%	92.8%
Year 7	99.7%	99.5%	99.2%	97.0%	84.3%	61.2%	32.7%	98.6%	74.0%	92.1%
Year 8	99.6%	99.4%	99.0%	96.4%	82.4%	58.2%	28.6%	98.3%	71.9%	91.4%
Year 9	99.5%	99.3%	98.8%	95.8%	80.5%	55.4%	25.5%	98.0%	69.9%	90.8%
Year 10	99.3%	99.2%	98.5%	95.1%	78.7%	52.6%	23.2%	97.7%	68.0%	90.2%

Source: Moody's U.S. Municipal Bond Rating Scale, Special Comment, November 2002, Report Number 76553. © Moody's Investors Service, Inc. and/or its affiliates. Reprinted with permission. All Rights Reserved.

Table A2.2

Probability of Meeting All Projected Cash Flows for Corporate Bonds, 1920–1999, Based on Cumulative Default Rates over 1 to 10 Years from Date of First Issue

	Investment Grade					Speculative Grade		
	Aaa	Aa	A	Baa	Combined	Ba	B	Combined*
Year 1	100.00%	99.92%	99.92%	99.70%	99.84%	98.57%	95.52%	96.65%
Year 2	100.00%	99.75%	99.73%	99.06%	99.51%	96.55%	90.84%	93.24%
Year 3	99.98%	99.59%	99.40%	98.27%	99.07%	94.43%	86.27%	90.02%
Year 4	99.91%	99.39%	99.03%	97.38%	98.57%	92.20%	82.44%	87.11%
Year 5	99.80%	99.03%	98.63%	96.49%	98.03%	89.96%	79.11%	84.43%
Year 6	99.69%	98.63%	98.22%	95.55%	97.46%	87.91%	76.32%	82.09%
Year 7	99.57%	98.19%	97.77%	94.66%	96.88%	86.10%	73.81%	80.04%
Year 8	99.38%	97.74%	97.37%	93.79%	96.32%	84.27%	71.68%	78.11%
Year 9	99.17%	97.33%	96.90%	92.88%	95.73%	82.69%	69.78%	76.41%
Year 10	98.91%	96.90%	96.39%	92.08%	95.15%	80.95%	68.10%	74.69%

*Combined includes all speculative bonds rated Ba, B, Caa, or lower.

Source: Moody's, Historical Default Rates of Corporate Bond Issuers, 1920–1999, January 2000 (www.moodyskmv.com/research/whitepaper/52453.pdf). © Moody's Investor Service, Inc. and/or its affiliates. Reprinted with permission. All Rights Reserved.

Figure A2.1

Trailing 12-Month All-Corporate Issuer Default Rate, 1920–1999

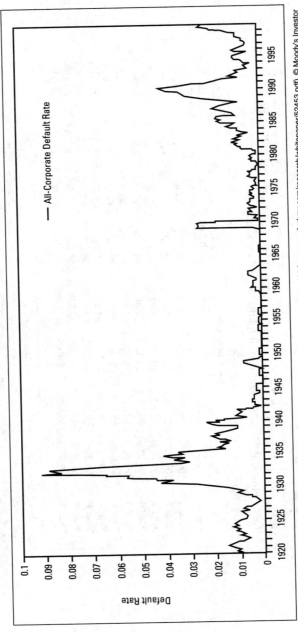

Source: Moody's, *Historical Default Rates of Corporate Bond Issuers, 1920–1999,* January 2000, p. 11 (www.moodyskmv.com/research/whitepaper/52453.pdf). © Moody's Investor Service, Inc. and/or its affiliates. Reprinted with permission. All Rights Reserved.

Figure A2.2

5-, 10-, 15-, and 20-Year Average Cumulative Default Rates,
Corporate Bonds, 1920–1999: Correlation between Ratings and Default Risk
for Holding Periods of Up to 20 Years

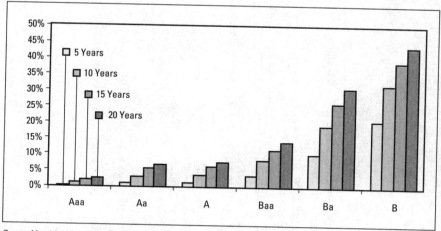

Source: Moody's, *Historical Default Rates of Corporate Bond Issuers, 1920–1999*, January 2000, p. 16
(www.moodyskmv.com/research/whitepaper/52453.pdf). © Moody's Investor Service, Inc. and/or its affiliates. Reprinted
with permission. All Rights Reserved.

MUNI BONDS

Table A2.3 on p. 296 shows the probability of meeting all projected
cash flows from 1970 to 2000, based on 28,099 separate issuers,
among whom 18 had any type of late payment of interest or less
than full payment of principal. None of the 18 was a general obligation, water/sewer, or public university issue.

Table A2.3

Probability of Meeting All Projected Cash Flows for Municipal Bonds, 1970–2000, Based on Cumulative Default Rates over 1 to 10 Years from Date of First Issue

	Investment Grade				Speculative Grade			Combined Invest. Grade	Combined Specul. Grade	All Munis
	Aaa	Aa	A	Baa	Ba	B	Caa-C			
Year 1	100.0%	100.0%	100.0%	100.0%	99.9%	99.2%	90.9%	100.0%	99.6%	100.0%
Year 2	100.0%	100.0%	100.0%	100.0%	99.8%	98.1%	89.5%	100.0%	99.3%	100.0%
Year 3	100.0%	100.0%	100.0%	100.0%	99.8%	97.1%	89.5%	100.0%	99.2%	100.0%
Year 4	100.0%	100.0%	100.0%	100.0%	99.7%	96.6%	89.5%	100.0%	99.0%	100.0%
Year 5	100.0%	100.0%	100.0%	100.0%	99.6%	96.0%	89.5%	100.0%	98.8%	100.0%
Year 6	100.0%	100.0%	100.0%	100.0%	99.4%	96.0%	89.5%	100.0%	98.7%	100.0%
Year 7	100.0%	100.0%	100.0%	100.0%	99.2%	96.0%	89.5%	100.0%	98.5%	100.0%
Year 8	100.0%	100.0%	100.0%	100.0%	98.9%	96.0%	89.5%	100.0%	98.3%	100.0%
Year 9	100.0%	100.0%	100.0%	99.9%	98.8%	96.0%	89.5%	100.0%	98.2%	100.0%
Year 10	100.0%	100.0%	100.0%	99.9%	98.7%	96.0%	89.5%	100.0%	98.1%	100.0%

Historical Comparisons by Decade—Middle Period (1947–1984)

Table A3.1

Asset Dedication versus Asset Allocation: Ending Portfolio Value Comparisons for Ms. Smith, 29 Ten-Year Spans, 1947–1984 ($600,000 Initial Investment, $30,000 Annual Withdrawal plus 4 Percent Inflation)

	Ending Values for Ms. Smith's Portfolio, Decades 1947–1956 to 1975–1984					
Decade	Dedicated Portfolios	Stk/Bnd 70/30	Stk/Bnd 60/40	Stk/Bnd 50/50	Stk/Bnd 40/60	Stk/Bnd 30/70
1947 to 1956	**$1,417,499**	$1,265,237	$1,060,090	$879,739	$721,789	$584,022
1948 to 1957	**$1,458,346**	$1,395,229	$1,171,691	$973,952	$799,673	$646,673
1949 to 1958	**$1,838,448**	$1,688,149	$1,379,990	$1,114,816	$887,859	$694,759
1950 to 1959	**$1,584,254**	$1,533,302	$1,272,436	$1,044,015	$844,953	$672,374
1951 to 1960	**$1,329,299**	$1,301,786	$1,111,123	$939,791	$786,355	$649,452
1952 to 1961	**$1,307,749**	$1,279,725	$1,098,582	$934,993	$787,725	$655,603
1953 to 1962	$1,128,882	**$1,167,948**	$1,023,525	$889,689	$765,999	$652,018
1954 to 1963	$1,287,740	**$1,353,481**	$1,166,006	$995,495	$840,920	$701,284
1955 to 1964	$1,031,862	**$1,051,482**	$931,552	$820,408	$717,629	$622,804
1956 to 1965	**$923,196**	$920,333	$829,316	$743,818	$663,632	$588,552
1957 to 1966	$856,386	**$890,988**	$814,688	$741,343	$670,956	$603,519
1958 to 1967	$915,982	**$961,535**	$861,422	$767,173	$678,602	$595,521
1959 to 1968	**$788,731**	$782,488	$726,294	$672,525	$621,135	$572,073
1960 to 1969	$651,802	**$698,281**	*$658,176*	$618,703	$579,918	$541,871
1961 to 1970	$653,507	**$694,506**	*$658,065*	$621,782	$585,719	$549,941
1962 to 1971	$643,621	**$670,920**	*$644,173*	$617,156	$589,922	$562,525
1963 to 1972	$743,192	**$764,315**	$717,930	$672,481	$628,020	$584,595
1964 to 1973	$539,084	**$582,506**	*$572,239*	*$561,002*	*$548,834*	$535,775
1965 to 1974	$386,662	*$429,421*	*$443,109*	*$456,164*	*$468,534*	**$480,170**
1966 to 1975	$491,604	*$497,421*	*$510,948*	*$523,206*	*$534,140*	**$543,698**
1967 to 1976	$533,851	*$569,655*	*$576,593*	*$581,942*	*$585,682*	**$587,803**
1968 to 1977	$458,117	*$490,672*	*$512,505*	*$533,493*	*$553,530*	**$572,507**
1969 to 1978	$483,875	$467,724	*$494,031*	*$519,440*	*$543,827*	**$567,073**
1970 to 1979	$693,354	*$703,907*	*$708,190*	**$710,139**	*$709,784*	*$707,168*
1971 to 1980	**$688,417**	$632,887	$627,596	$619,950	$610,076	$598,111
1972 to 1981	**$597,277**	$559,490	$563,796	$565,679	$565,175	$562,334
1973 to 1982	**$699,512**	$604,664	$622,489	$637,507	$649,676	$658,967
1974 to 1983	**$975,600**	$891,439	$872,572	$851,235	$827,604	$801,858
1975 to 1984	$1,302,627	**$1,314,309**	$1,234,717	$1,156,567	$1,079,968	$1,005,024

Note: Bold indicates highest value (see Chapter 4 for summary); italics indicate return higher than that on the asset dedication portfolio.

Table A3.2

Asset Dedication versus Asset Allocation: Total Returns (IRR) for Ms. Smith, 29 Ten-Year Spans, 1947–1984 ($600,000 Initial Investment, $30,000 Annual Withdrawal plus 4 Percent Inflation)

Internal Rate of Return for Ms. Smith's Portfolio, 1947–1956 to 1975–1984

Decade	Dedicated Portfolios	Stk/Bnd 70/30	Stk/Bnd 60/40	Stk/Bnd 50/50	Stk/Bnd 40/60	Stk/Bnd 30/70
1947 to 1956	**12.1%**	11.1%	9.7%	8.3%	6.8%	5.3%
1948 to 1957	**12.3%**	11.9%	10.5%	9.0%	7.6%	6.0%
1949 to 1958	**14.3%**	13.6%	11.9%	10.1%	8.3%	6.5%
1950 to 1959	**13.0%**	12.7%	11.2%	9.6%	8.0%	6.3%
1951 to 1960	**11.5%**	11.4%	10.1%	8.8%	7.4%	6.0%
1952 to 1961	**11.4%**	11.2%	10.0%	8.7%	7.4%	6.1%
1953 to 1962	10.2%	**10.5%**	9.4%	8.4%	7.2%	6.1%
1954 to 1963	11.3%	**11.7%**	10.5%	9.2%	7.9%	6.6%
1955 to 1964	9.5%	**9.6%**	8.7%	7.7%	6.8%	5.8%
1956 to 1965	**8.6%**	8.6%	7.8%	7.0%	6.2%	5.4%
1957 to 1966	8.1%	**8.4%**	7.7%	7.0%	6.3%	5.5%
1958 to 1967	8.6%	**8.9%**	8.1%	7.2%	6.4%	5.4%
1959 to 1968	**7.4%**	7.4%	6.8%	6.3%	5.7%	5.2%
1960 to 1969	6.1%	**6.6%**	*6.1%*	5.7%	5.3%	4.8%
1961 to 1970	6.1%	**6.5%**	*6.1%*	5.7%	5.3%	4.9%
1962 to 1971	6.0%	**6.3%**	*6.0%*	5.7%	5.4%	5.1%
1963 to 1972	7.0%	**7.2%**	6.8%	6.3%	5.8%	5.3%
1964 to 1973	4.8%	**5.3%**	*5.2%*	*5.0%*	*4.9%*	*4.7%*
1965 to 1974	2.7%	*3.3%*	*3.5%*	*3.7%*	*3.8%*	**4.0%**
1966 to 1975	4.2%	*4.2%*	*4.4%*	*4.6%*	*4.7%*	**4.8%**
1967 to 1976	4.7%	*5.1%*	*5.2%*	*5.3%*	*5.3%*	**5.4%**
1968 to 1977	3.7%	*4.1%*	*4.4%*	*4.7%*	*4.9%*	**5.2%**
1969 to 1978	4.1%	3.8%	*4.2%*	*4.5%*	*4.8%*	**5.1%**
1970 to 1979	6.5%	*6.6%*	*6.7%*	**6.7%**	*6.7%*	*6.7%*
1971 to 1980	**6.5%**	5.9%	5.8%	5.7%	5.6%	5.5%
1972 to 1981	**5.5%**	5.0%	5.1%	5.1%	5.1%	5.1%
1973 to 1982	**6.6%**	5.5%	5.8%	5.9%	6.0%	6.1%
1974 to 1983	**9.1%**	8.4%	8.2%	8.0%	7.8%	7.6%
1975 to 1984	11.4%	**11.4%**	10.9%	10.4%	9.9%	9.3%

Note: Bold indicates the highest return (see Chapter 4 for summary); italics indicate a return higher than that on the asset dedication portfolio.

Source: Table A3.1.

Historical Comparisons by Decade—Earliest Period (1926–1955)

Table A4.1

Asset Dedication versus Asset Allocation: Ending Portfolio Value Comparisons for Ms. Smith, 21 Ten-Year Spans, 1926–1935 to 1946–1955 ($600,000 Initial Investment, $30,000 Annual Withdrawal plus 4 Percent Inflation)

	Ending Values for Ms. Smith's Portfolio, 1926–1935 through 1946–1955					
Decade	Dedicated Portfolios	Stk/Bnd 70/30	Stk/Bnd 60/40	Stk/Bnd 50/50	Stk/Bnd 40/60	Stk/Bnd 30/70
1926 to 1935	$510,887	*$596,574*	*$612,574*	**$615,486**	*$605,796*	*$584,322*
1927 to 1936	$583,057	*$644,958*	**$657,746**	*$654,858*	*$637,420*	*$606,903*
1928 to 1937	$269,735	*$308,325*	*$357,298*	*$399,214*	*$432,492*	**$455,813**
1929 to 1938	$220,460	$147,260	$212,319	$275,017	$333,515	**$386,016**
1930 to 1939	$236,902	$187,440	*$249,688*	*$307,465*	*$359,067*	**$402,920**
1931 to 1940	$282,196	*$312,335*	*$357,449*	*$395,585*	*$425,611*	**$446,577**
1932 to 1941	$538,254	**$728,076**	*$716,842*	*$696,950*	*$668,595*	*$632,102*
1933 to 1942	$713,599	**$935,206**	*$880,342*	*$817,379*	*$747,623*	*$672,421*
1934 to 1943	$502,764	**$576,825**	*$574,388*	*$565,711*	*$551,130*	*$531,037*
1935 to 1944	$714,315	**$825,295**	*$772,292*	*$715,041*	*$654,657*	*$592,177*
1936 to 1945	**$630,638**	$589,550	$574,570	$554,247	$529,469	$501,073
1937 to 1946	**$423,653**	$358,479	$375,222	$386,895	$393,740	$396,023
1938 to 1947	$669,238	**$700,165**	$650,533	$601,346	$552,794	$505,055
1939 to 1948	$613,403	**$624,609**	$586,830	$548,648	$510,242	$471,784
1940 to 1949	$714,693	**$718,835**	$661,216	$604,715	$549,545	$495,902
1941 to 1950	**$1,102,893**	$1,072,727	$929,103	$798,056	$678,984	$571,276
1942 to 1951	**$1,389,738**	$1,328,701	$1,116,078	$928,043	$762,514	$617,516
1943 to 1952	**$1,275,251**	$1,211,635	$1,027,600	$863,426	$717,568	$588,547
1944 to 1953	**$1,103,910**	$1,072,447	$923,579	$788,257	$665,682	$555,070
1945 to 1954	**$1,353,711**	$1,227,398	$1,037,362	$867,804	$717,266	$584,329
1946 to 1955	**$1,161,155**	$961,411	$829,224	$709,277	$600,896	$503,405

Note: Bold indicates the highest value (see Chapter 4 for summary).; italics indicate a return higher than that on the asset dedication portfolio.

Table A4.2

Asset Dedication versus Asset Allocation: Total Returns (IRR) for Ms. Smith, 21 Ten-Year Spans, 1926–1935 to 1946–1955 ($600,000 Initial Investment, $30,000 Annual Withdrawal plus 4 Percent Inflation)

			Internal Rates of Return for Ms. Smith's Portfolio, 1926–1935 through 1946–1955			
Decade	Dedicated Portfolios	Stk/Bnd 70/30	Stk/Bnd 60/40	Stk/Bnd 50/50	Stk/Bnd 40/60	Stk/Bnd 30/70
1926 to 1935	4.4%	*5.5%*	*5.6%*	**5.7%**	*5.6%*	*5.3%*
1927 to 1936	5.3%	*6.0%*	**6.1%**	*6.1%*	*5.9%*	*5.6%*
1928 to 1937	0.6%	*1.3%*	*2.2%*	*2.8%*	*3.3%*	**3.7%**
1929 to 1938	−0.4%	−2.2%	−0.6%	*0.7%*	*1.8%*	**2.6%**
1930 to 1939	−0.1%	−1.2%	*0.2%*	*1.3%*	*2.2%*	**2.9%**
1931 to 1940	0.9%	*1.4%*	*2.2%*	*2.8%*	*3.2%*	**3.5%**
1932 to 1941	4.8%	**6.9%**	*6.8%*	*6.5%*	*6.3%*	*5.9%*
1933 to 1942	6.7%	**8.7%**	*8.3%*	*7.7%*	*7.1%*	6.3%
1934 to 1943	4.3%	**5.2%**	*5.2%*	*5.1%*	*4.9%*	*4.7%*
1935 to 1944	6.7%	**7.8%**	*7.3%*	*6.7%*	6.1%	5.4%
1936 to 1945	**5.8%**	5.4%	5.2%	5.0%	4.6%	4.3%
1937 to 1946	**3.2%**	2.2%	2.5%	2.7%	2.8%	2.8%
1938 to 1947	6.3%	**6.6%**	6.1%	5.5%	4.9%	4.3%
1939 to 1948	5.6%	**5.8%**	5.3%	4.9%	4.4%	3.9%
1940 to 1949	6.7%	**6.8%**	6.2%	5.5%	4.9%	4.2%
1941 to 1950	**10.0%**	9.8%	8.7%	7.5%	6.4%	5.2%
1942 to 1951	**11.9%**	11.5%	10.1%	8.7%	7.2%	5.7%
1943 to 1952	**11.2%**	10.8%	9.5%	8.1%	6.8%	5.4%
1944 to 1953	**10.0%**	9.8%	8.6%	7.4%	6.2%	5.0%
1945 to 1954	**11.7%**	10.9%	9.5%	8.2%	6.8%	5.3%
1946 to 1955	**10.4%**	8.9%	7.8%	6.7%	5.5%	4.3%

Note: Bold indicates the highest return (see Chapter 4 for summary); italics indicate a return higher than that on the asset dedication portfolio.

Source: Table A4.1.

5

IRS Rules and Regulations on Individual Retirement Accounts (IRAs)

The rules and regulations on IRAs are given in IRS Publication 590, a 100-page document. As legislation changes tax laws, this publication changes. That is why it is best to consult with a knowledgeable adviser in this field. Advisers of this type can provide real value for the fees they charge.

Figure A5.1 shows Table 1-2 from Publication 590, taken from the IRS web site. It indicates the rules associated with the deductibility of contributions to traditional IRAs for those people who are covered by a retirement plan at work. Figure A5.2 does the same thing for those who are not covered at work. Figure A5.3 provides the life expectancy table that is most commonly used to determine how much must be withdrawn from an IRA after age 70.5. For instance, a person aged 76 must withdraw $\frac{1}{22}$ or 4.5 percent of the value of her portfolio at the end of the previous year as taxable income.

Figure A5.1

Table 1–2. Effect of Modified AGI[1] on Deduction If You Are Covered by a Retirement Plan at Work

If you are covered by a retirement plan at work, use this table to determine if your modified AGI affects the amount of your deduction.

IF your filing status is ...	AND your modified adjusted gross income (modified AGI) is ...	THEN you can take ...
single or head of household	$40,000 or less	a full deduction.
	more than $40,000 but less than $50,000	a partial deduction.
	$50,000 or more	no deduction.
married filing jointly or qualifying widow(er)	$60,000 or less	a full deduction.
	more than $60,000 but less than $70,000	a partial deduction.
	$70,000 or more	no deduction.
married filing separately[2]	less than $10,000	a partial deduction.
	$10,000 or more	no deduction.

[1] Modified AGI (adjusted gross income). See *Modified adjusted gross income (AGI)*, later.
[2] If you did not live with your spouse at any time during the year, your filing status is considered Single for this purpose (therefore, your IRA deduction is determined under the "Single" filing status).

Source: www.irs.gov/pub/irs-pdf/p590.pdf.

Figure A5.2

Table 1–3. Effect of Modified AGI[1] on Deduction If You Are NOT Covered by a Retirement Plan at Work

If you are not covered by a retirement plan at work, use this table to determine if your modified AGI affects the amount of your deduction.

IF your filing status is ...	AND your modified adjusted gross income (modified AGI) is ...	THEN you can take ...
single, head of household, or **qualifying widow(er)**	any amount	a full deduction.
married filing jointly or **separately** with a spouse who *is not* covered by a plan at work	any amount	a full deduction.
married filing jointly with a spouse who *is* covered by a plan at work	$150,000 or less	a full deduction.
	more than $150,000 but less than $160,000	a partial deduction.
	$160,000 or more	no deduction.
married filing separately with a spouse who *is* covered by a plan at work[2]	less than $10,000	a partial deduction.
	$10,000 or more	no deduction.

[1] Modified AGI (adjusted gross income). See *Modified adjusted gross income (AGI),* later.
[2] You are entitled to the full deduction if you did not live with your spouse at any time during the year.

Source: www.irs.gov/pub/irs-pdf/p590.pdf.

Figure A5.3

At Age 76, the Owner of the IRA Must Withdraw ½₂ or 4.5 Percent of the Value of the Portfolio on December 31 of the Prior Year

Table III
(Uniform Lifetime)

(For Use by:
- Unmarried Owners,
- Married Owners Whose Spouses Are Not More than 10 Years Younger, and
- Married Owners Whose Spouses Are Not the Sole Beneficiaries of Their IRAs)

Age	Distribution Period	Age	Distribution Period
70	27.4	93	9.6
71	26.5	94	9.1
72	25.6	95	8.6
73	24.7	96	8.1
74	23.8	97	7.6
75	22.9	98	7.1
76	22.0	99	6.7
77	21.2	100	6.3
78	20.3	101	5.9
79	19.5	102	5.5
80	18.7	103	5.2
81	17.9	104	4.9
82	17.1	105	4.5
83	16.3	106	4.2
84	15.5	107	3.9
85	14.8	108	3.7
86	14.1	109	3.4
87	13.4	110	3.1
88	12.7	111	2.9
89	12.0	112	2.6
90	11.4	113	2.4
91	10.8	114	2.1
92	10.2	115 and over	1.9

Source: www.irs.gov/pub/irs-pdf/p590.pdf.

INDEX

A

Accumulation phase, 96–99
Active management, xi, 219
  by asset allocation brokers,
    23–30
  returns with, 7–8
ADV form, 209
American Stock Exchange (AMEX),
  214
Angels, 213
Annualized growth rate, 245–248
Antrim, Minna, 262
Appreciation, 233
Asset allocation, 5–17
  and active management by
    brokers, 23–30
  arbitrariness of XYZ formula in,
    20–21
  asset dedication vs., 39 (*See also*
    Historical comparisons)
  based on historical average
    returns, 9–14
  as dominant paradigm, ix, 5–6
  Dorfman's study of, 25–27
  flaws in, ix–x
  history of, 7–8
  illusion of science/objectivity in, 23
  investment policy committee
    recommendations for, 24–25
  redeeming qualities of, 30–31
  response bias in, 22
  risk-tolerance questionnaires for,
    22–23
  and volatility avoidance, 14–16
Asset dedication, 2, 33–60
  advantages offered by, 51–59
  allowing for inflation (step 3),
    42–43
  asset allocation vs., 39 (*See also*
    Historical comparisons)
  bond restrictions (step 4), 43–44
  bonds in, 36–37
  brokers' dislike of, x–xi
  cash and cash equivalents in, 35

Asset dedication (*Cont.*):
  in charitable foundation's
    portfolio, 188–191
  concept of, 6
  dedicated portfolios in, 34–35
  dedicating growth portion of
    portfolio (step 6), 48–49
  dedicating income portion of
    portfolio (step 5), 44–48
  forecasting income/cash flow needs
    (step 1), 39–40
  for irregular lump sum withdrawal,
    175–179
  for legal settlement, 179–188
  mathematics behind, 143–146
  perspective of, 35
  precision of, x
  for projected future income
    stream, 194–195
  reviewing, reloading, and repeating
    (step 7), 49–51
  risk with, 90
  with rolling horizon, 192–194
  software for, 203–205
  specifying planning horizon
    (step 2), 40–42
  stocks in, 37–38
  target income stream in, 38–39
  web site for, 44, 143 (*See also* "Do-it-
    yourself" retirement portfolio)
Athletes, 194
Average annual total return,
  245–248
Averages, 242–245, 267–269

B

Banking industry, 285–286
Bear markets, 41
Beardstown Blunder, 237, 278
Beta, 245
BHB study (*see* Brinson, Hood, and
  Beebower study)
Big Board, 214
Biggest days, 271

About the Authors

Stephen J. Huxley, Ph.D., received his doctorate in economics from the University of California at San Diego (1975) and a Bachelor's degree in business and statistics from Ohio State University (1966). He is a tenured Professor of Decision Sciences at the University of San Francisco, where he has been teaching full-time in the School of Business and Management since 1973. His courses include Data Analysis, Decision Modeling, and Operations Management, all at the graduate level. He has received awards for Outstanding Teaching, Outstanding Service, and Outstanding Research both within his department and universitywide. He has published in various academic journals, presented papers at international conferences, and in 1988 won the national Franz Edelman Award for Outstanding Achievement in Management Science (the highest award given by the profession) for his work in scheduling, which resulted in estimated annual savings of $14 million for the city of San Francisco. Applying his expertise in scheduling to investment portfolio construction led to the discovery of the asset dedication approach. He has provided legal testimony as an expert witness and project director for a variety of consulting projects, including personnel scheduling (for police departments), productivity and quality improvement (for the California Public Utilities Commission), and statistical process control systems (for a manufacturing company). He has also contributed voluntarily to the community through work in his church and by hosting a conference on intelligent design on the USF campus. He is married with six children.

Brent Burns received his MBA degree in finance from the University of San Francisco and a Bachelor's degree in Industrial Organization from the University of California at Berkeley. He began working with Stephen Huxley in 1997 at USF, where he was recipient of a coveted McLaren Research Fellowship Grant and member of the Beta Gamma Sigma Honor Society. His expertise in financial modeling became an integral part of the research confirming the advantages of the asset dedication approach. His investment management career began with a Wall Street buyout of his family's business in 1997, when he assumed management of the family holding company, which included managing real estate holdings as well as financial assets within the portfolio. After graduating with his MBA, he took a position with a major stock brokerage company and then began consulting with other investment advisors while continuing research on asset dedication.

Balancing academics and athletics, Brent is a former world-class track and field athlete, competing in the pole vault. A two-time All-American while an undergraduate at Cal, Brent went on after graduation to become a member of the United States National Track and Field Team, representing the United States in international competition. He also won the USA Track and Field indoor grand prix series in 1994. Brent was a three-time finalist at the United States Olympic Trials (1992, 1996, and 2000) and retired from active competition in 2000 following a sixth-place finish at the Trials.